CFO Insights

CFO Insights

Achieving High Performance Through Finance Business Process Outsourcing

STEWART CLEMENTS
MICHAEL DONNELLAN
IN ASSOCIATION WITH
CEDRIC READ

John Wiley & Sons, Ltd

Published in 2004 by   John Wiley & Sons Ltd, The Atrium, Southern Gate, Chichester,
West Sussex PO19 8SQ, England
Telephone   (+44) 1243 779777

Email (for orders and customer service enquiries): cs-books@wiley.co.uk

Visit our Home Page on www.wileyeurope.com or www.wiley.com

Other Wiley Editorial Offices

John Wiley & Sons Inc., 111 River Street, Hoboken, NJ 07030, USA

Jossey-Bass, 989 Market Street, San Francisco, CA 94103-1741, USA

Wiley-VCH Verlag GmbH, Boschstr. 12, D-69469 Weinheim, Germany

John Wiley & Sons Australia Ltd, 33 Park Road, Milton, Queensland 4064, Australia

John Wiley & Sons (Asia) Pte Ltd, 2 Clementi Loop #02-01, Jin Xing Distripark, Singapore 129809

John Wiley & Sons Canada Ltd, 22 Worcester Road, Etobicoke, Ontario, Canada M9W 1L1

Wiley also publishes its books in a variety of electronic formats. Some content that appears in print
may not be available in electronic books.

British Library Cataloguing in Publication Data
A catalogue record for this book is available from the British Library

ISBN 0-470-87086-9

Typeset in 11/13pt Rotis by Sparks, Oxford – www.sparks.co.uk
Printed and bound in Great Britain by CPI Bath Press, Bath

This book is printed on acid-free paper responsibly manufactured from sustainable forestry
in which at least two trees are planted for each one used for paper production.

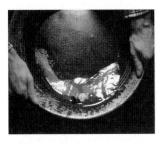 # Preface

In writing this book, we've witnessed a global phenomenon: Executives around the world have shown an insatiable appetite for information on business process outsourcing (BPO). This enormous interest is being fuelled by a surge in the outsourcing of back-office functions: Every week, somewhere in the world, for example, a major new finance and accounting outsourcing deal is being completed. What began as a trickle of activity by a handful of pioneering companies in the 1990s, with BP leading the way, has become a huge wave – a corporate tsunami.

Today, many leading companies are actually in a race to use business process outsourcing as a means to achieve market leadership and redefine their competitive position in the global economy. The CFOs of these companies have made a strong commitment to BPO and moved aggressively to exploit the benefits that it offers. Some see BPO primarily as a cost-reduction tool, others as a path to radical business transformation.

Many CFOs, however, are still considering outsourcing as an option. Whatever their goals or industry, we found that they were asking the same fundamental questions: 'I've seen so much in the news about outsourcing – what's it all about?' 'Can you tell me who's doing what? I hear a lot and I want to know the truth.' 'What's behind the rush to India?' 'We already have a shared service program or we're thinking about one – why should we outsource?' 'Won't I lose control if I take this route?' 'Where do I actually start and how far do I go?' 'Can you give examples of companies that have outsourced or even gone offshore with sophisticated areas of their business?'

CFO Insights was written with precisely these questions in mind. It traces the entire lifecycle of the outsourcing process, from building a business case, achieving stakeholder buy-in, and selecting the right outsourcing partner to pricing and shaping the deal, choosing where to locate outsourced business services, managing implementation, reducing risk, and keeping the deal working. By drawing on the experience of high-performance companies with well-established programs, our goal is to assist CFOs in moving up the outsourcing learning curve as quickly as possible. The practical, timely information offered here provides a strong foundation for planning a cost-effective outsourcing strategy, winning success quickly, and avoiding the mistakes of early adopters.

This book breaks new ground in charting the outsourcing landscape. As our case studies show, the path to success is surprisingly well traveled. BP, for example, offers the classic case of a company that has adopted a 24/7 'follow the sun' F&A outsourcing strategy. Procter & Gamble has gone global by outsourcing its IT, HR, and property management functions. In North America, BC Hydro has outsourced HR and payroll. Canada's BC Hydro has outsourced its entire back office. Neptune Orient Lines, one of the largest logistics companies in the world, is now served from a thriving multi-service global hub based in Shanghai.

In interviewing the CFOs of these and other leading-edge companies, we were impressed by the innovative, far-reaching ways in which they have used business process outsourcing as a tool to enhance overall corporate performance. Among our most important findings are the following.

Many companies have progressed well beyond using outsourcing simply to reduce costs; today they are using it as a tool to promote enterprise-wide change. Companies like BP and Thomas Cook have turned to business transformation outsourcing, which is one step along from BPO, as a way to generate sustained profitability and attractive returns so that they can invest back in their core business. In fact, mature players don't view outsourcing as a commodity cost play, but as a means to revitalize their businesses and as a strategic weapon for transformational change.

Many companies are concerned that outsourcing will lead to less control over their business and therefore expose them to greater risk. However, the opposite is true. Our research clearly reveals that, far from diminishing control, outsourcing actually increases it. A company that outsources selected functions doesn't give anything away; instead, it is buying a set of defined, measurable outcomes and a predictable service that leads to greater control and transparency, not less.

The outsourcing industry has reached a surprising level of maturity in its service delivery model – and emerged as an industry in its own right. Today's mega-service providers have at their disposal truly interconnected delivery networks that provide a full spectrum of services, global sourcing, resilience and disaster recovery backup, and consistent, high-quality support. We're now seeing the death of the 'captive' in-house shared services model and the rise of a global one-to-many delivery service model, in which multiple clients and multiple industries are being served by a network of centers.

By 2007, the outsourcing industry will double in size, driven by the rapid innovation and large-scale investment of mega-service providers. This rapid growth will prove enormously beneficial to clients. It will enable them immediately to reap the economic advantages of scaled shared services and next-generation technologies. Companies will no longer invest in improving back-office administrative productivity and will expect enterprise benefits far beyond cost reduction. Some very sophisticated enterprises are even outsourcing their business analytics. Soon, mega-service providers will create a new branch of finance BPO around decision support and complex business analysis.

The bottom line? More and more companies will use outsourcing as a path to greater profitability and leaner capital consumption. They'll redirect their capital into areas that excite their customers and lead to faster growth and more innovation than they could achieve with the drag of a back-office anchor. By cutting the links of that anchor, they will release valuable energy and time – and free themselves so they can become far more entrepreneurial.

CFO Insights: Achieving High Performance through Finance BPO has been written not only to help finance executives, but all decision makers, as they embark on their outsourcing journey. It offers original research, hands-on advice from the CFOs of leading companies, detailed case studies, and a wealth of best-practice data – everything necessary for planning and implementing a successful outsourcing strategy.

Writing this book was both challenging and rewarding. We wish to thank and acknowledge the talented CFOs and senior finance executives who generously shared their insights and ideas with us: Alan Eilles of BP, Lauralee Martin of Jones Lang LaSalle, Clayton Daley of Procter & Gamble, Bob Davis of Dell, Dennis Kooker of BMG, Ron Dykes of Bellsouth, Wolfgang Reichenberger of Nestlé, Gary Chan and James Dollive of Kraft, Michel-Marc Delcommune of MOL, Lim How Teck of Neptune Orient Lines, Ian Ailles of Thomas Cook, David Harrison of Accenture Business Services of British Columbia (ABS-BC), Pierre Prot of Rhodia and Paul Van Beveren, formerly of Rhodia and now Accenture, Thomas Buess of Zurich Financial Services, John Palmer of Sainsbury's, John Coghlan of Exel, and Peter Moore of Lincolnshire County Council.

From Accenture, we wish to thank the following people for contributing their expertise and experience: Michael Sutcliff, Chapter 2; Adam Johnson, Chapter 3; David Rowlands, Chapter 4; Daniel Lipson, Chapter 5; Stephen Ferneyhough, Chapter 6; J. Scott Laughner, Chapter 8; Alan Healey, Chapter 9; Anoop Sagoo, Chapter 10 and Jane Linder; Susan Cantrell; Justin Jenk; and Alison MacKenzie.

We must also give special acknowledgement to our external advisors and contributors and to the team that helped us put this publication together. Special thanks go to Christy Kirkpatrick who produced the diagrams for CCR Partners, and who contributed substantially to the research and coordinated the individual chapter contributions into a cohesive end product. In addition, we would like to thank Sarah Thomas, Accenture Finance Solutions marketing director, and her team for their tireless efforts on our behalf. This book would not have been completed without their help. Finally, thanks also go to our editor, Karin Abarbanel, and the team at John Wiley, especially Rachael Wilkie and Chris Swain.

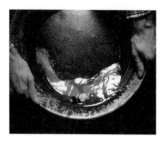

Contents

Contents

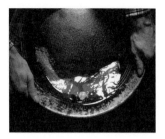

Abbreviations

AP	Accounts Payable
AR	Accounts Receivable
BHQ	Business Headquarters
BPO	Business Process Outsourcing
CFO	Chief Financial Officer
CoA	Chart of Accounts
DSO	Days Sales Outstanding
EDI	Electronic Data Interchange
EMEA	Europe, Middle East and Africa
ERP	Enterprise Resource Planning
EU	European Union
EVA™[1]	Economic Value Added
F&A	Finance and Accounting
GL	General Ledger
IAS	International Accounting Standards
IFRS	International Finance Reporting Standards
JV	Joint Venture
KPI	Key Performance Indicator
M&A	Merger and Acquisition
NPV	Net Present Value
OHQ	Operational Headquarters
OLA	Operating Level Agreements
Q&A	Question and Answer
R&D	Research and Development
RFID	Radio Frequency Identification

---

[1] ™ Stern Stewart & Co.

RFP	Request for Proposal
ROI	Return on Investment
SG&A	Sales, General and Administration
SLA	Service Level Agreement
SME	Small to Medium Sized Enterprise
SSC	Shared Service Center
T&E	Travel and Entertainment Expenses
TRS	Total Return to Shareholders
VAT	Value Added Tax
VP	Vice President
WIP	Work in Progress
WRC	World Rally Championship

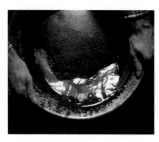

CHAPTER 1

The Finance Outsourcing Landscape

TRANSFORMING THE FINANCE FUNCTION THROUGH OUTSOURCING

Alan Eilles, Vice President Group Financial Infrastructure
BP

BP plc is one of the largest oil companies in the world. The company first outsourced its European upstream accounting services 15 years ago in a groundbreaking contract worth $20m a year. By 2002, the outsourcing of finance and accounting (F&A) had been extended to other businesses in the group and elsewhere in the world – and the value of the contracts had risen to $1.5bn. The BP deal is the largest and most enduring F&A outsourcing arrangement ever. Undoubtedly, one of the biggest successes BP has achieved has been the smooth integration of five major acquisitions into its outsourcing arrangements. Alan Eilles credits BP's usage of outsourcing and its outsourcing suppliers with contributing to this success.

Alan Eilles is responsible for managing F&A outsourcing contracts across the BP Group. He has also been involved in the global restructuring of many F&A deals as they matured and in renegotiating outsourcing scope as circumstances changed. He comments:

'As we demonstrated success through outsourcing and became confident in other service providers, these relationships broadened across BP. Initially, this was

1

seen as a financial transaction for accounting outsourcing. Now, it encompasses a broad spectrum of services including: systems, technology, tax, property management, HR services, construction, and procurement.

'Clearly we've received benefits over the past several years that were only aspirational when we first began outsourcing. If you only partially outsource, you can never completely access the potential economies of scale. We have seen cost reductions every year for each of the 13 years of our outsourcing experience. In fact, in the first seven years, the volume of work in the outsourcing centers doubled, due to taking on new oil fields, but our F&A costs were halved.'

When BP merged with Amoco, its scale of operations radically changed overnight. Alan Eilles says:

'Consolidation of acquisitions was the key agenda point – in accounting, we wanted to up the level of materiality and bring down the clerical workload! The business case for outsourcing was revitalized by our acquisitions. Our new scale made it even more compelling.'

Based on BP's size and the complexity of its various businesses as well as the immaturity of the outsourcing market in 1998, BP decided to minimize the risks involved by dividing upstream and downstream F&A operations between two outsourcing partners, Accenture and IBM. Alan comments:

'Today, we have two very engaged and serious firms. After much deliberation, we decided to go with a two-supplier model because we wanted to encourage a competitive dynamic and reduce risk. We split upstream and downstream between Accenture and IBM in both Europe and North America to ensure that we had resilience across the board.'

BP's suppliers have outsourcing F&A centers in Houston, Tulsa, and Alaska in the United States, and Calgary in Canada. In Europe, the F&A outsourcing centers are in Aberdeen, Rotterdam, and Lisbon. Recently, both BP outsource partners have chosen to migrate and consolidate a portion of the F&A operations in low-cost locations, such as Bangalore in India, and Krakow in Poland. As Alan notes:

'The main benefit of moving location is labor arbitrage; however, we have found benefits in both labor quality and embedded process improvement skills. How critical is location? Well, the move to India and offshoring generally in F&A outsourcing will drive change, as companies in the western world shift from considering the "which city" issue and look deeper into collaborative practices. We need to turn our

attention toward moving our business processes from being oil-centric to being cross-industry to gain further scale globally. This means that we don't necessarily want to own the process; ultimately the supplier should.' While location is important and feeds change into the equation, transition management is also critical to success. Eilles says:

'You want things to happen smoothly and peacefully. Otherwise, the relationship gets off to a bad start from which it is tough to recover. I am delighted to say that our outsource partners have done a good job in transition management.' BP's initial strategy was to get key employees to transfer to the outsourcer because their knowledge, skills, and corporate history go with them.

'But we also want a balance,' notes Eilles. 'We also bring in people from the outside in order to help create a new culture and do things differently. With transition to new geographies the old paradigm of moving existing employees had to be broken. Of course, this places even greater importance on transition management. Where and how do you cut the process for outsourcing? Our practice at BP is to retain in-house matters of judgment, policy, and interpretation.'

The company F&A services now being outsourced include general accounting, joint venture accounting, retail site accounting, hydrocarbon accounting, inventory accounting, accounts payable, and in some cases preparation of financial management information. While BP has pushed the envelope on what has been outsourced it still believes in its original premise that transactional services should be outsourced, and analysis and decision-making remain BP internal activities.

Drawing from experience, Alan notes that any business will change over time. Accordingly, outsourcing deals need to change. In one outsourcing location, BP has been through multiple contract renewals. It started as a fixed price deal, and then became open book, and finally cycled back to fixed. Alan says he would not be surprised if it moved back to open book again. He comments:

'Structuring involves many variables, including the preferences of the individuals managing the deal. Sometimes it is about achieving the next level of benefits. The first round gives you the low-hanging fruit; later, it's about change and realignment. You have to focus your people on continuous improvement. We still have not yet achieved lights-out back-office processing for accounting. We'll get there, but it's a few years away. With all our acquisitions, we are still consolidating and standardizing. For example, we are implementing a SAP platform in North America and Europe *to simplify and standardize our infrastructure.'* Eilles advises companies considering an outsourcing initiative for the first time:

'You should invest serious time and energy in developing and maintaining the relationship. Both parties must be treated fairly. There will always be changes and difficult times, but at the end of the day, the quality of the partnership and the relationship will have a significant impact on the financial success of the deal.

'The original outsourcing scope was the North Sea story. The challenge by John Browne, the chief executive of BP, was: "I want you to provide a more holistic approach." This didn't mean that the outsourcers had to do more work for BP around the world. Rather, he wanted them to understand BP's business at the strategic level and to focus their offer where they could add value.' In keeping with the vision of the CEO for the organization as a whole, BP's first outsourcing initiative was a truly forward-thinking arrangement. Alan explains:

'Creating an internal shared service center would not have driven internal transparency. People at BP were used to spending significant effort on internal allocations. Outsourcing allowed BP to gain a complete understanding of its accounting costs. Now we have an open book on cost, quality, and metrics. I can honestly say we have never looked back!' Alan continues:

'This deal was perceived as innovative and years ahead of its time. It was courageous and it took strong, committed leadership to actually make it successful. For me personally, one of the biggest challenges was making sure that the transitions to our service provider's new outsourcing centers were managed successfully.'

In this initial outsourcing arrangement, BP centralized the organization into a single location in Aberdeen; it brought together accounting people from Glasgow, from accounting centers in England, and from two offices in Aberdeen. So essentially, it combined some 6 accounting groups from these locations. Alan points out:

'In terms of cost reductions, we had a target of at least 30%. We've delivered more than 50%, a very solid performance. In terms of being a catalyst for BP and for the industry, we have evolved from a single-service center into a multiclient site in Aberdeen. Part of our initial vision was the availability of industry-wide accounting services in the North Sea. And we are very pleased that the outsourcer and other oil companies have come together. They can learn and quickly transfer ideas from one company to another. Today the service provider owns the people, processes, and

SAP systems technology. This has created what I would call a community of value.
Alan Eilles summarizes:

'Would we ever bring this back in-house? My answer would be no! First, we are finally seeing the outsourcing market mature. The advancement of multiclient centers will create new value. Second, as new low cost centers spring up around the world I want to have easy access to these opportunities. If BP were to insource now we would be doing so at the wrong time. You do need the full and continuing support of the CEO. It took us several years to build up the necessary experience and confidence. In the longer term we seek robustness, with centers that provide service on a rolling basis through time zones around the world. We want the ability to shift services across locations to reduce the risk of service disruption and to take benefi- cial economies. This flexibility will be a significant benefit of increased outsourcing scale.'

BP has the largest F&A outsourcing program in the world. They see out- sourcing as a fundamentally new way of doing business. In their view, outsourcing has offered benefits that extend far beyond the enormous cost savings they have reaped. BP's outsourcing relationships have had a transforming effect, not only on accounting practices, but also on the managerial style of the company itself. By outsourcing financial opera- tions and increasing control – the heart of every business – John Browne and Alan Eilles believe that the enterprise as a whole has been encour- aged to be more innovative.

BP's experience underscores three powerful advantages that out- sourcing offers:

- **Radical transformation:** Outsourcing is not just a tactical weapon, but a strategic one. BP has successfully deployed its outsourcing model to stimulate broad structural change. Outsourcing has been key to creat- ing value without compromising corporate objectives.

- **Growth through business partnering:** Outsourcing is about partner- ing, not merely service provision. BP, for example, has worked vigor- ously to develop long-term strategic relationships with suppliers who are prepared to invest both expertise and resources in BP's business.

- **Increased innovation:** By moving priority non-differential processes (whether they be deemed to be core or non-core) and activities outside the enterprise, BP has released internal resources to focus on its strategic agenda – *a key source of competitive advantage.* Deploying its outsourcing model on a global scale has helped BP to fast track this shift of internal resources from operations to innovation.

Most of the executives we interviewed for this book have not had the benefit of BP's experience. Among the advantages that BP has reaped from outsourcing are: powerful economies of scale, standardized processes, advanced technology, and continuing investment in the back-office. As more and more companies of all shapes and sizes consider the outsourcing continuum that BP has pioneered, CFOs and their finance team members have many questions:

- How does a sophisticated, successful enterprise with all its complexity and global spread achieve tangible results from finance business process outsourcing (BPO)?

- How do you ensure you're working with the right outsourcing partner to achieve a step-change, sustainable improvements, and a good cultural fit over the longer term?

- How relevant is the BP experience to other companies?

In this chapter, we look at the *evolutionary shift of the finance function* from the late 1990s trend towards in-house shared services to the current phenomenon of finance BPO. We survey *who is doing what.* We capture current thinking and describe the new business model that is emerging, powered in part by innovative outsourcing techniques. We go on to examine the drivers behind this trend and the value proposition they deliver.

THE IMPACT OF FINANCE BPO ON THE CORPORATE AGENDA

The overwhelming finding of our research is that the outsourcing promise is both tantalizing and tangible. Outsourcing suppliers pledge to perform front- and back-office functions, including F&A, far more cheaply and efficiently than companies can do on their own. Our research shows that outsourcing delivers powerful economies of scale by using standardized processes and leading-edge technology. It also makes continuing investment in back-office improvements affordable for companies of all shapes and sizes. This adds a completely new dimension to the traditional outsourcing model: an intriguing market dynamic in which minnows can compete on the same terms as industry giants.

Higher quality service at ever-lower prices is irresistible, particularly when outsourcing allows companies to focus on the true competitive core of their businesses. The logic is simple: If someone else can perform mission-critical processes cheaper, faster, and better while ensuring the highest standards of security, integrity, and control – then why not make the leap into outsourcing?

Sophisticated technologies that automate routine tasks and connect far-flung corporations via a single platform are fuelling an unstoppable trend. Furthermore, locations are emerging that can provide highly skilled workforces at very low cost. Prime examples are Bangalore in India, Prague in eastern Europe, Shanghai in China, Curitiba and Sao Paulo in South America. A mature network of multilingual service delivery centers linked across the globe is now a reality. Many of the CFOs we interviewed expressed both surprise and shock at the speed with which this industry has come into being.

Business process outsourcing – contracting with an external organization to take responsibility for providing part or all of a business process or function – is not new in F&A. Companies have a long history of buying standard, discrete processes such as payroll, credit checking, debt factoring, check printing, and regulatory reporting from external service providers.

During our wide-ranging discussions with senior finance executives, we discovered an obsessive interest in the broader role that outsourcing is assuming. But why – and why now? Simply because operating costs are too high, huge investments are being made in undifferentiated, non-competitive areas, and everyone is still searching for the Holy Grail: the ability to out-compete everyone else. Restoring growth in profits is an absolute necessity, but we have found that this is sustainable only if it is based on a *radical* transformation of the current business model.

Senior finance executives have continued to ask a number of common, recurring questions:

> *'We have read that company XYZ is deep into outsourcing; what's the story? They have a reputation for being in the upper quartile for efficiency; what contribution has outsourcing made and where does it fit in?'*

> *'We hear others are outsourcing accounting; can they be serious? With tighter and tighter regulation, isn't there a control risk? Will we lose control and won't it be more difficult to achieve regulatory compliance? I cannot reconcile this with the fact that so many are going into outsourcing; what's the story?'*
>
> *'What's this I hear about shared services centers that are located in Costa Rica, Shanghai, and Manila? I know another company that's moving its finance function to India. What should we be doing? Why are companies doing this?'*

In the wake of explosive business scandals and the erosion of public confidence, a new corporate agenda is emerging. Investors, the media, regulators, and governments insist on transparency, honesty, and trust. The stock market now has unprecedented access to more accurate data underlying the drivers of corporate performance. Finance and industry analysts regularly meet with CEOs and CFOs. The result? More realistic and meaningful investment information that regulators such as the SEC are scrutinizing constantly with a stream of new regulations in the pipeline that are intended to make decision-making more transparent. CFOs do not work in isolation. They, together with their boardroom colleagues, are addressing the challenges posed by new market dynamics and accountability demands:

- **Growing interconnectedness**, through global capital flows, geographically transferable technology, and increased transnational trade – all supported by international treaties and protocols

- **Increased organizational scale and complexity**, with wider asset deployment, ever-more complex reporting structures, and tensions between control and flexibility

- **Pervasive low-cost technology**, creating the opportunity for a technology environment that is always on, always active, always aware, always changing

- **Increased scrutiny from financial markets**, regulatory bodies, and the public – magnifying every aspect of an enterprise's financial and operating performance

- **New roles for knowledge and intangible assets** – drivers of today's economy, in which brand, intellectual property, reputation, loyalty and, perhaps most important, a commitment to innovation, have become key competitive weapons

- **Changing workforces,** with new capability development, motivation, and retention issues raised by diverse employee populations.

Our research confirms the fierce competitive battle being waged for scarce investment resources to pay off corporate debt and recapitalize balance sheets to fund the next phase of growth. It also reveals a radical rethinking of conventional business wisdom. As described in Chapter 2, a process of strategic renewal and innovation is now under way that will produce a new operating model – lean in asset consumption and heavy on growth in revenues and cash margins.

In the past, companies sought pure cost reduction from outsourcing; better service at lower cost was the goal. Today, forward-looking companies are moving beyond this. We have discovered numerous examples of strategically focused outsourcing partnerships based on long-term commitments between service provider and client companies that have produced radical new business models. Such alliances commonly pool the very best assets and capabilities of both partners to create new sources of competitive advantage and spur step-changes in economic performance. Similar in their impact to disruptive technology, such arrangements promise to reshape whole industries. Although cost reduction remains a key objective in today's climate, for most companies, the real prize is rapid transformation of the business model leading to higher market valuation.

Once a company's top-level team has selected the operating model that will shift its business into a higher shareholder-value creating gear, it then faces the next serious challenge: acquiring the capabilities needed to implement the changes required. This is where transformation and BPO (distinct from pure commodity-based outsourcing) come in.

THE CFO AND FINANCE TRANSFORMATION

Recently, the finance function has undergone major changes in response to two distinct, but converging forces:

1 **Transparency:** Finance has never been under so much scrutiny – or faced so much pressure for change. Although adherence to proper accounting principles and disciplines is part of the answer, it is not

the entire picture. Communicating to stakeholders the economic *value* of the business is still important, but conveying how this *value* is *changing and why* is equally so. Finance must broadcast this not just internally, but externally, to investors and other stakeholders.

2 **Technology:** Most companies have invested heavily in ERP. Many CFOs tell us that they have no choice but to continue with their programs of simplifying and standardizing business processes; but there remains much to do. In addition, CFOs now wish to beef up their *decision support capabilities, but they can only do this is if they free up time from the routine daily grind of transaction processing and bookkeeping.* Their problem? The explosive growth of technology has created what we call *systems spaghetti.*[1] The only way to cut through this is to simplify and streamline unnecessarily complex business processes, systems, and structures.

Propelled by these two forces, the role of the CFO is changing from score-keeper to strategist. Finance, accounting, corporate strategy, and economics have all converged as never before. As Figure 1.1 demonstrates,

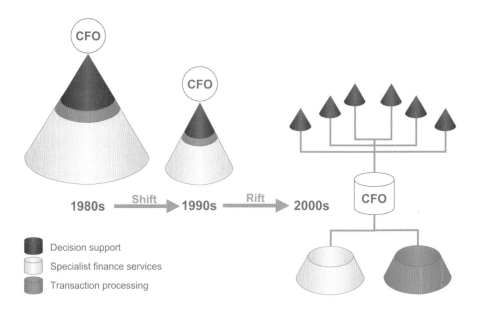

Source: eCFO: Sustaining Value in the New Corporation, Wiley 2001

Figure 1.1 *The changing shape of finance*

today's CFOs are shaping the futures of their finance functions at an accelerated pace.

In Figure 1.1, the finance function of the 1980s is portrayed as a relatively fat pyramid, emphasizing transaction processing and lightly promoting decision support. In the 1990s, finance leveraged ERP systems and became more compact, with a leaner transaction processing operation and greater focus on performance management. By the late 1990s, the Internet had made its mark. As explored in the book, *eCFO: Sustaining Value in the New Corporation,*[2] the CFO became the center of a web of relationships managing the value of the extended enterprise. The finance function was fragmented, with transaction processing operated remotely in shared services or possibly outsourced. Decision support was embedded in business units. Today, the success of this more fragmented model depends on the CFO's ability to maintain the integrity of processes and systems.

WHY MOVE TO SHARED SERVICES?

Effective shared service centers (SSCs) are not about maintaining the status quo of the in-country, federated business model; they are about unremitting innovation. They need to be supported by strong corporate commitment to investment in leading-edge solutions. Our research and interviews with hundreds of organizations worldwide have led us to conclude that the decision to enter into outsourcing arrangements rather than adopting the in-house shared service option is motivated by six factors:

1 **Efficiency:** Multiple business units operating with independent support organizations and systems are being closely scrutinized for cost-effectiveness

2 **Growth:** Intent on growing through acquisitions/joint ventures, companies are concerned about efficiently absorbing acquisitions

3 **Scale:** Large transaction volumes and/or above-average processing costs are pressuring large companies to improve operating performance, while small- and medium-sized businesses want access to economies of scale

4 **Location:** Companies are seeking new geographic opportunities to cut costs without compromising skills

5 **Capability:** Outdated legacy processes/systems and the need for change are tempered by concern over previous failures to build new capabilities

6 **Reputation:** Internal and external pressures are mounting to increase the finance function's service and value, and to improve controls and transparency.

As companies fine-tune their approaches, feedback about what works and what doesn't is rapidly accumulating. Some distinct shared service trends are evident:

- **They are expanding in scope** ... Economies of scale are being achieved by bringing more countries and business units into the fold. More processes are included, such as IT, finance, human resource management, procurement, and customer relationship management (CRM).

- **They are becoming more and more automated** ... Better technology, less human intervention, and greater speed are close to making 'lights-out processing' a reality.

- **They are increasingly serving more than one client** ... Mega players, such as BP, who have used large, dedicated regional centers for the past decade are being joined by agile, fast-growing smaller companies. The age of multiclient service centers has arrived, giving small- and medium-sized companies access, for the first time, to scale economies that only their larger brethren have been able to enjoy.

- **Businesses are being pushed towards greater flexibility** ... Companies are being driven to decide more quickly whether to perform services internally or to outsource them. Why? Mainly because they must move faster than ever before to absorb new acquisitions, handle disposals, and manage corporate restructurings.

- **Businesses are working hard to drive down investment and operating costs** ... They are using new technology to process transactions in lowest-cost locations, wherever they might be. They are partnering with suppliers, customers, and competitors – and, in some cases, they are sharing non-strategic support services. The leading outsource providers continue to invest in next-generation, high-performance technologies, freeing client companies to redirect their investment programs to spur innovation and create competitive advantage.

OUTSOURCING: WHO IS DOING WHAT?

Despite the growing attractions of outsourcing, finance remains a function that executives handle with care. There is far greater interest in outsourcing low-risk, routine tasks than the more analytical, value-added ones. 'If you have a high-volume, repetitive transaction, you are leveraging economies of scale and it works well,' says one executive. 'You can't outsource thinking, but you can outsource brute force,' quips another. 'We keep the role of the orchestra conductor and outsource the rest,' explains a European finance director.

Consider the results[3] shown in Figure 1.2 of a survey in which more than two hundred senior finance executives were asked which processes they were already outsourcing and which ones they intend to in the future.

The first outsourcing candidates are typically 'commodity' processes, such as payroll. Such processes require limited company knowledge and do not add competitive advantage. Some pioneers are moving beyond basic service provision to include performance reporting and business analytics. Other companies plan to broaden their programs down the road

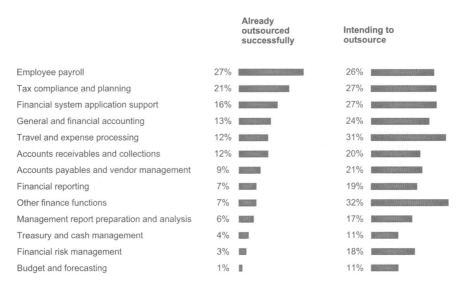

	Already outsourced successfully	Intending to outsource
Employee payroll	27%	26%
Tax compliance and planning	21%	27%
Financial system application support	16%	27%
General and financial accounting	13%	24%
Travel and expense processing	12%	31%
Accounts receivables and collections	12%	20%
Accounts payables and vendor management	9%	21%
Financial reporting	7%	19%
Other finance functions	7%	32%
Management report preparation and analysis	6%	17%
Treasury and cash management	4%	11%
Financial risk management	3%	18%
Budget and forecasting	1%	11%

Source: Accenture and Economist Intelligence Unit Research, 2003

Figure 1.2   *What companies outsource now and plan to outsource in the future*

as they gain experience. One chemicals company, for example, intends to expand its outsourcing program from accounts payable and receivable to general accounting and treasury. Companies tend to retain in-house finance policy formulation and management judgment.

CASE STUDY
Thames Water

Thames Water is a typical example. Its director of finance and support services describes the company's finance function as a pyramid with four tiers. The first tier at the bottom covers transactional activities, such as payroll and accounts payable; the second handles financial and management accounting; the third covers finance decision-making; the fourth is responsible for strategy and policy. Tiers one and two account for 80% of Thames Water's finance headcount. Most of the first tier is outsourced, while second-tier activities – cash management, reconciliation of cash, statutory reporting, and management accounts – are run through a shared service center. The CFO of Thames Water would consider outsourcing the second tier as well, but he draws a line there. 'When you look to outsource management judgment,' he says, 'you cannot hold the business manager responsible.'

Jones Lang LaSalle (JLL) is well acquainted with the complex issues involved in choosing how far to commit corporate resources to the care of outside suppliers. It has a dual involvement in outsourcing. As a service provider, it offers property-outsourcing services to its far-flung clients around the world. As a user of external suppliers, the company has gradually expanded into outsourcing. Along the way, it has learned first-hand some major lessons about managing and negotiating outsourcing programs.

CASE STUDY
Moving from IT to F&A outsourcing

Jones Lang LaSalle is one of the world's leading global real estate services and investment management firms, managing 735 million sq. ft. of real estate properties and facilities, with $20.5bn in real estate investment under management, and 7000 *professionals. It provides strategic advice to major companies owning, occupying, and investing in property around the world.*

The company was formed as a result of a recent merger between a leading partnership in London (Jones Lang Wootton) and one in Chicago (LaSalle). These partnerships were merged and floated on the NYSE (JLL) in the late 1990s. Lauralee Martin, the company's global CFO, says:

'The transition from two country-based partnerships, albeit with multinational coverage, into one global publicly listed company, has provided us with strategic advantage. But the transition has also confronted us with many internal management challenges. Although we are a global corporation, we still recognize the importance of the partnership ethos in our management culture – in pursuit of excellent client service, we encourage entrepreneurial flair and incentivize our best people. Although we wish to be fully aligned globally, we do not believe in standardization for standardization's sake.' JLL sees its strengths today as:

- *Global reach, with consistent culture and service*
- *Global best practices and infrastructure*
- *Investment in technology and research.*

As Lauralee Martin notes, 'We are an outsource service provider ourselves because we offer property outsourcing services to our clients.'

DRIVING IMPROVED PROFITABILITY

In its drive to improve profitability, JLL is creating new revenue opportunities by capitalizing on the outsourcing trend. Its recent most prestigious outsourcing win was Procter & Gamble, which has outsourced global facilities management to JLL. This involved the transfer of over 600 people from P&G to the JLL property service, with over 40 million square feet of property under management.

Stakeholder management is probably the single most important factor in ensuring the success of an outsourcing deal the size and complexity of P&G's. Security of employment for those employees being transferred from one organization to another – their compensation and incentives, and their alignment with business objectives are all high on the early transition agenda.

Having experienced outsourcing as a supplier, Lauralee comments on some of the learning points gathered from her company's recent P&G success:

'We believe P&G chose us above our competitors for the quality of our people – their temperament, their attitude, their deep experience, and excellent references – which combined to produce a good cultural fit. P&G's challenge was to secure a positive reaction from its in-house property staff to the outsourced deal. In return, we had to provide the senior level of management we have taken on from P&G with even more attractive career opportunities.'

JLL sees the skills and sequencing required for outsourcing deals the same way it sees any M&A (merger and acquisition) transaction. First, due diligence; second, post-acquisition planning, and third, deal negotiation. Governance of the ensuing contracts is high on the agenda. Lauralee comments:

'You have to connect responsibilities for decision-making with accountabilities for results. How decisions are made, who's responsible for delivery – these issues all need formalizing and documenting. Our experience shows that if you have to revert to detailed change control evidence and the contract itself to resolve disputes, then governance can become a nightmare. What you need is a sound set of business and governing principles that allow for flexibility and relationship-based dialogue. Confronting the difficult issues face to face is much better than resorting to legal documentation and data.'

The drive for improved operating efficiency at JLL has led them to focus on cost management and streamlining their back-office. JLL also decided to take some of its own medicine and experiment with outsourcing some of its own administrative infrastructure.

INFRASTRUCTURE OUTSOURCING

The company has adopted a 'tactical, evolutionary' approach to outsourcing its own infrastructure rather than going down the 'big-bang' route. Soon after its merger, JLL had some early challenges with IT in terms of the need to connect its huge new global platform. Lauralee comments:

'We thought that by outsourcing IT we were going to solve many of our internal management process problems following our merger; our outsourcers were encouraging us to believe in a vision, a dream, rather than reality. IT outsourcing was only part of the solution; we also needed to streamline and standardize our systems and processes. We also underestimated the workload for us internally. Outsourcing places more, not less, demand on your internal management to manage both the

outsource supplier as well as the transition. My experience shows that you have to work twice as hard when working with an outsourcing consultant through the transition phase, but it pays off in the end.' JLL's IT outsource contract has had to be re-negotiated twice, but is now delivering results.

The complexities of the company's business processes in Europe provided the next greatest opportunity for savings.

OUTSOURCING PROCUREMENT

JLL believes in establishing a solid base line for service management on outsourcing contracts. Service contracts are based on two key monitoring principles:

1 Metrics – where possible work outputs are quantified and measures established.

2 Judgment – even with the most precise measures, subjective judgment is still required to evaluate performance and, as such, strong current relationships and well-documented performance review dialogues are essential.

The key to success in any outsourcing deal for JLL is to bring these two principles together in a way that improves both service quality and efficiency. As Lauralee points out:

'In the USA, we have already outsourced some of our back-office processes, such as travel and expenses (T&E), HR and benefits, and IT support for desktops. We retain inside our organization customer-related activities, including client accounting. However, in Europe, we are starting our outsourcing program with indirect procurement. This evolutionary approach is aimed at picking the low-hanging fruit first – activities with relatively low risk – for example, procurement savings in stationery of 30% of spend are already being achieved. We are starting with the UK and working through, country by country. As our confidence grows, we shall then potentially expand the scope from indirect procurement to client-related property spend (direct) and to other related finance processes such as accounts payable.' The outsourcer on this contract is incentivized for a basic service level with a base fee, supplemented with a success fee based on savings achieved. A scorecard monitoring key performance indicators (KPIs) monthly has been developed to manage the contract as a whole; quarterly contract performance reviews are carried out during the year.

DEFINING PRIORITY F&A PROCESSES TO OUTSOURCE

This CFO defines the following non-core finance activities as suitable for outsourcing:

- *Payroll and benefits*
- *Procurement, payables and T&E*
- *Fixed assets*
- *Credit vetting, debtors and collections.*

Lauralee does not believe that activities such as budgeting and forecasting, and contact activities related to client contracts, should be outsourced since they require judgment and JLL core skills. She says:

'We wish to retain in-house those activities that require our specialist knowledge and where we run the risk of making business-critical errors or exposure to regulatory risk. The Sarbanes-Oxley regulations should be good for the outsourcing business, since both processes and risks will have to be fully documented. In a good outsourcing contract, you should map your processes, document your decision rights, define your service management framework, and insist on regular internal control audits. However, before I move significantly up the food chain in outsourcing my finance function, I would like to know more about what works well for other companies in outsourcing finance and what the benefits would be if we were to do things differently. I would also like to know more about outsourcing situations that haven't gone so well and the lessons learnt.'

More and more companies are choosing to source corporate functions with external business partners. An Accenture report developed in collaboration with the Economist Intelligence Unit, *Outside Upside: Finding focus through finance outsourcing*, draws these main conclusions:

- **Finance outsourcing is gathering momentum:** Of the survey respondents, 71% expect finance outsourcing to increase over the next three years, 30% are currently outsourcing their F&A function – and a majority of these think the arrangement has been very successful (8%) or successful (57%).

- **Outsourcing reduces costs:** Companies with metrics in place report significant savings from outsourcing their F&A functions. For example, Rhodia, the French specialty chemicals company, reduced spending by 30% in two years. Overall, 66% of survey respondents saw 'lower costs' as outsourcing's major benefit.

- **Outsourcing supports core competencies:** Reduced costs are not the only – or always the most significant – benefit. Outsourcing relieves finance managers of repetitive or generic business tasks, letting them concentrate on high-level, value-added activities. By enabling companies to review and reshape entire business processes with an outsider's discipline, outsourcing can help companies execute ambitious transformation plans. Some 55% of survey respondents saw a sharper focus on core competencies and 32%, increased business productivity, as outsourcing benefits.

- **Awareness of potential risks is high:** Outsourcing is often *perceived* as risky. Many executives worry that it involves surrendering control over vital business functions. More recent surveys undertaken by IDC and others show that most executives actually report increased control having entered into outsourcing arrangements.

- **'Commodity' tasks are first in line:** Executives are keener to outsource repetitive, generic finance processes than they are to hand off operations requiring higher analytical capability. Payroll is a common starting point. It is the activity outsourced by the single greatest proportion (27%) of survey respondents. Niche and specialist areas, such as tax planning and compliance, are other natural outsourcing candidates.

- **Precise deliverables are essential:** To keep outsourcing arrangements on track, contracts should detail both client needs and outsource provider responsibilities. Fees should be performance-based and incentives structured to ensure continuous improvement. Metrics should be unambiguous. Alarmingly, 82% of survey respondents had no system to measure outsourcing benefits. Faith in providers may offer an explanation: 71% of respondents cited mutual trust as key to successful finance outsourcing.

- **Outsourcing can cause discord:** Even if F&A staff are transferred to the outsourcing provider, short-term upheaval is inevitable. Resistance is to be expected from employees and departments whose jobs are transformed or eliminated; only firm management will ensure that outsourcing providers receive information for the processes inherited. Explicit timetables and well-designed severance packages help.

- **Sustained management is crucial to success:** Two of the main barriers to outsourcing cited by survey respondents were 1) cultural resistance (50%) and 2) vested interest in defending jobs, budgets, and power (40%). Company leaders must remain committed and involved to overcome such obstacles as they arise.

- **Outsourcing reinforces transparency:** A surprising 73% of survey respondents felt that finance outsourcing could improve disclosure by creating a healthy separation between managers trying to achieve performance and accountants charged with measuring it.

- **Shared services can be the first step:** By standardizing and centralizing F&A operations – and integrating disparate IT systems onto a single platform – SSCs can help reduce headcount and consolidate regional or country back-offices operations. SSCs are tricky, time-consuming, and often costly to set up. Yet they can ease the integration of acquisitions, speed change, and promote cost-saving innovation. Many companies that pioneered SSCs are now leading the way in finance outsourcing.

Despite the accelerating trend towards F&A outsourcing, there are still some doubters. Some executives worry about losing control over sensitive financial operations. But by examining the outsourcing proposition more closely, such executives will quickly discover that they have more control rather than less.

CFO CONCERNS

Some of the concerns that CFOs raise on this issue are shown in Figure 1.3.

The risk of proprietary data falling into competitors' hands was a potential outsourcing drawback cited by more than half of survey respondents. Nurturing in-house knowledge and expertise is another concern. Still other companies feel that they are too big to use outsourcing. A disinclination to standardize is another obstacle cited by those surveyed.

% (Respondents could choose more than one answer)

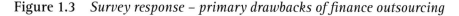

Risk of valuable data falling into competitors' hands	52%
Risk that cost of outsourcing exceeds expectations	48%
Level of in-house knowledge and expertise erodes	45%
Risk that quality of service deteriorates over time	42%
Difficulty of switching provider if need be	35%
Difficulty of monitoring ongoing relationships with provider effectively	27%
Governance & compliance issues more difficult to address with organizations outside direct control	24%
Risk that outsourcing provider goes bankrupt or changes ownership	23%
Difficulty of measuring gains in performance effectively	19%
Level of innovation on the part of the provider is lower than expected	9%
Other	4%

Source: Accenture and Economist Intelligence Unit Research, 2003

Figure 1.3   *Survey response – primary drawbacks of finance outsourcing*

Proponents of outsourcing are quick to counter that many of the reservations cited above dwell on perceptions rather than on the track record of outsourced projects. Veterans of successful arrangements stress that outsourcing does not entail loss of control, but offers an enhanced form of control. 'It's very difficult to convince people that they are actually gaining control because outsourcing will free up valuable resources and time to really focus on the things they want to focus on,' explains Peter Salerno, Ingersoll-Rand's enterprise-program and BPO-relationship manager.

Confidentiality is another worry that outsourcing advocates are eager to lay to rest, arguing that outsourcing providers offer the same levels of professionalism and confidentiality as banks, with which most companies share sensitive internal financial data. There are also good examples of competitive companies that share a common outsourcing platform yet maintain confidential results. As shown in Figure 1.4, the overwhelming majority of companies that have tried finance outsourcing are satisfied with the benefits they receive.

Only 7% called the experience unsuccessful or extremely unsuccessful, while 65% were satisfied. These upbeat results suggest that perceived risks are less daunting than many executives imagine. The list of complaints about suppliers from dissatisfied survey respondents included insufficient expertise, high costs, and poor service! If nothing else, the skeptics provide a helpful catalogue of doubts that must be overcome to win a green light for outsourcing.

Outsourcing has been extremely successful	8%
Outsourcing has been successful	57%
Outsourcing has brought no significant improvements on in-house arrangements	28%
Outsourcing has been unsuccessful	5%
Outsourcing has been extremely unsuccessful	2%

Source: Accenture and Economist Intelligence Unit Research, 2003

Figure 1.4 *How successful has your experience been with F&A outsourcing?*

While some doubt, others do! In Figure 1.5, we list the wide range of companies that have signed F&A outsource contracts between 2001 and 2003 (publicly announced).

While the list is long, remember that there are at least as many companies again who have signed F&A outsourcing contracts in this period who choose not to publicly disclose the fact.

Company*	Provider	Company (cont.)	Provider (cont.)
Outokumpu Oyj.	Accenture	Slovnaft	Accenture
Northern Arizona Healthcare	Perot Systems	GrafTech	CGI
Olivetti Tecnost	Accenture	BC Hydro	Accenture
East Sussex County	ITNet	Regions Bank	Fiserv
General Motors Europe	ACS	BT	Xansa
Gateway	ACS	Ingersoll-Rand	ACS
Mount Sinai	Perot Systems	University of Phoenix	Andersen (now ACS)
Allegheny Technologies	ACS	Resort Condominium International	Accenture
Dairy Farm	CGE&Y	Airgas	Accenture
La Rinascente	Accenture	Thomas Cook	Accenture
AT&T	Accenture	Metromedia Restaurant	ACS
NetStar	Vsource	HP EMEA	Equitant
Visanet	EDS	DTI	Amey
Fortis Commercial Finance	EDS	Cable & Wireless	Accenture
Magnet	Liberata	Comcast Cable Com.	Unisys
O2	Xansa	BP	Accenture
Lucent Technologies	Equitant	U.S. Navy	CSC
Neptune Orient Lines	Accenture	MOL	Accenture
Air France	ACS	BP	PwC (now IBM)
Exel	Accenture		

Source: Accenture Analysis, 2004
* In date order, most recent first

Figure 1.5 *Publicly announced F&A outsourcing contracts 2001 through 2003*

Here are some salient facts and figures drawn from a recent analysis of leading outsource contracts in 2003:

- The average contract value is $217mn

- The average contract length is 6 years

- F&A and HR continue to be most commonly outsourced.

The scale and breadth of the largest contracts signed in 2003 is typified by BC Hydro in Canada who signed a single outsourcing contract covering customer billing services, IT, HR, purchasing, financials, and property management. This contract is worth $1bn ($1.45bn CDN) over 10 years.

We interview the CFOs of BC Hydro later in this book to garner insight into their business cases and the value they have created by enhancing capabilities through the innovative use of outsourcing.

The F&A market – including administration and payment services – is rapidly growing. Today, when taken together, this represents a $33bn market[4] that is expected to increase at approximately 10% annually until 2005, as some outsource providers offer processes with significantly higher content skill and customer interaction. Services such as multiple process back-office transaction processing, management reporting, planning and forecasting, and decision-support analysis are also being provided. This total F&A market has three major segments:

1 **Payment services:** check clearing, credit card authorizations and clearing, electronic funds transfers.

2 **Compliance services:** tax reporting, financial statements, regulatory reporting, and transaction processing.

3 **Analytic services:** corporate payables, receivables & collections, general accounting, payroll, claim, order & customer administration, management reporting, performance reporting, and risk management.

The F&A outsourcing market is currently fragmented and service providers come from different backgrounds and build on different platforms of strength. The market includes traditional IT outsource players, pure-play BPO providers, vertical solution providers, and process specialists. Offshore service providers are entering the market by aggressively leveraging IT and call center capabilities to cross-sell F&A services.

Executives can choose from a variety of BPO providers that either focus on a number of different processes, or that present themselves as multi-process suppliers. In some instances, these vendors can execute globally, while others are focused solely on niche or regional markets. The competitive landscape has changed dramatically due to the Sarbanes-Oxley Act, which bars audit firms from providing BPO services to their clients.

Later, in Chapter 3, we deal with the issue of how to choose the service provider that is right for you.

THE OUTSOURCING PROMISE

CFOs tell us that they are keen to use outsourcing as a vehicle for achieving cost reductions so they can make capability improvements elsewhere in the business. They are attracted to transformational outsourcing because it is faster, requires less capital, and offers reduced risk than the alternatives. So what is the value proposition? There are several aspects to business process outsourcing's appeal:

- **Financial control and visibility:** Companies with distributed systems, processes, and infrastructures can move to consistent, well-defined best practice models with increased transparency of information and process controls. This is crucial as companies pursue new operating models in order to increase their competitive capabilities.

- **Speed to market:** Companies interested in rapidly building new business capabilities, expanding into new geographic markets or changing internal systems and processes to support new business models can exploit BPO services to enhance the speed of delivering business benefits. For example, Thomas Cook is leveraging outsourcing capabilities to create a world-class finance organization and implement new ERP technologies to stimulate transformational change across the enterprise.

- **Competitive capabilities:** Outsourcing service providers can improve a company's competitive position. Highly effective organizations like BP and Exel have used long-established service providers to achieve superior capabilities through standardization, centralization, and technology enhancements.

- **Operating cost savings:** Every company is interested in lowering operating costs by improving process efficiencies, accessing lower wage rates, and leveraging technology to increase automation and enhance decision-making. In many cases, they can achieve these results more quickly and with less risk by accessing external consulting skills, intellectual property, assets, and service delivery networks. F&A BPO contracts typically generate from 20% to 40% in operating cost savings (across all industries).

- **Financing & fiscal cost reductions:** BPO contracts can help companies slash costs, such as working capital, eliminate bad-debt expense, improve tax efficiency, and lower financing costs. One telecommunications company received $90m in cash-flow improvements within four months of outsourcing its receivables management service.

Multiple outsourcing models exist to support the CFO in striving for radical change and increased value. Outlined here are three types of outsourcing relationships:

- **Conventional outsourcing:** This entails using a niche outsource supplier to provide a narrow set of services through a contractual relationship. Most frequently, companies use the outsourcer's own standard processes to minimize costs. They may or may not transfer people and assets to the outsourcer.

- **Collaborative outsourcing:** This involves a cooperative, flexible relationship with outsource providers that offer a broader scope of services. The company and its outsourcing partner frequently define these services jointly. Again, the company may or may not transfer people and assets to the outsourcer.

- **Business transformation outsourcing:** This high pay-off outsourcing initiative involves a deep commitment between the firm and its outsourcing partner to radically transform the firm's enterprise-level performance and outcomes. The two companies jointly define a broad range of processes they will use and may also share in a joint venture that manages assets and employees.

Figure 1.6 covers the outsource delivery models available in the market today. These range from conventional consulting and outsourcing, to forms of collaborative outsourcing (such as co-sourcing and global sourcing), through to transformational models.

Organizations have a better chance of success with process outsourcing when they craft a relationship that specifically meets their needs. In

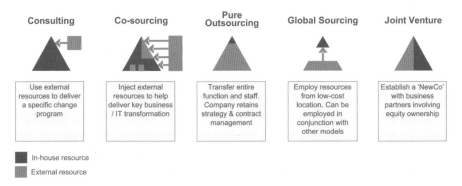

Figure 1.6   *Spectrum of outsourcing delivery models*

fact, we have found that there is no 'one-size-fits-all' approach that guarantees good results. A variety of initiatives are equally valid. We provide a table[5] here for evaluating different approaches to process outsourcing.

Outsourcing Models			
	Conventional	Collaborative	Business Transformation
Objective	Hand off support to specialist provider to cut costs and focus managers on core issues	Upgrade non-core processes to cut expenses and provide flexibility to respond to changing business needs	Transform the way a business works to achieve dramatic, sustainable enterprise-level performance improvement
Partner Role	Run support function	Re-engineer and run non-core processes	Collaborate to transform the business
Approach	Standardized services Transaction-based fee for service pricing Narrow scale and scope of services	Flexible, tailored services Output-based, gain-share pricing Services scaled to meet changing business needs	Integrated services to radically change business Outcome-based, risk-share financial structure Accelerated delivery
Typical Benefits			
Inputs	20–50% cost savings Access to best practices Improved career opportunities Improved management focus	50% cost savings Access to competitive skills Improved career opportunities Improved management focus	50% cost savings Access to critical skills Improved career opportunities Improved management focus
Outputs	Same, consistent service level Shared financial risk	Higher, consistent service level Improved flexibility, speed Shared operating risk	Higher, consistent service level Improved flexibility, speed Shared strategic risk
Outcomes			50% Market-increase Revenue doubled Basis of competition changed

There are major additional benefits to be reaped from collaborative and business transformation outsourcing. The most valuable are greater cost savings, increased flexibility and speed, and higher service levels. Consider the following advantages that more sophisticated outsourcing relationships can provide:

- **By turning an existing asset over to an outsourcer, an organization can turn fixed costs and capital into variable expenses.** This applies to people, too. The organization no longer has to invest in recruiting, training, motivating, and managing the people who staff these operations.

- **Outsourcers can share assets among multiple clients to improve cost and handle capacity fluctuations.** Sharing common application platforms, staff, and facilities spreads fixed cost. For example, in four years, one high-tech firm achieved a 35% cost saving in its call center, despite a fluctuating workload. This was possible largely because its outsource provider had the flexibility to shift staff to other clients when the high-tech firm's call volumes changed.

- **The need for integration can override other considerations.** One oil company, for example, outsources F&A to a shared service provider. However, it maintains ownership of its own software to avoid potential integration problems. The outsourcing provider performs standardized financial processes through a direct link to the oil company's SAP financials module.

This chapter has served as an overview of outsourcing trends and provided an overview of 'who is doing what?' The rest of this book is intended to serve as a guide to outsourcing for the CFO, senior finance executive, and the C-level team. It is based on real case studies and first-hand experience.

In Chapter 2, we analyze the characteristics of high-performing businesses and examine the impact of *changing business models* on the case for business transformation through outsourcing. Chapter 3 explores in detail the *outsourcing supply market* and how to choose between suppliers.

Chapter 4 deals with *scoping* – what to outsource to maximize benefits, infuse new skills, build core capabilities, and streamline business processes. The issue of scoping is fundamental to long-term success. In the two subsequent chapters (5 and 6), we cover the issues vital to *global sourcing* and *shaping the deal.*

Chapter 7 focuses on *stakeholders* – how to achieve buy-in and motivate your people through the transition. Chapter 8 provides frontline advice on how to manage *change and implementation.* It conveys the issues of transition timing, culture, communication, and building a robust service management framework.

Chapter 9 explores the full range of *risks inherent in outsourcing* and the governance structures necessary to manage the route to success. In Chapter 10, we look at how to *keep the deal working* and how to secure continuous improvement.

In the final chapter, we *fast forward* to explore where the outsourcing phenomenon is leading – envisioning a new world where physical organizational boundaries cease to be relevant; where companies in the same industry share a common infrastructure for non-strategic functions; where an outsourcing industry has transcended national boundaries on a global basis; and where technology has made business transactions truly virtual. The competitive landscape is changing rapidly and the dynamics that are driving this are permanent!

Here are some insights that other finance executives have shared with us.

CFO INSIGHTS

- CFOs are becoming more and more comfortable with the outsourcing of routine, transactional processing; they are more concerned about outsourcing complex responsibilities – including matters of principle, judgment, and decision support.

- The BPO model has matured around interconnected global service delivery, rather than any single country or region. Outsource providers should be given process ownership to create cross-industry capabilities.

- Companies are increasingly adopting process outsourcing to help drive strategic transformational change – for example, leveraging post-acquisition synergies.

- Finance BPO provides CFOs with more control, not less; creates greater transparency, not less; and compliance with new statutes like Sarbanes-Oxley is easier and cheaper to achieve than the alternative in-house option.

- Outsourcing finance shared services is a more attractive option than the in-house option – it is lower cost, enables scarce investment to be redirected towards core innovation and provides superior scale benefits.

- An outsourcing arrangement should be viewed as a long-term partnership, with shared risks and rewards – and should include well-structured mechanisms to keep the deal fresh.

FROM INSIGHT TO ACTION

ARTICULATE YOUR BUSINESS MODEL OF THE FUTURE

Outsourcing can be a powerful enabler. Analyze your value drivers. Identify those components of your business that create value and those that destroy value. Decide to retain only those core competencies that make you truly distinctive and provide real competitive advantage.

CONSIDER THE OUTSOURCING SERVICE DELIVERY OPTIONS AVAILABLE TO YOU

Decide between conventional outsourcing, a collaborative joint venture, or the potential benefits of major transformation. Do your research thoroughly to identify the best external partner for what will be a major corporate transaction. Cultural fit will be key. Establish a strong foundation for trust – you shouldn't have to resort to contract struggles later down the line.

DEFINE SCOPE CLEARLY

Consider carefully how and when you should release one or more business functions. Are the trade-offs between integration and segregation well understood? Negotiate service-level agreements that meet baseline requirements and then use incentives to drive improved performance.

CREATE NEW CAPABILITIES!

Don't see outsourcing as a situation where you are relinquishing assets, but rather as an opportunity to build new capabilities to transform your competitive position. This is the chance to revolutionize your operating model. Seize it!

SHAPE THE DEAL TO SUIT YOU

With your chosen outsource partner, develop a robust and mutually beneficial value proposition. Align your goals with those of your outsource supplier to motivate optimum performance and maximize shareholder value. Work with your supplier as a strategic business partner – you will be surprised at how much you can achieve together.

UNDERSTAND YOUR STAKEHOLDERS' NEEDS AND ASPIRATIONS

Be honest. Communicate clearly a well-argued business case and involve the right people in the transition. Be decisive! Achieving buy-in means being bold.

DON'T UNDERESTIMATE THE CHANGE MANAGEMENT REQUIRED

Is the timing right for an outsourcing deal, in terms of both your company's business cycle and changes within your industry? Take steps to minimize the potential for cultural trauma. Avoid the mistakes of others; learn from the past!

TAKE THE RISKS INVOLVED SERIOUSLY

Analyze the downside and build structural flexibility into your outsource contract. Clearly define your method for adjusting existing arrangements. But also treat risk as an opportunity. For example, acquisitions may provide you with opportunities to achieve valuable leverage and scale economies.

TREAT OUTSOURCING AS AN M&A TRANSACTION

Do your due diligence in a specific timeframe. But don't drag your organization through a long period of uncertainty. And don't allow 'scope creep' to unnecessarily prolong the negotiation process and delay benefits.

> KEEP THE DEAL WORKING!
>
> As you start on the outsourcing journey, think of the future. There will always be new and better ways of operating. Renew, and if necessary, re-negotiate your outsourcing contract as your business strategy evolves. Look to refresh the deal: Take advantage of step-changes and major advances in technology, labor cost arbitrage, and the structure of your industry.

REFERENCES

1 Cedric Read, Hans Dieter Scheuermann and the mySAP Financials Team, *The CFO as Business Integrator*, Wiley, 2003.

2 Cedric Read and the PwC financial management consulting team, *eCFO: Sustaining Value in the New Corporation*, Wiley, 2001.

3 Accenture in cooperation with Economist Intelligence Unit, *Outside Upside: Finding focus through finance outsourcing*, 2003. www.accenture.com/financesolutions

4 *Gartner Focus Report*, July 2003.

5 Jane Linder, Alvin Jacobson, Matthew D. Breitfelder and Mark Arnold, *Business Transformation Outsourcing: Partnering for Radical Change*, Accenture, 2001. www.accenture.com

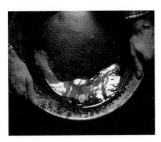

CHAPTER 2

Creating an Operating Model for High Performance

CHANGING TO A GLOBAL BUSINESS MODEL BASED ON BRANDS AND TECHNOLOGY

Clayton Daley, CFO
Procter & Gamble

Procter & Gamble (P&G) is one of the world's largest consumer goods companies. Two years ago, A.G. Lafley was appointed CEO and charged with spearheading the company's return to consistent high performance. By the end of the 1990s, P&G had been in danger of becoming a once-great company that had lost its way. Clayton Daley, CFO of P&G, comments on performance at the time:

'Sales on most of our 18 top brands were slowing; the company was being out-performed by more focused rivals such as Colgate-Palmolive and Kimberley-Clark. The only way we had kept profits growing was by cutting costs. At the same time, the dynamics of the industry were changing as massive retailers, such as Wal-Mart, Tesco, and Carrefour were emerging.'

The first thing that Lafley told P&G's top managers when he took over was to 'focus on what you do well – selling the company's major brands such as Tide,

Pampers, and Crest – instead of trying to develop the next big thing.' Now those old and reliable products have gained so much market share that they are again the envy of the industry. So is the company's stock price, which has climbed to $103 a share since the turnaround started, while the S&P 500 stock index has declined by 32%. P&G's profits for the current fiscal year (2003) rose to $5.2bn based on an increase in sales to $43bn. Volume growth has averaged 7% over the past 6 quarters, excluding acquisitions – well above the company's goal and the industry average. Daley comments:

'As a branded products company, our challenge is always to add value for our consumers. The core of that challenge lies in technology – developing and marketing products that are demonstrably better to the consumer than competitive offerings. With P&G's price-to-earnings ratio (P/E) at about 25, we are still regarded as an industry leader, but we have more to do.'

Despite P&G's emphasis on technology, it retains a very heavy focus on the consumer. The CEO coined the slogans 'the consumer is boss', and 'the first moment of truth is where consumers first see the product on the shelf; the second moment of truth is the consumer's experience at home.' The P&G leadership hasn't made grand announcements on the company's future; instead, they spent an enormous amount of time patiently communicating how they want P&G to change. Lafley, Daley, and their team are focused on how to make P&G relevant in the 21st century, now that speed and agility are so crucial. Recently, the company made two of its largest acquisitions ever – Clairol, in 2001 for $5bn and Wella in 2003 for $7bn. More than half of the company's top 30 officers have turned over and more than 9,500 jobs have been cut. Yet the revolution is far from over.

P&G uses stakeholder value as a unifying concept. It is trying to get everyone – from people in finance, marketing, R&D, and product supply to those who deal with customers – to understand that their activities should be directed at improving value for the stakeholder. To sustain good financial performance over time, P&G must keep its franchises strong. This requires the discipline to invest in R&D and the marketing mix.

The CFO goes on to say:

'Some four years ago, we had the most significant reorganization in our history, converting our company from a geographic profit-and-product model to a global product-and-profit model. We have moved to a global product management struc-

ture because we view ourselves today as a technology company, not just a market-ing company. As such, our R&D dollars must create technologies that introduce and enhance brands with broad application across the world, in both developed and developing markets.'

The global re-structuring has had a significant impact on finance and back-office operations. Most of the IT, finance and accounting, HR and employment services are now in a shared service organization with only a small element of local infrastructure in the geographic markets. Daley is a strong believer in the value of shared services:

'We now have a shared service center in Costa Rica to support our North American and Latin America operations; one in Newcastle, England for continental Europe; and one in Manila for Asia-Pacific. We have made great progress in benefiting from labor cost arbitrage – in the case of Costa Rica, a 70% reduction in unit labor cost. But, perhaps the biggest benefit has been in the increased focus of our market and product management, both globally and on a country-by-country basis in creating shareholder value. We have also managed to achieve standardization in our busi-ness processes and systems across the world.'

The CEO wants a more outwardly focused, flexible approach. This has implica-tions for every facet of the business, from manufacturing to innovation. For exam-ple, during 2003 all the company's bar-soap manufacturing – including Ivory, P&G's oldest surviving brand – was outsourced to a Canadian contractor. Subsequently, P&G outsourced their IT operations to Hewlett-Packard.

Clayt Daley comments on the future shape of the company: 'We are in the busi-ness of creating and building brands. We don't see ourselves as generalists, trying to do everything on our own – we see ourselves as specialists with core competencies in brands and product innovation.'

P&G has already taken the 'low hanging fruit' from shared services – which, in itself, is treated as a large business in its own right. Daley goes on to say:

'Through outsourcing, we could take even greater advantage of the competence of outsourced specialists and their economies of scale. Our outsourcing experi-ence to date is not seen as a big-bang approach, but a more tactical evolution of our operating model. We look at the feasibility of outsourcing specific parts of our infrastructure – for example, property management and facilities, which recently has been outsourced to Jones Lang LaSalle on a worldwide basis. We're careful to keep our outsource suppliers to a manageable number and to capture the benefits *of best of breed. But, we don't want a huge organization internally to manage the outsourcers – every time you outsource something you have to consider the effort that goes into purchasing and contract management. If you are not careful, you end up spending your savings on managing the outsourcer!'*

The increasing trend inside P&G toward specialization and outsourcing processes considered to be non-core is extending into finance and accounting. The CFO goes on to say:

'We started by outsourcing our employment services, which includes the payroll function. Some of the other parts of our finance function may also be outsourced in the future – for example, accounts payable and accounts receivable are both possibilities – but we need to consider the high risks in today's corporate governance environment. We need to satisfy ourselves that there is a well-developed market out there for outsourced services offering reasonably low risk. The outsourcing of our IT should not only provide us with an IT service, but we hope to leverage the economies of scale through the purchasing of hardware and the software updates. Our internal organization has been very successful in the past, but in the future, our company will succeed because we are better focused.'

Clayt concludes with his views on the changing business model at P&G, a reflection on his personal contributions, and how he sees the role of the CFO and the finance function changing in the future: 'The world out there says that the tenure of the CFO shortens every year! My view of the CFO's role is relatively simple: How do you add value? That is what I think the challenge has been and will continue to be. Do I think that there will continue to be a finance function with all this talk of outsourcing? Absolutely. I can certainly envision, though, that it will be very different from its role in the past. Recently, I have been personally and intimately involved in the larger outsourcing deals. The CFO has to be in the forefront in understanding at a strategic level the relative economics of different parts of the business model – and vitally play a decisive role in deciding what should be insourced and what should be outsourced. Just as crucial is using the skills and expertise of the finance function in negotiating the outsourcing deals and in setting up disciplined, but flexible, contractual management frameworks.'

Even perennially successful companies like P&G are finding it more difficult to deliver consistently superior returns. They often respond with new leadership – in P&G's case, a new CEO – with a revitalized strategy. This strategy involves a new focus on core brands and the consumer. Such companies often break with tradition to seek innovation from outside the organization and, as in P&G's case, endeavor to decrease new product time-to-market. Inevitably, such strategies involve programs for improving operational efficiency and outsourcing.

Of course, enormous value still resides in having loyal customers, well-known brands, deep industry know-how, preferential access to distribution channels, proprietary physical assets, and a robust patent portfolio. But these forms of value have steadily eroded. Technological discontinuities, regulatory upheavals, industry disintermediation, abrupt shifts in consumer tastes, and non-traditional competitors have all undermined the advantages that incumbents once enjoyed.

In today's turbulent age, the only dependable advantage is a superior capacity for reinventing your business model before circumstances force you to. According to Gary Hamel[1] a turnaround is 'transformation tragically delayed'! Strategic resilience is not about rebounding from a setback. It is about continuously anticipating and adjusting to trends that can permanently impair the earning power of a core business. It is about having the capacity to change before the case for change becomes desperately obvious.

In this chapter, we consider the ways in which companies like P&G are radically changing their business models to improve performance. We articulate the reasons why some companies are moving towards outsourcing. *And why even high performers who choose to retain their functions in-house keep their eyes and ears open to the developing outsourcing industry and other revolutionary new ideas just around the corner.*

WHAT IS A 'HIGH-PERFORMANCE' COMPANY?

A high-performance business is one that delivers the greatest possible total return to stakeholders over an extended period of time. World-class leaders are revisiting and adapting their operating models. How? By increasing flexibility and adopting a single-minded focus on innovation, strategy, and core competencies.

How does a company rise to the highest level in its industry?[2] Accenture research into what constitutes a high-performance business has identified five vital qualities:

1 They have the vision and determination to identify the most important *industry drivers of present and future value.* High performers have an uncanny ability to sense and respond to major environmental shifts.

2 High-performance businesses are masters of action. They create *adaptable and executable strategies* that can weather uncertain economic conditions. Their leadership teams build flexible, fast-learning organizations.

3 High-performance businesses know which of their *core competencies are critical to driving value.* They master these core competencies and compete based on them, yet they also know when and how to extend their mastery by partnering in areas both inside and outside their core. *Outsourcing supports this mastery process.* Industry by industry, companies and governments are looking at outsourcing as a strategic change weapon – one that provides strong performance and flexibility.

4 High-performance businesses are obsessive about *winning the battle for the customer.* They know that connecting with customers unlocks real business value. They use their insight and expertise to create highly satisfied, lifetime customers who generate powerful economic benefits.

5 Every high-performance business has something uniquely its own... a cultural bias toward winning ... a *'high performance business anatomy' that is difficult to replicate.*

High-performance companies are also extremely effective at managing paradoxes. They know how to balance seemingly contradictory values: *present and future strategic agendas... lean, flexible workforces and employee loyalty ... globally driven change imperatives and local empowerment ... aggressive new market entry and highly disciplined risk management.* And successful businesses know how to harness technology and invest with a focus on long-term success, not just short-term cost maximization.

The key building blocks of a high-performance business – understanding value drivers, mastering core competencies, and developing a *difficult-to-copy high-performance anatomy* – which includes a unique business operating model – are illustrated in Figure 2.1.

Dell has many of the characteristics of a high-performance business – its *direct* business model has been outstandingly successful in captur-

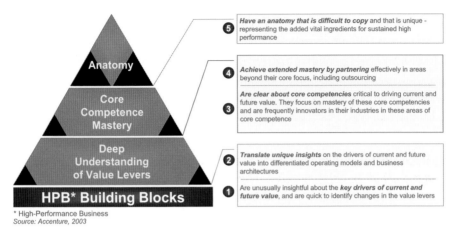

Figure 2.1 *The five characteristics of high-performance businesses (HPBs)*

ing market share in the fiercely competitive PC market. Having ridden the extreme highs and lows of the technology stock markets in recent years, Dell's sustained financial performance also makes it a market leader. Much of this success can be attributed to its operating model – relatively low physical asset intensity, strategic partnerships with suppliers, and a core competence in delivering *velocity* through a streamlined supply chain. And, central to its high performance, is Dell's obsession with customers and pursuit of innovation.

CASE STUDY
Building a direct business model

Dell is a premier provider of products and services that enable customers worldwide to build IT resources and Internet infrastructures. Through its direct business model, Dell designs, customizes, and manufactures products, and provides services to customer requirements while offering an extensive selection of software and peripherals.

Results announced at the end of the third quarter of 2003 showed company revenue up 40% over that achieved two years ago. Sales for the rest of the industry were essentially flat over the same period! Year on year, Dell achieves 22% volume growth and more than a 20% increase in net income. To quote Michael Dell, chairman and CEO:

'Customers and investors get the best value over time from companies like Dell – companies that are growing and are financially very healthy. The market should insist on both. It is a credit to our teams and a better way of doing business that we are consistently meeting those expectations.'

Customer perceptions of Dell's performance are equally strong. In 2003, for example, Technology Business Research (TBR) ranked Dell number one in UK customer satisfaction in servers, notebook computers, and desktop computers. The company also holds the same distinction for all three product categories in France and Germany.

Dell's business model is predicated on building value through direct delivery. It focuses on a positive customer experience, moving goods in a compressed time period, shrinking distance, and reducing cost. Dell's overall finance objectives are threefold:

- Being nimble, and supporting the general managers in the business; for example, with fast cycle customer segmentation
- Granular reporting real-time, for example, profit pool analysis and fine tuning product strategy
- Driving a low-cost structure, which includes migrating certain functions to less expensive locations.

Online penetration and driving customers to purchase over the Internet is still a very strong focus. To quote Bob Davis, the Vice President and Chief Accounting Officer:

'The Internet is a great extension of the direct model for one-on-one customer segmentation. It leads to almost perfect information, in almost perfect time, and at almost perfect pricing. For some time we have used "fast cycle segmentation" at the customer level. After all, it is the customers who buy the products that create the value. We look for trends or common characteristics across customer sets, and as businesses grow larger, we split them into smaller units. I think the industry is only beginning to understand the true drivers of value creation in today's Internet-based economy.'

Dell is in a good competitive position, but Michael Dell and his team recognize that they must continue doing things differently. To quote Jim Schneider, the senior vice president and CFO, on strategic direction:

'We leverage our timely information flow to grow market share with stabilized margins and improved profitably. The combination of our direct model and real-time *information flow enables us to move quickly and precisely to deliver outstanding results in any environment. We manage segment profitability down to the most granular level. For corporate consumers, we track deals and profitability daily by customer and by product. This enables us to quickly and accurately identify profitable accounts and bid accordingly. For domestic consumers, Dell's knowledge of prospect demand and preferences is unparalleled. We track ROI of price movements and promotions in real-time. We respond in hours, even minutes, and are more nimble in response to our customers than competitors are.'*

Bob discussed finance's relationship with the business: *'Our finance executives today are creative people, who are open to creative solutions – they are customer-focused and metrics driven. We have an excellent partnership with the business – helping to make customer segmentation decisions and providing input to pricing propositions. Less than 10 years ago there were only three main product lines, but now there are 15 different product initiatives that all need real-time reporting. Finance is very integral to measuring and managing performance real-time at Dell – the business general managers rely on us to help them execute.'*

As Dell has grown, non-core processes have migrated to low-cost locations, both on and offshore. Dell International Services, the company's internal organization, that provides customer technical support, customer care, and shared services for accounts payable, HR, IT, and product development. So far the organization has centers in Slovakia, Panama, China, Morocco, and India because – with Dell's considerable internal scale – these services can be more economically provided offshore without sacrificing quality. The growing number of centers enables good redundancy and disaster recovery ability. Service can be transferred should one center fail. Dell also uses outsource service providers to increase capacity in non-core areas at busy times of the year. Bob considers:

'We do use outsource providers, particularly when we receive high call volumes over Christmas – there are times of the year when we are more dependent upon outsourcers than others. There is a very fine line that divides what we should retain, and what should be outsourced. For example, we would not outsource the supply chain, manufacturing, or distribution – our areas of core competence. We are keen to protect our valuable skills and expertise in the way that we service and develop intimacy with our customers.'

Ever keen to look at more efficient and cost-effective alternatives, external partners add value to other parts of the Dell value chain. For example, they partner with Intel, Microsoft, and EMC (a Boston-based information and storage management company) to jointly leverage research and development. This partly explains why revenue seemingly grows faster than R&D investment. Bob explains:

'You need to figure out your core competencies. For example, we partner with EMC, who have good storage products and other intellectual property, while they leverage our manufacturing expertise and sales force.

'Ten years ago, Dell had at least 300 suppliers providing 80% of its building materials; today 30 suppliers account for those materials. This created closer relationships between Dell and its suppliers. We help our suppliers by letting them leverage our procurement strength. Most of our top suppliers embrace an extranet relationship with Dell. Internet negotiation has provided considerable transparency, and, therefore, better pricing.'

Dell's growth rate continues to surpass all but one or two companies. In its market, it is the fastest-growing, lowest-cost, most profitable open systems vendor. Dell took advantage of the Internet to relentlessly achieve ever-greater efficiencies and exploit scaling opportunities. Now it concentrates on building strong alliances. By giving a great share of commitment to a limited number of partners, Dell is able to benefit profitably from sharing information on design, quality, product, and pricing; via a continuous feedback loop.

While beating market competitors in revenue and earnings growth, Dell seems to grow in a disciplined manner. It claims it does not chase unprofitable business in any customer segments. Dell was number one in the worldwide PC market when its performance was reviewed for this book because its business model is structurally advantaged. Dell is also focused on growth opportunities. Emerging products, new services, and international market strategies are expected to drive growth and profitability, and ensure the company's long-term success.

A business model like Dell's is central to its core logic for creating value. The term 'business model' can mean very many different things – everything from how a company earns money to how it structures its organization. In this book, we define a business model[3] as:

1 The set of value propositions an organization offers its stakeholders

2 The operating processes it employs to deliver its value propositions

3 A *coherent* business system, that both relies and builds on assets, capabilities, and relationships to create value.

DIFFERENTIATED OPERATING MODELS

A business model should enhance a company's special strengths and core competencies: how it wins customers, woos investors, and earns profits. Effective business models are rich and detailed; their components reinforce each other. Change any one and you have a different model.

In the past, executives had the luxury of assuming that business models were stable and enduring! Companies always had to work to *get better,* but they seldom had to *get different* – not at their core, not in their essence. Today, *getting different and staying so* is the imperative.

Traditionally, players in the global market configured themselves as multinationals, with relatively independent entities in each country bound into a corporate structure. These country-based businesses were (and are still) often organized by region and then globally. Due to statutory and national policy frameworks, country-based businesses often have an independent P&L statement, but are governed by an overall corporate strategy. Typically, country-based operations have independent approaches to marketing and relatively separate supply chains.

Over time, trade barriers have come down and capital markets have become more integrated and interdependent. Companies like Dell and Nokia began to move to a *global product model*, in which the P&L businesses were recast around global products, with global supply and demand chains. These more coherent global strategies benefited from improved product development, marketing focus, and supply chain efficiency.

More efficient supply chains have allowed companies to concentrate on multidimensional segmentation of their customer bases, products, and services. In turn, global markets evolved and experienced the disruptive effects of disintermediation and reintermediation. Customers learned how to exploit the disruption in these global networks by using newly available Internet technology. As these reconstituted supply networks responded to *customer-of-one* pressures, businesses were forced to become more responsive to the customer.

Growing industry consumer and industry sophistication are triggering the development of differentiated operating models – and, increasingly, outsourcing is emerging as a powerful mechanism for delivering change fast. Consider these value drivers:

1 Global brand-led, innovation-oriented companies are *promoting greater customer intimacy* by expanding relationships with the rapid introduction of new products and services.

2 *Ownership of physical assets is declining in importance.* The decapitalized nature of brand-owning companies allows them to shift direction quickly, not only into new markets, but also into new sectors. This creates entirely new options within the global marketplace.

3 *Increased flexibility to reconfigure and redirect capacity quickly,* as technology is exploited to optimize continuous supply and demand chains. This improves physical and working capital efficiency and supports high-speed communications – leading to an erosion of pricing power.

4 *Disintermediation of non-value added processes* is also driving down overall costs and enabling a closer interface between the customer and the supplier. Additional revenues are generated as low-cost discount retailers, such as Aldi in Europe, sell premium brand products at significantly lower prices than competitors.

The trend towards *decapitalizing* business – moving away from a focus on physical asset investment to a focus on intangible asset investment – is illustrated in Figure 2.2.

The evolution of global markets is creating new options for leading players, enabling them to rapidly reconfigure their business models and take advantage of advancing technology and outsourcing as the business environment changes.

Companies that are skilled at exploiting this dynamic growth – like Wal-Mart and Nokia – have a right to feel confident. Such companies continued to innovate during the 1990s downturn and were therefore well-positioned for success when the upturn arrived.

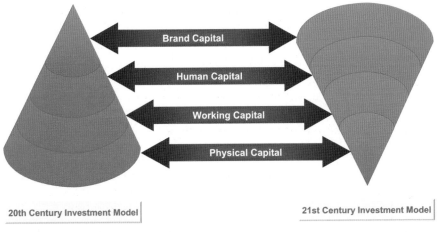

Source: The CFO as Business Integrator, Wiley, 2003 by Cedric Read, Hans Dieter Scheuermann and the mySAP Financials Team

Figure 2.2   *Trend toward intangible asset investment*

INNOVATION IN CONSUMER GOODS AND RETAIL

As we move into the advancing stages of the next upturn, history is repeating itself. A select group of high-performance companies, identified by Accenture's high-performance business research, have distinguished themselves from their competitors by delivering consistent shareholder returns.

Consumer goods and retailing clearly illustrate this accelerated pace of change and rapid development. In Figure 2.3, we show how this group has performed in the *home and personal care* and *superstore* segments against their peers in the Standard & Poor's 500 (S&P 500).

The key dimensions these businesses demonstrate superior performance upon, include:

- Consistently strong returns to shareholders

- Ability to drive revenue growth above industry norms

- Create value over the cost of capital

- Managing for today and for tomorrow.

Wal-Mart is a good example of a company that operates like a high-performance business with a clear strategic intent, an obsession with cus-

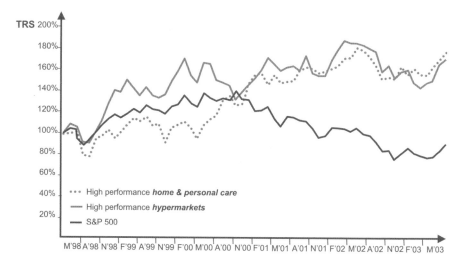

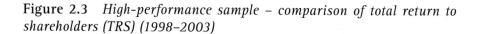

Sources: Factset, Accenture analysis, 2003

Figure 2.3 *High-performance sample – comparison of total return to shareholders (TRS) (1998–2003)*

tomers, and a focus on innovation. It also is acknowledged as a leader in operational excellence and a shaper of alliances between consumer goods manufacturers and retailers.

In the consumer products sector, the barriers as to who does what are fading between the manufacturer, the distributor, and the retailer. Organizations are repositioning themselves to take advantage of the greater profit pool made available to them by extending their value chain. Some companies are going as far as 'valuing their value chain' – examining where they create value and where they destroy value.

In Figure 2.4, we illustrate how some companies have mastered the management of these dimensions in their business.

New technologies are making their presence felt, opening up new opportunities, and closing down others. Increased communications and two-way information flows are breaking the mold. Suppliers and customers are collaborating and sharing information across previously impenetrable barriers; in some sectors competitors are joining forces in what once would have been unthinkable combinations.

Who will be the winners and the losers? Consider the significant impact of 'mega-retailers' on their industry. For example, Wal-Mart's

Competencies	Example
Clear Strategic Intent	• **Wal-Mart:** "Lowering the cost of living for everyone"
	• **Avon:** Best understand & satisfy the product, service & self-fulfillment needs of women globally
Talent Management	• **Colgate:** Key criteria of long-term managerial incentive plan is a 90% retention of all "high potentials"
	• **Target:** Offer flexible staffing, menu benefits, more balanced scheduling & family support to attract & retain the best employees for their stores
Obsessive Customer Focus	• **Loblaws:** Unique private label products, extensive array of lifestyle and convenience offerings, and community building through "Upstairs at Loblaw"
	• **Target:** First US retailer to offer Smart Visa Card, where smart chip captures increased shopper insights & enables personalized rewards tied to the card
Innovation & Execution to Value	• **Beiersdorf:** Core brand (Nivea) successfully extended into new categories, e.g. suncare, babycare, face care, and Nivea Men
	• **Alberto Culver:** Successful new product launches (e.g. Alberto VO5 Herbals and TRESemme Hydrology) rely on insights and trends gleaned from professional customers of Sally and Beauty Systems Group
Operational Excellence	• **Avon:** Well defined, continuous programs for driving cost improvements to help fund strategic investments
	• **Colgate:** Intense focus on productivity improvements helped Colgate reap higher profits without increasing price of tube of toothpaste in the US for the past decade
	• **Wal-Mart:** Supply chain and Information Technology leader
Alliances and Partnerships	• **Target:** Designer partnerships, exclusive product lines from major manufacturers, partnerships with Amazon for eCommerce and with famous chefs for SuperTarget
	• **Costco:** Joint ventures in the UK, Taiwan, and Mexico; partnerships with major manufacturers
	• **Alberto Culver:** Exclusive relationships with salon brands and other vendors result in 90% of product range not being available in Food / Drug mass channels

Source: Accenture analysis and secondary research, 2003

Figure 2.4 *High performance competencies – examples in action*

constant willingness to reformulate its business model – including logistics and purchasing strategy – and to fulfill evolving customer needs is legendary, driving its recognition throughout the industry as an innovative pioneer.

CASE STUDY
Wal-Mart –technology pioneer

Wal-Mart found that within its price-sensitive consumer segment, customers want to purchase almost the same products available elsewhere, but more cheaply and in bulk. Their stores have little display or floor help. The prices are lower, the margins thinner, but the customers are loyal – and the company has a resilient operating model that is highly resistant to attacks from competitors.

Wal-Mart owns and operates more than 108 distribution centers in the US alone. These distribution centers are at the heart of the company's success; by strategically locating retail outlets near distribution centers, the company can resupply its stores directly – often on a daily basis. Wal-Mart recently issued a stunning edict: By 2006, the company wants all its suppliers to place radio frequency identification (RFID) tags on all cases and pallets shipped to its distribution centers. Unlike traditional bar codes, which rely on line-of-sight technology, RFID tags – which are microchips with antennae – emit signals that are read by electronic readers. These readers, in turn, are integrated with the company's enterprise applications, such as inventory management. RFID tags will provide precise information on the whereabouts of merchandise as it moves along the company's supply chain.

The RFID tag is just the tip of the iceberg. Manufacturers will have to change their packaging lines and their finished goods warehouses. Problems may abound with the technology, but it is doubtful that many consumer goods manufacturers will want to disappoint Wal-Mart!

In Chapter 11, we go on to describe the impact of this and other emerging technologies on the finance function. Innovation in its widest sense includes developing new products and services, new ways of working, and new commercial arrangements, such as outsourcing. Companies should take a fresh look at their industry's sources of value – especially customer value. They can then change their products, services, delivery platforms, assets, and capabilities to provide value in the most profitable way.

Companies – be they high performers or weaker performers who are currently on the journey to high performance – all seek the same competency characteristics. Specifically, they have an appetite for innovation and new technology – and are capable of forming alliances and industry collaborations. This provides them with structural flexibility. *In some cases they incorporate outsourcing arrangements into the heart of their operating models.* Key examples include: BP in the oil industry; P&G, and Nestlé in consumer goods; BellSouth in telecommunications.

Outsourcing is similar in its impact to a disruptive technology; it can have far-reaching effects on the make-up of whole industries. Think about the influence that broadband and wireless technology is having on working methods in both large and small companies. The disruption occurs as companies embed the outsource solutions into their operating model and pressure increases on the retained organization to improve related internal processes.

COPING WITH MAJOR UPHEAVAL

In today's volatile economy, responding to market changes with the wrong business model can be fatal. But it happens all the time. How can you be sure that your company will still be around five years from now – or next year, for that matter? Simple – by nimbly adjusting your business model as markets change. Easier said than done! While it is hard enough to make the right strategic decisions, it is just as important to avoid making the wrong ones. Consider the current upheaval in the music industry.

CASE STUDY
Revolution in the music industry

This industry is evolving rapidly, presenting traditional players with serious survival challenges. Dennis Kooker, the head of North America Finance at Bertelsmann Music Group (BMG) Entertainment explains:

'The music industry topline has decreased by 25% and at some point in the future, companies will reach a critical survival point.' Yet the challenges faced by the music industry – ranging from production and publication to retailing – cannot be entirely attributed to piracy over the Internet. While piracy is eroding music sales, this is merely symptomatic of the collapse of many of the barriers to entry that protected traditional players in the past. The industry's historic value proposition is being undermined by:

1 Better, cheaper product technology: *Customers have access to improved and affordable technology, such as MP3 players, that facilitate electronic music downloads and reduce the demand for physical CDs. Opportunities to experience free music have left consumers unconvinced that a retail tag of $12.99 for a CD is fair market value.*

2 Improved domestic production technology: *Artists are less dependent upon the financial sponsorship and investment of big music companies, which traditionally behaved as banks. Today's artists can produce their own music at a reasonably high standard using easily available technology. They also have access to industry know-how via Internet communities. Taking this non-traditional route releases artists from the obligation to repay record companies for their R&D investment prior to making a profit.*

3 Disintermediation: *Uninhibited by the need to develop physical assets, competitors can easily enter the market. Facilitated by the Internet, they can quickly establish worldwide customer channels. Without the overhead of production and development, these companies have a significant pricing advantage.*

4 Pressurized artist and repertoire (A&R) budgets: *As revenues fall, music companies are taking a more conservative R&D approach, preferring to focus on established artists. The decision to play it safe has a negative impact on established industry players by pushing up-and-coming artists into the arms of new entrants. But without the infusion of fresh talent, a record label's brand can quickly lose value.*

5 Aggressive protection of intellectual property: *Incumbents have found themselves in an aggressive fight to protect artists against piracy. Unfortunately, this stance has adversely affected the mega-players' once-loyal customer base.*

6 Funding media, marketing, & promotion: *Hard-hit revenue streams are making marketing – the lifeblood of entertainment companies – more difficult to fund. This is weakening the industry's traditional value proposition. Artists now have a rich array of market channels to choose from. Thriving online music communities also provide alternative means of promotion.*

7 Packaging & presentation: *The value of presentation in the consumer experience has changed. For example, consumers who can download a digital reproduction have no need to spend money on a pre-packaged CD.*

8 Sales & distribution: *Teenagers are visiting retail outlets less and less to buy their music. As this traditional channel is overtaken by its alternatives, established music players are being forced to re-evaluate market access.*

Everyone knows that the music industry is under siege from piracy. Music and entertainment are rapidly becoming commodities. Although the volume of music consumed has increased, prices have decreased due to music downloads and CD burning. Consumers can now readily access CD burning technology; a child can go to school with up to 50 CDs in his bag and sell them. Historically, most of the music value chain was kept in-house. Companies owned their own studios and artwork was handled internally, along with back-office activities. This previously insular industry is now having to look at new ways of doing business – potentially with new partners.

In Figure 2.5, these changes are correlated to the music industry value chain. The segment of the value chain that covers the storing, packaging, and retrieval of music

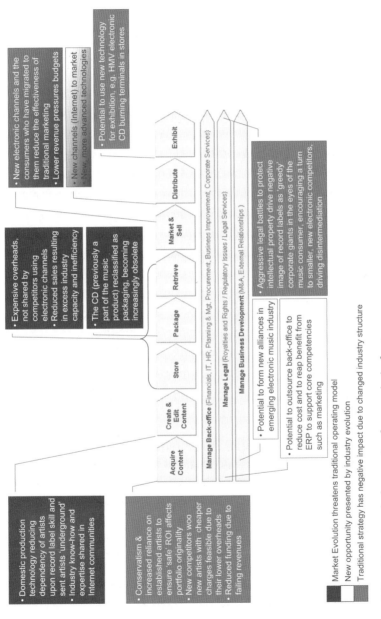

Figure 2.5 *Structural change in the music industry*

using on-line technologies is having a profound impact on the industry. Similarly, traditional marketing and selling approaches are experiencing significant competitive attack.

Dennis Kooker of BMG comments: 'In the music industry manufacturing and physical distribution are no longer considered core, but they are substantial fixed costs that limit our flexibility moving forward.'

Clearly, outsourcing can be used as a cost-reduction mechanism by increasing efficiency and freeing up cash for investment. Some music companies have found that by joining with the right outsourcing partner, they have been able to reinforce their marketing function – a core capability. As one CFO explains:

'We were facing a serious challenge. Although we had a traditional shared service center, our systems were not standard, so we introduced a new management system that enabled us to interpret data consistently. We now have high-quality data for decision support. For example, we can now correlate airplay data with follow-on sales information; this has helped us market more effectively.

'We also wanted to centralize our accounting globally. We benchmarked our process performance against companies in the pharmaceutical industry, which has much in common with the music industry, including a strong focus on intellectual property and R&D. Since introducing global standards, we have improved spending control through centralized purchase ordering. Outsourcing has given us the opportunity to find a partner who could help generate process efficiency improvements in order-to-cash management.'

As the current state of the music industry clearly demonstrates, there are a number of business-model traps that companies must avoid. These range from clinging to an outdated business model, despite dramatic market shifts, to rushing to alter existing business models in the wrong direction!

So, how do you evaluate whether or not you have the optimum business model? The components you need to analyze range from revenue models and value propositions to organizational structures and trading relationships. To assess the overall effectiveness of your organization's business model, follow these four steps:

1 **Identify your sources of revenue:** What is current and what is in development?

2 **Identify your value propositions:** What drives your ability to generate and sustain each revenue stream?

3 **Identify your delivery model:** What enables you to realize your value propositions profitably and consistently?

4 **Identify your leverageable assets:** What are your capabilities, resources, and relationships?

The results of this exercise should be mapped to your company's value chain. Each component of the business model – or value chain – should be assigned revenues, costs, and investment figures. When taken together and expressed in terms of future cash flow, these components represent total shareholder value. This should provide the economic blueprint for deciding what to *insource* and what to *outsource.*

A strategic question regularly asked by finance executives is where to cut business processes – and what the timing of the outsourcing program should be. They want to know whether the outsourcing arrangement should start small and grow in progressive steps or whether a more radical, aggressive stance should be taken. The answer depends on the health of the business, the sustainability of current strategy, and the strength of executive leadership. These and other criteria depend upon a company's individual circumstances. These questions are examined more fully in Chapter 4 – deciding what to outsource.

THE PHARMACEUTICAL NETWORKED MODEL

The pharmaceutical industry offers examples of companies with integrated value chains in which economics vary substantially from one value chain component to another. To quote the CFO of a leading US-based global pharmaceutical company: 'If you take the market capitalization of our company at $50bn, a *third* is tied up in existing products which are currently on the market, a *third* in drugs in our pipeline which have yet to reach the market, and a *third* in the market's perception of the value of our future R&D.'

- **R&D:** *Much of the value of a pharmaceutical company is tied up in pipeline activity and intangible assets – products that are on patent and* *expected to go to market. Drugs at various stages of development have a future value – although this is difficult to determine on a cost basis – and can be traded as assets before they reach the market.*

- **Manufacturing:** *This activity is tied to strict quality standards regulated by the Federal Drug Administration (FDA). However, some companies choose to insource and others to outsource various parts of their supply chain. Such outsourcing decisions are made on quality, security of supply, and economic benefits.*

- **Sales and distribution:** *One pharmaceutical company may have a competitive advantage with its sales network in North America, for example; another may dominate this area in Europe. Competitors in the industry often cross-license their products to take advantage of relative sales and distribution strengths.*

By analyzing the value of each of these components and the cost effectiveness of the integrated value chain as a whole, decisions are taken as to how much to invest, where, and when. This financial discipline and rigor is also applied to processes that support the value-creating core – such as finance, legal, IT, HR, and facilities.

Pharmaceutical companies are beginning to use outsourcing not just to cut costs, but to gain strategic benefits. Ken Lacey, the UK-based managing partner of Accenture's global health and life sciences practice, comments:[4]

'To determine how pharmaceutical firms are using outsourcing to become high-performing businesses, Accenture recently surveyed some 160 senior healthcare executives across the US and Europe. An overwhelming majority – 87% – said that outsourcing had increased their control of business results in a variety of critical areas, especially in planning. While these executives wanted outsourcing to deliver traditional benefits, such as cost reduction and containment, they also sought strategic results. These included better focus on core activities, access to innovation, faster response time to support internal information needs, and ongoing process improvement.'

Pharmaceutical companies regularly take their lead from other industries in outsourcing best practice. Yet few sectors have as much experience in contracting with service providers to achieve tactical business outcomes. Many of the industry's executives use outsourcing to achieve greater consistency and cohesion in their sprawling global networks of manufacturing, packaging, formulation, clinical trial, and sales organizations.

In fact, 42% of companies outsource IT, information learning and training (31%), supply chain (22%), human resources (20%), finance and accounting (18%), and customer relationship management (8%).

These results illustrate that when pharmaceutical companies grow, merge, and acquire they move from their original *'ownership'* model – in which they maintain in-house control over most functions to a *'partnership'* model – in which they outsource responsibilities for specific functions. Others, however, are increasingly using outsourcing as a strategic tool and are adopting a *'networked'* model.

Some pharmaceutical companies are exploring the potential of broader outsourcing, keen to make massive leaps in efficiency and effectiveness. With a determination to focus on their core capabilities, they are pursuing increasingly far-reaching arrangements to reap both strategic and tactical benefits.

Industries that are increasingly investing in intangible assets, such as R&D in pharmaceutical firms, or brands in consumer goods, are primary candidates for outsourcing parts of their physical supply chain and back-office processes. This trend is illustrated in Figure 2.6.

SO WHAT DO YOU OUTSOURCE – AND WHY?

Outsourcing can affect an existing business model in many ways: by reducing cost or adding competency, by improving or extending the model or by radically transforming it. For example, in the telecommunications industry, the growth of shared services, the need for internal

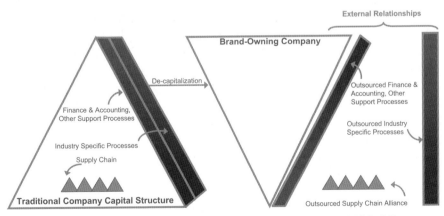

Source: "Meta-Capitalism: the eBusiness Revolution and the design of 21st-century companies and markets", Grady Means and David Schneider, PricewaterhouseCoopers, John Wiley & Sons, 2000

Figure 2.6 *Business model migration to outsourcing*

cost transparency, and the drive for overhead cost reduction have all combined to provide a solid, organic foundation for outsourcing. Increasingly, telecommunications carriers are building new outsourcing supplier relationships, not only to reduce costs, but also to gain flexibility and market access – and refocus in-house resources on their core business capabilities. Consider the comments of Ron Dykes, CFO of BellSouth.

CASE STUDY
Making the decision to extend outsourcing

'Most of our business value resides in our core competencies around technology, network operating, and customer service. BellSouth has invested very heavily in shared services. We have two massive customer call and bill processing centers which service 25m customers a month. These centers also support our internal processes and affect some 60,000 or more employees. We use shared services for other parts of our transaction processing, such as accounts receivable, payables, HR, and even the general ledger. We have achieved economies of scale and believe our service and cost performance to be in at least the upper quartile of external benchmark comparisons. We are already experiencing the benefits of more clearly defined credit policies and improved collections.

'The next step might be to consider outsourcing and possibly offshoring to benefit from labor cost arbitrage. Wage rates are still relatively high in Atlanta, where we are headquartered. We do already have experience in outsourcing the IT function. Generally this was a good strategy; some things went well, others not so well. It was the right thing to do and we are continuing to upgrade our IT capability by following the outsourcing route. For the finance function, I would not outsource value-adding activities such as planning and analysis or decision support. We would, however, consider outsourcing some of the more routine transaction processing activities.'

Over the last two decades, the structure and nature of the telecommunications industry have changed dramatically. But, the operating models of its leading players have not. Slowing growth, severe price-based competition, and high customer acquisition costs mean that both the landline and wireless industries are struggling to return their cost of capital.[5]

The transition to a lean, strategically focused structure represents a dramatic break from the past for an industry with traditionally heavy physical assets. The corporate headquarters must shift its focus from just running the business to developing the capabilities necessary to support its new operating model. Roles, responsibilities, and relationships within the organization must all be redefined.

The merger wave of the late 1990s taught the telecommunications industry an important lesson: 'You can buy size, but you have to *engineer* scale.' In addition to improving cost structure, customers are more demanding. They want bundled offerings, customized solutions, and 'single channel' service. Customer intimacy will be the prime source of competitive differentiation. To strengthen operating economics and business unit linkages, telecommunications service providers will need to change the way that they do business.

Generally, companies can change their operating models in various ways, as illustrated in Figure 2.7.

While organizational choices and configurations differ across the telecommunications industry and there are many sectors (local, long distance, and wireless) – the basic elements of the new operating models are consistent:

- Business units formed around market segments with clear value propositions
- Support services that provide internal clients with responsive, competitive services
- Lean corporate centers
- Partnerships with outsource providers to leverage scale, expertise, and flexibility
- Decision support to bring organizational elements together in executing strategy.

STRATEGIES FOR CHANGE AND INNOVATION

A change model provides the core logic for how a firm can evolve to remain profitable in a dynamic environment – and potentially deploy outsourcing as a mechanism. The Accenture Institute for High Performance has identified four change strategies:

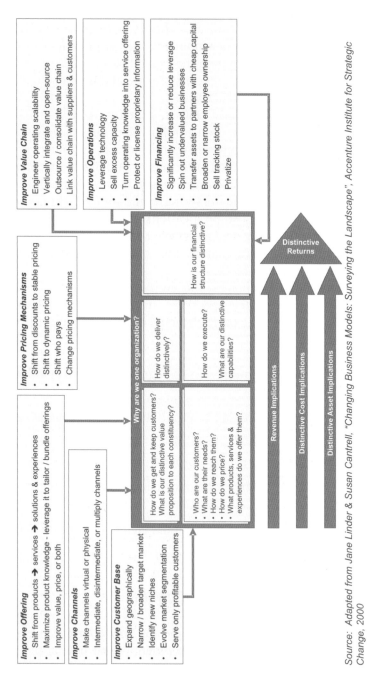

Source: Adapted from Jane Linder & Susan Cantrell, "Changing Business Models: Surveying the Landscape", Accenture Institute for Strategic Change, 2000

Figure 2.7 *Examples of business model choices*

1 **Realization:** Companies use this type of strategy to maximize the returns from their existing mode of operating. They exploit the potential of their current business model to grow and profit.

Microsoft consistently ranks as a company with one of the highest value-adding business models in its industry. It has been supremely successful in maximizing its global market position through a steady stream of software product releases, related technologies, and services. External contractors contribute a high proportion of Microsoft's flexibility and capabilities.

2 **Renewal:** Companies that change through renewal consistently and consciously revitalize their products and services, brands, cost structures, and technology bases. A renewing firm leverages its core skills to create new – *sometimes disruptively new* – positions on the price/value curve.

Fast-moving consumer goods companies like Diageo – the world's leading branded spirits company – have succeeded by treating renewal as both an art and a science. Diageo expanded its traditional drinks brands into 'alcopops' – an entirely new, premium value proposition aimed at reaching younger consumer groups. Smirnoff Vodka, for example, has been reincarnated as Smirnoff Ice. Diageo is following a shared services strategy for its back-office functions. Outsourcing is high on its agenda, starting with IT and applications support.

3 **Extension:** These strategies expand businesses to cover new ground. An extending company stretches its operating model to embrace new markets, value chain functions, product and service lines. New business lines don't replace – *but add to* – existing operations.

Philip Morris, for example, formed a new holding company (Altria) and remains one of the world's leading branded cigarette manufacturers. It also built an entirely new food business, Kraft, via acquisition to diversify away from the increasingly litigious tobacco industry. Recently, Kraft International investigated the feasibility of outsourcing F&A as a way of integrating into shared services and consolidating the support functions from its acquired businesses.

4 **Reinvention:** This involves truly radical transformation. Unlike an extension strategy, the company moves deliberately and purposefully to an entirely new operating model and never returns.

Clearly, this strategy lies at the far end of the change spectrum. Nokia offers a prime example; the company shed its traditional roots in pulp and paper entirely and now focuses on mobile phone technology. Electricity utility companies are choosing between two fundamental strategic options: a focus on customers or a focus on engineering. Companies in the same integrated industry have been known to 'swap' customers for physical assets in pursuit of their strategic focus. Customer call centers and network engineering services are good examples of outsourcing vehicles used in such circumstances.

As companies change their operating models in pursuit of high performance, the CFO and the finance function will need to play their part in constructing the business of the future. If transaction processing is a candidate for outsourcing – standardized, seamless, and automated until human intervention is no longer required – *then how is the finance function of the future to add value?*

Michael Sutcliff, managing partner of Accenture's Finance & Performance Management group, considers, for illustrative purposes, the future role of the CFO – extrapolating current trends in the finance function and speculating on the form it will take in ten years' time.

 ## CASE STUDY
Fast forward to the CFO, ten years hence

Back in 2004, international accounting standards and regulation were dealing with the problems caused by accounting scandals such as Enron, Worldcom, and Parmalat. The reaction engendered by Sarbanes-Oxley was only an initial wake-up call. Something had to be done to better connect the outside world of the stakeholder with the inside world of management.

More than 80% of the value of the typical company in the Fortune 500 was not accounted for in the balance sheet. And the situation was deteriorating. Why? Because more and more of a company's shareholder value was made up of intangible assets – things like brands, R&D, intellectual property, and customers – while the financial world was only generally required to report on the state of physical and tangible assets. The pursuit of ultimate transparency in financial reporting became an obsession among the world's leading finance professionals.

Yes, one set of accounting standards were adopted worldwide. But, legitimate variations in these standards to cope with the varying requirements of different industries overcame the 'one-size-fits-all' approach previously advocated. For example, R&D represents such an overwhelming proportion of a pharmaceutical company's value that reporting standards had to be introduced for the drug devel-opment pipeline. Another example: Brands represent such a significant proportion of a consumer goods company's value that they, too, were subjected to valuation guidelines for reporting purposes.

Perhaps the most controversial change that happened was the requirement for companies to publish their value drivers – those indicators of future cash flow that support investors' current views of shareholder value. Basel II, and subsequent accords in the banking industry, greatly assisted this transition. Under Basel II, financial institutions had to analyze their varying risks for different customer and product combinations to assess their capital adequacy. This exercise was not just useful for capital regulatory requirements, but also opened up a whole new field of value analysis which was later adjusted and adopted for use in other industries. Understanding where value is created or destroyed – and crucially what is driving that value – at this level of granularity has led to a level of transparency today, in the year 2014, which wasn't dreamt of back in 2004.

The corporate world of the CFO and the finance function is dramatically different from that of ten years ago. The old world financial disciplines governing transaction processing have diverged from the new world financial disciplines governing value creation.

The traditional accounting legislation and standards are now hard-coded and 'shrink-wrapped' into global standard processes and systems. The F&A outsourcing market has matured and consolidated – the previously independent shared service centers of many of the world's leading companies have now been combined to lever-age scale and process specialization. Three leading outsource providers dominate the supplier landscape – each competes using its global network of delivery centers to balance workload with risk.

The role of senior finance executives has shifted, with more attention focused on developing capabilities across the business. This is necessary to target and deliver value as new opportunities arise. As transaction processing and controls have become more stable and efficient, senior finance executives have led the develop-

ment of enterprise-level risk management and performance management capabilities. As a trusted business advisor across the enterprise, the finance organization has developed new capabilities in value chain economics and value reporting.

Value management is now the discipline connecting the management team's decisions and actions as they respond, with flexibility and innovation, to constantly changing business conditions and opportunities. Speaking a common language and using a common set of information tools, the management team is finally able to rapidly assess and respond to changes in the competitive environment.

Unlike the CFO of old, the new CFO is more concerned with 'resource attraction' than 'resource allocation'. The goal is to attract the right people to execute new value-creating strategies and resolve value-chain bottlenecks. Human, not financial, capital is the real key to exploiting innovation and achieving superior performance. The CFO has truly become the internal venture capitalist – resourcing the ideas that work, and abandoning the ideas that fail.

Inside corporate organizations, the traditional functional boundaries between finance, HR, and IT have blurred. Specialist IT expertise is provided externally by the technology industry. Self-service and online analytics build on data warehouses information to provide seamless decision support.

A new information industry has grown up around the increased collaboration between suppliers and customers, and the increased transparency between business partners. This explosion in information has in itself become regarded as a 'disruptive technology' – disrupting the configuration of value chains both within and between organizations. The achievement of shareholder value – as it migrates from one industry to another, one part of the world to another – means organizations have to reconfigure faster, transform more radically, and focus on innovation more fiercely than ever before. Information transparency has exposed the inefficiencies of the world's economic systems as we knew them – only true business partnerships built on trust and long-lasting, real relationships will provide the necessary flexibility and resilience to resist the resulting competitive pressures on value.

The finance professional is now much closer to filling the accounting black hole and to becoming the true business partner. He or she is also much closer to the ultimate finance vision – increased structural flexibility, dramatically reduced physical investment, near-to-complete transparency, well-managed risks – all while the business is under absolute control!

CFO INSIGHTS

- High-performance businesses are those that deliver the greatest possible total return to stakeholders (TRS); high returns on invested capital; revenue growth above industry norm; and are managed for today and managed for tomorrow. They are becoming lean and mean in their use of capital.

- High performers consider which core competencies are critical to driving value and know when to extend their capabilities by partnering in areas both inside and outside their core. Outsourcing is emerging as a mechanism that can deliver change *fast*, while minimizing risk.

- Outsourcing is similar in its impact to a disruptive technology; it is having far-reaching effects on the make-up of whole industries. The evolution of global markets is creating new options for leading players, enabling them to rapidly reconfigure their business models and take advantage of advancing technology and outsourcing as the business environment changes.

- Companies are increasingly investing in intangible assets and innovation – product, process, and service. From entertainment, to travel, to research-based companies – they are all prime candidates for outsourcing and want to unlock the invested capital tied up in physical assets and in non-differential, back-office service functions.

- Current trends in globalization of accounting standards and regulations are accelerating standardization in processes and systems. As the F&A outsourcing market matures, previously independent shared service delivery centers are now combining together to create global networks that are able to balance workload and risk.

FROM INSIGHT TO ACTION

CONSIDER THE CHARACTERISTICS OF HIGH PERFORMANCE
Understand which core competencies are critical to driving value. Do you truly understand your industry's value drivers, both current and potential? Ensure your leadership team adapts quickly and flexibly to change.

REVIEW YOUR ORGANIZATION'S CORE LOGIC FOR CREATING VALUE
Can you define your company's value propositions for your stakeholders? Define what is best in class for the crucial operating processes in your industry. Single out assets, capabilities, and relationships that will create the most value in supporting your business model.

AVOID COMMON TRAPS
Responding to market changes with the wrong business model can be fatal. Don't cling to a weak value proposition; don't choke on physical assets. Focus on customers who will create the most value over the longer term. Adjust your business model and align your pricing policies with it.

REFLECT ON YOUR ORGANIZATION'S BUSINESS ANATOMY
Winning business models are hard to imitate. Ask yourself, *honestly,* whether your organization offers unique value. Ensure that your business model has sufficient barriers to entry to protect future profit streams.

VALUE THE VALUE CHAIN!
Segregate and evaluate individual business model components. Which create value, which destroy value? Identify the economics of each business component – their future revenue, cost, and investment. Benchmark externally. Make well-informed, conscious decisions on sourcing – what to insource, what to outsource.

DON'T CHANGE YOUR BUSINESS MODEL FRANTICALLY OR WITHOUT DIRECTION!
Carefully chart and follow a course for change. Decide on the right change strategy. Is it: maximizing your existing operating model? Creating new positions on the price/value curve? Extending the business to cover completely new ground? Moving to an entirely new business model?

> IMPROVE YOUR ORGANIZATION'S FOCUS
> Do the people in your organization understand the operating model and
> how they contribute to it? Do they know what makes your firm distinctive
> and how it makes money? Make sure that decision-making everywhere in
> the organization – from the corporate ivory tower to the front line – sup-
> ports the value-creating agenda.

REFERENCES

1 Gary Hamel and Liisa Valinkangas, The Quest for Resilience, *Harvard Business Review*, 2003.

2 Jane Linder and Susan Cantrell, What Makes A Good Business Model Anyway? Can Yours Stand The Test Of Change? *Outlook Point of View*, 2001. www.accenture.com

3 Jane Linder and Susan Cantrell, Business Models: Cautionary Tales, *Outlook*, January 2001. www.accenture.com

4 Ken Lacey, High Performance Outsourcing: Gaining Control Through Outsourcing, *Scrip Magazine*, PJB Publications, December 2003.

5 Stefan Elkemann, Michael Fritsch, Monique Ouduk and Michael Stomberg, *Outsourcing Trends in European Telecom Industry*, Booz Allen Hamilton, 2003.

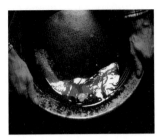

CHAPTER 3

Suppliers: Options for Service Delivery

CONSIDERING FUTURE BUSINESS PARTNERS

Wolfgang Reichenberger
EVP Finance, Nestlé

Nestlé, one of the world's leading consumer products companies, employs more than 250,000 people. Its market capitalization is approximately $100bn, and it has an industry-leading portfolio of brands, many of which hold top market positions. Wolfgang Reichenberger, the group CFO, talks about the company's strategy:

'*Increasingly, we are focusing on sophisticated, high-margin, value-adding products that affect the well-being of our consumers, contribute to longer, better lives for them – and create enjoyment. This strategy puts special emphasis on research and innovation. As CFO, I see my role as that of an internal venture capitalist – financing good ideas, evaluating risks, and identifying opportunities.*'

One of Nestlé's strategic objectives is improving margins. This presents Wolfgang with a dilemma: how to fund increasing demand for research and development (R&D), while generating more profit. He says:

'*We believe in brand diversity and adapting to local markets. Our business strategy and planning is focused on products. Two years ago we launched a venture capital fund to explore fresh avenues for innovation. In no way has all invention to come from within the company. Research and development costs should not be a drain on profit. We treat such cost as an investment, and demand a return on the investment. If R&D can not deliver higher margins, I question its value.'*

Nestlé is a complex company. Its many different product categories have many geographic variations. Chocolate in France, for example, is very different from chocolate in neighboring Switzerland. To manage these complexities, Nestlé is aligning its global supply chains and making its back-office operations more efficient. Wolfgang goes on to say:

'Our priorities in finance? Driving functional excellence, setting standards, developing KPIs for risk management and decision support. We are implementing initiatives to help us act as a global company, rather than as a series of national companies. Where appropriate, we operate as a global product/market organization – in servicing companies such as Wal-Mart, for example. We are developing a global business approach, aligning our business processes to best practice with our Project GLOBE and the worldwide roll-out of SAP, our ERP implementation. Gradually, it will give us more global standardization, better customer and product profitability information on a global basis, and global efficiencies in purchasing and supply. We will become faster, more efficient and more flexible.'

The benefits Wolfgang is seeking for Nestlé include purchasing reductions, lower IT costs, shared services, low supply chain costs, and increased efficiencies: ' We are making considerable progress in our quest for a world class finance function. We are honest enough to admit that we don't have all the answers; we are always searching for better tools and techniques. We want to centralize everything that we can in the back-office: whatever the consumer cannot taste, smell, touch, eat or drink. The answer lies in improving operational efficiency. We are changing our mind-set at Nestlé. Our new global operating style lets us overcome country-based silos. We are working more interactively – sharing knowledge and support services.

'We have already removed many financial and support competence areas from the individual responsibility of many markets, such as Treasury, Legal, Intellectual Property, Tax Planning and Strategic Purchasing. Those functions operate today as virtual, or even physical insourced shared services.

'Nestlé is considering the merits of insourcing vs. outsourcing. Shedding non-core activities is not a new phenomenon for us. For example, while cocoa powder, cocoa butter, or basic milk production are not part of Nestlé's core business, it is important to have innovative and interactive relationships with our suppliers. Infor-

mation needs to be shared across the extended value chain, but it is not important to own all the assets involved and perform all processes in-house.'

But what are the implications of this for the finance function? Wolfgang believes a key benefit of going outside could be the increased speed at which you can make change happen:

'We have some areas where we are exploring the opportunities and seeing the benefits that outsourcing can bring. We have found it can accelerate change and bring in new expertise. At the moment we are asking ourselves what our core competencies are. Treasury and pensions, for example, are central to risk management, which materially affects our group results. But there are functions in transaction processing areas that are non-core; with control parameters, they could possibly be outsourced.' Wolfgang is open to new ideas for structuring new, shared service centers.

'We are considering all kinds of capital participation, including joint venturing on shared services. Part of my job is directing capital efficiently to achieve our strategic priorities. The value proposition for outsourcing is based as much on the assets that our outsourcing partner brings to the table as it is on our internal savings potential.'

The business case for outsourcing is interesting, perhaps the biggest benefit being the chance to standardize and re-engineer business processes by using the expertise of a seasoned outsourcing provider. Wolfgang also hopes to leverage investment in the company's Project GLOBE SAP implementation.

Supplier selection is important to get right. When evaluating potential outsourcing partners Wolfgang establishes clear selection criteria:

'We look for an outsource provider that can offer a good cultural fit with Nestlé. Like us, they should have a strong global understanding – and they should have the resources needed to work in our local markets.' He continues:

'Our key concern is the probability of success. We chose to run an outsourcing pilot with one partner because we were impressed by their ability to provide the necessary leadership to make it happen – and get it right first time.'

The key requirements, for choosing our outsourcing partners, were as follows:

- High probability of success – *including good service continuity and economic benefits*

- Strong cultural fit – *resources should be aligned to work in specific local markets*
- Assured benefits – *a fixed price until the arrangement stabilizes, with shared risk and reward mechanisms*
- Flexibility in operations – *to allow for short-term volume fluctuations, and a governance structure that allows for the swift resolution of issues and change management*
- Local service capability – *experienced leadership and staff responsible for local countries.*

The pilot arrangement between Nestlé and its outsourcing provider stresses value creation. Nestlé signed contracts and commenced the pilot arrangement in late 2003. The first wave of outsourcing pilots took place in Denmark and Norway, followed by Sweden and Finland. This pilot project is monitored carefully, to assist decisions on future moves.

Success will depend, in part, on the provider's proven approach to planning, work shadowing, and stabilization. The primary focus on people changes is supported by a technology program incorporating a highly sophisticated virtual private network (VPN) with connectivity between Nestlé's intranet and the shared service center. The VPN offers flexibility across the provider's global delivery center network. It also provides resources to manage demand peaks and back-up service in the event of disaster recovery. Risk analysis, mitigation, and management are being given top priority. Wolfgang considers the relationship:

'We are very open and prepared to consider all kinds of alliances that bring capital participation or expertise that we do not have in-house, including joint ventures. Outsourcing is a key question that we must address and there is no simple or clear-cut solution. An arrangement will have to make good economic sense. The Nestlé GLOBE best practice program and the internal efficiency improvement program (dubbed FitNes) are already streamlining our transactional processes and generating cost savings, so we will be even more demanding when we evaluate the business case for outsourcing.'

In this chapter, we consider the range of outsourcing options available to the CFO, examine the relative merits of each, and provide guidance on how to select the right business partner for your organization. Having helped you choose the right business partner, we then outline the stages of business diagnosis and solution design. Our goal? To help match your needs with what is available in the outside market – and build the best possible service delivery model for your company.

TRENDS IN BUSINESS PROCESS OUTSOURCING (BPO)

BPO is not new; some leading-edge relationships are more than a decade old. But what exactly is it? Simply defined, BPO involves: Contracting with an external organization to transfer primary responsibility for providing a business process or function. The key to success, in embracing BPO, is understanding the dynamics of your organization and being very specific about what you want to achieve from outsourcing. The outsourcing decision has three facets: vendor capabilities, cost and benefits, and cultural fit. Each of these must be evaluated in the context of your organization and its requirements. Your objective is straightforward: Craft the solution that positions your organization for long-term success.

In today's economy, BPO extends beyond technology infrastructure or even application maintenance. The outsourcing service provider takes responsibility for ensuring that the process works, interfaces effectively with other company functions, and delivers the outcomes intended. Traditionally, organizations applied a simple rationale when considering BPO: Outsource non-core activities to niche providers who offer best-practice processes to achieve cost savings and focus on strategic issues. Today, although this rule still applies, the issue of control and how it is managed is much higher on the CFO's agenda. So is radical performance improvement.

Furthermore, the potential reach and impact of BPO has changed significantly. Some companies still contract out narrow processes to achieve cost savings. But more enterprising businesses have begun to use BPO creatively for very different goals. Trailblazing leaders are:[1]

1 **Raising the bar:** Organizations are moving beyond using BPO as an operational lever aimed at cost reduction and deploying it as a strategic tool to gain and sustain competitive advantage.

2 **Outsourcing several processes to one supplier:** Although 95% of current BPO spending is still for discrete processes such as billing or payroll, 61% of organizations use a single provider to handle multiple processes to simplify relationships and improve integration.

3 **Outsourcing strategic as well as tactical processes:** Only 35% of companies now limit outsourcing to processes of low strategic value; 65% outsource processes of medium-to-high strategic value.

4 **Expanding operational boundaries to drive value:** Organizations are looking beyond the attractions of inexpensive labor. They are now open to sharing their delivery logistics with direct competitors to increase scale efficiencies without compromising the competitive attributes of their core business. Netsourcing (outsourcing applications that run on the Web) offers the benefits of self-service processes and accelerated technology roll-out.[2]

The bottom line? Two trends are occurring simultaneously. One is a shift from transactional processing to strategic BPO. The other is a shift from single-process engagements to comprehensive, multiprocess outsourcing to gain greater synergies and benefits. The integration of collaborative applications and Web-based technologies into BPO offerings has accelerated the shift toward multiprocess outsourcing. Since data from multiple-process interactions can be integrated seamlessly, the delegation of several processes to one provider generates much stronger synergies.

In the past, corporates would outsource individual processes to different providers (for instance, payroll to one provider and benefits to another). Today, more and more companies are combining several BPO engagements into one. Providers now deliver BPO services across a range of processes or act as integrators, overseeing multiple BPO providers for their clients.

Traditionally, the evolution towards multiprocess outsourcing in one location occurs in a phased approach: through several contract extensions, rather than 'big bang' outsourcing engagements. More recently, where state-of-the-art service centers are the destination, the change to multiprocess in one location can be made in one move – the accelerated approach. Figure 3.1 contrasts these two implementation strategies.

The best candidates for multiprocess outsourcing are companies that are already outsourcing individual processes and now want to outsource additional processes, either to their current provider(s) or to an integrator.

In Chapter 1, we identified three principal outsourcing options:

1 **Conventional outsourcing:** Companies off-load their support functions onto specialist providers to cut costs and enable managers to focus on core issues.

3.1 a Traditional two step approach: solution implementation and location change are *stepped*

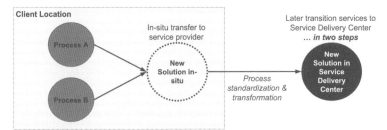

3.1 b Accelerated one step approach: solution implementation and location change are *simultaneous*

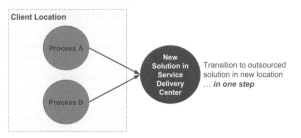

Figure 3.1   *Traditional versus accelerated implementation*

2 **Collaborative outsourcing:** Companies partner with outsourcing providers to upgrade their processes with the dual goals of cutting costs and gaining flexibility.

3 **Business transformation outsourcing (BTO):** Companies join with their partners to transform the way their businesses work in order to achieve dramatic, sustainable improvement company wide – often based on new IT capabilities and business processes.

In our research, we've found that companies are employing these outsourcing options in a host of ways, some traditional and some innovative:

An Internet search engine company successfully uses a conventional approach to outsourcing, with the sole objective of reducing the cost of its e-mail customer support division. Executives turned to a niche provider, an India-based customer service outsourcer, for help. By taking advantage of India's lower wage rates, the firm substantially reduced service costs. It needed only minimal interaction with the provider to manage the relation-

ship because both companies clearly spelled out responsibilities, service levels, and pricing structures in their contract.

A specialty chemicals firm worked with an outsourcing provider to improve finance and accounting processes, *which ran on five different systems. Executives were looking for better management information and decision-making in addition to cost improvements – and they've crafted an approach that gives them both. To gain management information benefits, they needed an integrated process, so they turned to a solutions integrator rather than a portfolio of niche providers. Transferring their processes to the provider's shared service center located in Prague should generate substantial cost savings – a 35-to-40% wage rate reduction on top of a 10% headcount cut. They've struck a cooperative relationship to accommodate the significant organizational changes they anticipate.*

A German bank is using an outsource provider to gain expertise that increases in value *when tailored to its specific needs. It works cooperatively with a niche provider under a long-term 'gentleman's agreement.' The director of global leadership development asserts that the cooperative customization approach contributed directly to his organization's successful transformation from a commercial bank to a leading European investment bank.*

HOW FAR SHOULD YOU GO WITH OUTSOURCING?

How far should you go with outsourcing? Many companies are quite satisfied with the conventional approach in driving cost down. However, the full transformation proposition is becoming more attractive. The full *business transformation outsourcing* value proposition, referred to in point three above, is simple but powerful; efficiency and productivity benefits plus the acquisition of new capabilities both within and beyond the finance organization to create incremental economic value. This, in turn, funds strategic initiatives and drives earnings growth.

One of the companies we spoke to, a consumer products company with sales of £600m a year, has outsourced to gain access for the first time to the economies of scale of its pan-European shared services. It has resulted in deep cost savings and has generated significant reductions in working capital. Some of the cash released has been reinvested to create new capability that gives managers unique insights into customer profitability and marketing channel effectiveness. Business transformation outsourcing quite often requires investment – usually in IT and change management. The money has to be found, and if you want to do it quickly, then this year's budget will always be the problem. This is one of the reasons why there is intense interest in working creatively with an outsourcing partner to craft a deal shape that delivers a compelling combination of cost reduction; increased process effectiveness; profitable growth rather than empty growth; and investment in IT – all of which increases the fundamental competitiveness of the business.

When considering which option to pursue, carefully analyze the degree of change you want to make and the increase in value that you seek. Use Figure 3.2 to help assess your company's appetite for change and the potential for value creation that outsourcing can offer.

In our research, we found many cases in which executives used collaborative outsourcing to transform a support function or process. But the radical change stopped there. Business transformation outsourcing sets a higher standard. It is a comprehensive approach designed to create new capabilities and use them to achieve a clear strategic objective (see Figure 3.3).

Is transformation right for you?

Given an option, most executives will avoid huge disruptions, preferring incremental change instead. But in today's volatile business environment, companies are called upon to revamp their business operating

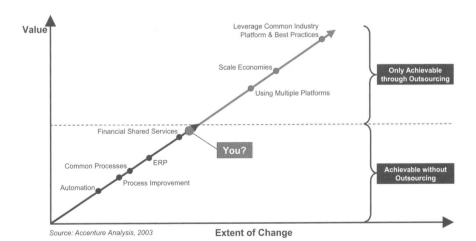

Figure 3.2   *Where are you on the change/value continuum?*

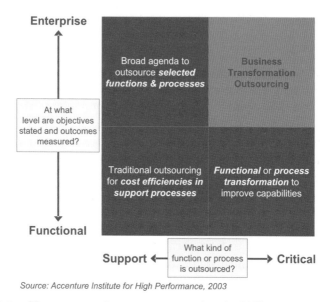

Source: Accenture Institute for High Performance, 2003

Figure 3.3 *How companies use outsourcing in different ways*

model much more frequently than ever before. Not surprisingly, even industry leaders often don't have all the skills and capabilities they need in-house to handle such intense and accelerated change.

Companies that have performed less well against peer group competitors should seriously consider using business transformation outsourcing to regain their position. Such companies are usually looking for a comprehensive service, trying to get the basics right, yet seeking to boost innovation as well. They need stability, security, and reliability.

Is your company in this situation? If you answer yes to most of the questions below, transformational outsourcing may well work for you. Even if you're not quite ready to fully commit to transformational outsourcing, you can start taking steps in that direction:

- Is speed a critical factor in implementing this radical change?

- Is the scale of transformation required challenging?

- Do you need more people and skills in order to accomplish it?

- Are you willing to share some of the potential benefits with your partner?

- Do you need capital to fund it? Is it high on your capital allocation priorities?

For companies with an appetite for radical change, business transformation outsourcing is a powerful tool. A pioneering executive recently said: *'This is like using one of those new, high-tech golf clubs. They definitely give you an advantage. But the golf community hesitates to embrace them because they are unconventional. As far as I am concerned, while they sit around debating, I'll move forward. I can use the edge.'*

In Figure 3.4, we show how companies can break through capability and scale barriers to create value by climbing the innovation curve!

THE MOVE TO MULTISOURCING

Integrated solution or best of breed? This argument has been around since the birth of the IT industry. In the IT services market, the pendulum originally swung towards the integrated outsourcing solution – the so-called 'mega deal' – in which the prime contractor takes responsibility for everything. The largest of these agreements can run to over $1bn per year, or $5bn over a typical five-year term.

We believe that this era is coming to an end. IT 'mega deals' have caused thorny problems for both customers and suppliers. The pendulum is now swinging back to either best of breed or to multifunctional, transformational outsourcing. The purely **cost-driven** approach is being replaced by **value-driven** multiprocess deals. We call this 'multisourcing' as opposed to 'single-sourcing'.

One-sourcing is on the way out because it doesn't always benefit the customer. Initial contracts tend to be overly binding; outsourcers have used change control to make up margins they gave away during the bidding process by committing themselves to unsustainable service charges. We believe that CFOs need to understand that this kind of situation creates significant risk when choosing a partner.

Another approach is emerging: Contracts can be procured on a best-of-breed consortium basis. Royal Mail, for example, has considered outsourcing IT to a consortium led by CSC in which Xansa will handle application management and British Telecom will perform network management outsourcing. To avoid putting all its eggs in one basket, the user plans to retain a strong relationship with each of its contractors. Similar solutions are appearing more frequently, some more far-reaching than others. In certain cases, the multisource approach may spread the risk

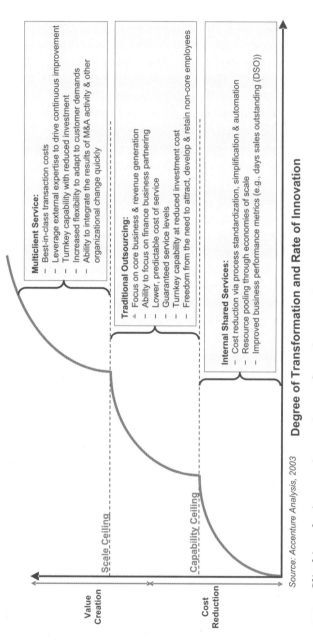

Multiclient Service:
– Best-in-class transaction costs
– Leverage external expertise to drive continuous improvement
– Turnkey capability with reduced investment
– Increased flexibility to adapt to customer demands
– Ability to integrate the results of M&A activity & other organizational change quickly

Traditional Outsourcing:
– Focus on core business & revenue generation
– Ability to focus on finance business partnering
– Lower, predictable cost of service
– Guaranteed service levels
– Turnkey capability at reduced investment cost
– Freedom from the need to attract, develop & retain non-core employees

Internal Shared Services:
– Cost reduction via process standardization, simplification & automation
– Resource pooling through economies of scale
– Improved business performance metrics (e.g., days sales outstanding (DSO))

Scale Ceiling

Capability Ceiling

Value Creation

Cost Reduction

Degree of Transformation and Rate of Innovation

Source: Accenture Analysis, 2003

Figure 3.4   *Climbing the innovation staircase for value creation*

and even reduce the cost, but not necessarily achieve the goal of organizational transformation.

Of course, overseeing a consortium approach requires more management resources. If poorly structured, it can create serious headaches! One government agency had so many outsourcing vendors that integration became nearly impossible. To integrate data, it often had to resort to batch processing interfaces, which undermined responsiveness to changing conditions. The agency recently ended its existing vendor arrangements to pursue a new more focused strategy. Not a happy situation!

Not all outsourcing agreements pose significant integration challenges. Firms that choose to host their own applications on someone else's servers, for example, can integrate them fairly smoothly into their existing portfolio of applications. As one manager explained: 'It's still the same system. The fact that parts of it physically reside outside our firewall in different locations doesn't make much difference.'

For example, ConocoPhillips, one of the oil companies participating with BP in Accenture's delivery center in Aberdeen, decided to maintain ownership of its own software to avoid potential integration problems. Outsourcing staff members are now directly linked to ConocoPhillips' SAP R/3 Financials module in order to perform ConocoPhillips' financial processes. The outsourcer is also required to maintain ConocoPhillips' standards and upgrade schedules.

Companies wanting to transform, rather than just cut costs, need to be even more discriminating in choosing their outsource providers. When outsourcing to multiple vendors, carefully consider three major issues:

1 **Technical complexity:** Use outsourcing to standardize applications and processes; the more customization involved, the harder it is to achieve desired cost efficiencies.

2 **Organizational interdependencies:** To help ensure that multiple vendors work together to promote your enterprise solutions, carefully structure their contracts up front and provide incentives.

3 **Integration planning:** Make integration a top priority and put solutions in place to support it. BP, for example, uses an integration hub to coordinate financial information. Each application inputs business results in standard format to the hub, where a consolidation tool integrates them. Having installed the technology to integrate its various best-of-breed applications, it was a simple step for BP to extend it to external applications as well.

In general, the fewer outsourcers you have, the easier it is to integrate them. True *business transformation outsourcing* is a strategic partnership between the company and its outsourcer. The outsourcer may subcontract to other best-of-breed suppliers, but fundamentally it's a one-to-one relationship. If you outsource inter-related processes to a single provider, make sure you find the right one. Today, the industry is awash with highly fragmented specialist vendors offering leading-edge practices for individual processes.

CHOOSING YOUR SUPPLIER COMBINATION

The number of outsource providers has mushroomed over the last few years – and, according to industry forecasts, this growth will continue. Inevitably, at some point the industry will consolidate. The trick will be to select providers that will survive the shakeout. When interviewing promising candidates, remember that they must satisfy your needs in three distinct outsourcing areas:

1 Business processes

2 IT hardware

3 Application support.

As a first step, assess the *capabilities* that the providers you are considering can bring to your organization. Look beyond proposal presentations and carefully analyze their ability to deliver the resources and skills you require – not just currently, but over time. During the selection process, establish 'show and tell' meetings at their sites and talk with some of their existing clients.

Next, consider *cultural* fit. As you meet individuals from each provider, continually ask yourself if these people can succeed in supporting your organization. Are their working styles and personalities compatible with yours? Do their values align with those of your organization? Will the provider bring the 'right' policies, procedures, and management disciplines? Will its team have the courage and maturity to implement the necessary processes and disciplines? Can the outsourcer be trusted as a long-term partner?

Sorting all this out won't be easy. Whatever your needs, you'll have a bewildering variety of BPO providers to choose from. Some have a single-process focus; others offer limited support for inter-related processes;

and still others operate more broadly, as multiprocess providers. Some vendors execute globally; others are equipped to implement in national markets or regional niches.

Figure 3.5 segments an illustrative grouping of outsource suppliers between those that provide full service globally, such as Accenture, CSC, and IBM, and those that are more specialized.

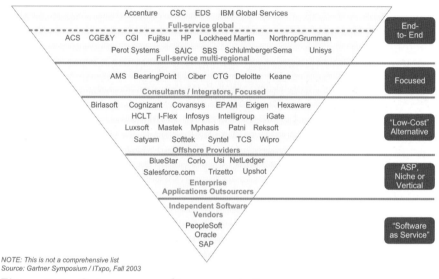

NOTE: This is not a comprehensive list
Source: Gartner Symposium / ITxpo, Fall 2003

Figure 3.5 *Outsource supplier segmentation*

Depending on the business process, the competitive landscape is more or less consolidated. For instance, in payroll, there are just a few players, whereas there are several hundred in recruiting. In the offshore provider segment, several local IT providers are reviewing the feasibility of offering BPO services as a way to create new revenue streams beyond existing consulting, development, and integration service lines.

Over time, it is likely that all this competition will lead to cross-border collaboration. US-based BPO providers, for example, may partner with offshore BPO players to reduce operational costs and standardize service delivery. Alternatively, offshore providers may seek commercial front-ends for their transaction processing. These are among the key factors differentiating BPO offerings:

- Target market (small, midsize, and large)

- Geography (local and global)

- Level of process ownership (application management and process management)

- Level of process transformation (transaction processing and strategic outsourcing)

- Process bundling (one process and multiprocess)

- Delivery (on-site and remote).

A survey by Gartner[3] of the selection criteria that companies use reported the following:

'When deciding to outsource the control of their business processes, users' foremost criteria in selecting a BPO provider are process expertise, level of customer service, and the ability to act as a trusted partner. Proven experience and strong references from existing accounts were the primary selection criteria and a shift away from these factors shows that BPO is becoming more mainstream and that users don't need so much education as to the viability of outsourcing anymore. However, clients now expect a high level of customer service, which goes hand in hand with the expectation that their provider will act as a trusted partner. Technical ability and industry expertise are less important factors to users than process expertise. While focus on business benefits is critical, the most successful BPO providers must not overlook the basic values of proven solutions and technical expertise as their core competencies.'

The CFOs interviewed for this book agreed that an 'established track record' and 'business process expertise' were by far the most important criteria for buying BPO. In short, among a sea of competitors, buyers are looking for outsource providers with proven capabilities and references. Indeed, the failure of some high-profile start-up BPO companies underscores the importance of solid track records.

Process expertise is also more important than industry/vertical expertise. Why? Mainly because BPO involves administrative functions that differ little across verticals and providers often specialize in vertical process expertise, such as health claims processing. As BPO matures, providers' abilities to provide *both* process and industry expertise will become critical, especially as they penetrate the midmarket.

In any accounting outsourcing arrangement, the quality and quantity of information offered are critical; so are speed and accuracy. As a result, a CFO should focus on an outsourcing provider's information management, access tools, and software expertise rather than on processing details, which will change over time.

Outsourcing an accounting function is a long-term commitment. It requires a true partnership and the 'right fit.' In a traditional software evaluation scenario, the provider sells its products and the company acts as the cautious, reluctant prospect waiting to be convinced. In F&A outsourcing, the parties are true equals; they must work together from the start.

In light of all these factors, CFOs faced with the challenge of identifying the most valuable provider attributes must take extra care. This is vitally important to both high-quality service and a smooth transition. The following checklist[4] should prove helpful in selecting your preferred outsourcing supplier:

- Demonstrated competencies: In terms of people, methodologies, technologies, innovation, industry experience, and track record

- Overall capabilities: In terms of financial strength, infrastructure, resources, management systems, and scope and range of services

- Relationship dynamics: Compatibility of vision and strategy, cultural fit, flexibility, quality of relationship management, and the relative size of your contract within their portfolio

- Quality of solutions: Benchmark performance, assess the relevance of services to your requirements, evaluate risk management and sharing capability, review quality of contractual terms and conditions

- Track record: Analyze service-level quality attained, financial value created, and commitment to continuous improvement.

Many organizations incorporate this type of information into their request for proposal (RFP) documents, specifying their evaluation criteria and weighting system. This ensures that providers are fully informed of their potential clients' outsourcing goals and expectations. Using the RFP as an evaluation tool can make it easier for you to select the right provider(s), but beware the difficulty of making direct comparisons in an RFP process when choosing an outsourcer for complex business processes; it's not the same as buying a piece of software.

Don't treat this as a procurement process, treat it as a *corporate transaction*. Quite often, outsourcing involves a 5-to-10 year contract; it is a strategic decision, not an operational one. There should be a clearly articulated, robust value proposition and any deal you strike should have an attractive risk-adjusted ROI. As a corporate transaction, an outsourcing agreement involves a sophisticated negotiation process – and requires access to legal, contractual, and corporate finance expertise.

SHAPING THE OUTSOURCING RELATIONSHIP

CFOs interviewed for this book expressed mixed views on their outsourcing suppliers:

'At different times and at different levels within the organization, we have a range of relationships with our outsource supplier. For example – intermittently a **strategic** *dialogue at the C-Level; a* **professional** *discussion, for example, in terms of best practice at the functional level; a service-oriented dialogue, almost at a* **commodity** *level in our shared service operations; and, unfortunately a sometimes* **adversarial** *relationship at the contractual level.'*

'Primarily due to a poor cultural fit, the relationship is certainly not good and at times, it borders on the adversarial.'

Research has shown that different suppliers have a tendency to pursue different types of relationships. When comparing providers or selecting multiple outsourcers, decide which of the following relationship types are most important to you – or what combination best meets your evolving needs:

- **A strategic partnership:** most suitable for transformation, sharing risks and rewards, focused on innovation

- **A professional relationship:** ideal for achieving standardization and best practice goals, focused on sharing expertise

- **A commodity supplier:** appropriate for a lowest cost, vanilla service, focused on delivering the basics with a shared incentive

- **An arms-length, contractual (can easily become adversarial) relationship:** short-term and aimed at inducing the supplier to make concessions, typically in a fixed price environment.

Clearly, a company is going to have severe problems with the fourth, adversarial option. The contract is a management tool; it should not be used as a weapon. If an outsourcing relationship has sunk purely to a contractual level, it is unlikely to succeed over the long term – failure has already been written into its future. It's important to stress once again that a successful outsourcing agreement is built on partnership. While the terms of a contract are valid when they are written, inevitably, circumstances will change. As partners, you and your provider can and should weather these changes without disrupting services.

PLANNING A DELIVERY STRATEGY

The CFO has a choice to make between having outsourced services provided on site or at an off-site shared service center run by its external provider. There is also a new option: remote delivery of BPO over the IT network. The choice of delivery mode depends on the four factors listed below:

1 **Technology components:** If the BPO contract includes applications outsourcing and significant systems development, requirements are usually delivered remotely from the provider's service center. If the contract involves few technology components and significant human support (some administration services, for instance), then services can be delivered on site.

2 **Number of clients:** If the provider serves several clients requiring the same process or similar processes, then creating a shared service center becomes relevant. Using this approach, the provider leverages its staff and technology from a central location.

3 **Number of sites served:** If the business process is streamlined across several geographical sites, the offering can be centralized at the provider's service center and remotely serve all sites, thus creating significant economies of scale.

4 **Nature of services provided:** High-volume transactions or repeatable processes lend themselves to shared service delivery better than consulting-oriented or high-touch, BPO-related services (some types of training, career consulting, and so on).

In fully exploiting the promise of ERP, corporate users quickly realized that they could not achieve competitive differentiation with standard applications. As a result, BPO providers are now playing the role of technology aggregators, augmenting packaged ERP applications with best-of-breed e-business applications and Web services. The transfer of this risk to the BPO provider, whose role it is to invest in the best technology mix for a particular process, is at the core of the BPO value proposition.

Web delivery of BPO services enables outsource providers to offer more flexible service options. Some of the changes introduced by Web delivery include:

- **Real-time upgrades in technology:** Instead of upgrading applications once a year, portal releases are delivered instantly over the Internet

- **Increased speed:** Transactions can be completed online and sent via the Internet to the BPO provider for processing

- **Integration:** Web delivery supports integration across processes (for example, HR, procurement, and finance)

- **Personnel efficiencies:** Labor-intensive activities, such as claims processing or call centers, are now migrating to the Web. In some cases, call centers are transforming themselves into help desks for consulting inquiries.

BPO providers are acutely aware that their survival depends on continually improving their business model – and technology is clearly a major tool in achieving this goal. If outsourcers can reduce the number of people needed in finance operations by automating their own internal activities, then they, like their clients, will enjoy better margins.

Ultimately, the niche outsource supplier market is unsustainable; the forces of globalization are simply too strong. Providers without the resources to invest in service improvements will not be able to keep pace with the rapid changes in technology. Few providers are content to be small niche players.

As new players, such as IT service companies, enter the BPO market, it is inevitable that once-distinct service categories will converge. Figure 3.6[5] plots the emerging BPO landscape across the dimensions of delivery and service.

Once you have selected a provider you feel comfortable partnering with, your focus should shift to execution. This means working with your provider to develop a blueprint for making the transition from in-house services to outsourcing. During this process, the following questions should be addressed:

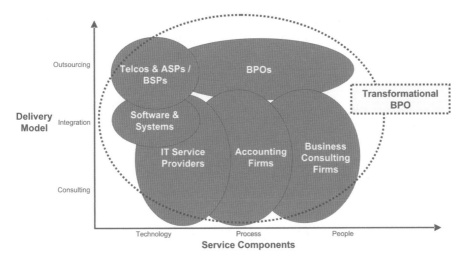

Source: IDC, Worldwide Business Process Outsourcing Forecast and Analysis, 2002

Figure 3.6   *BPO services competitive landscape*

1 What to outsource?

2 Where to source from?

3 How to structure the contract?

4 Can the outsourcer promote strategic change?

5 How will you encourage continuous improvement?

Identifying your value proposition lies at the heart of your outsourcing strategy. This value proposition provides the foundation for a productive relationship with your outsource provider. It will also point to the development approach you must jointly pursue to craft the best solution to your outsourcing needs.

It is important to be clear about who is doing what during this planning phase. Leading outsource service providers have methodologies to support this process and will help you achieve the optimum service delivery model. In Figure 3.7, we set out the solution planning approach developed by Accenture.

This deal-driven approach to establishing the right solution for both the client and the service provider starts with the value proposition and

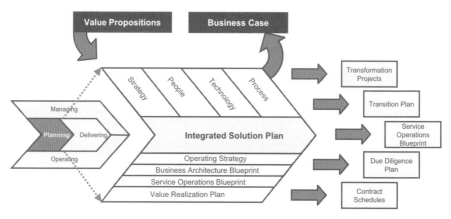

Figure 3.7   *A solution planning framework*

ends with the intended business outcome. The integration solution plan is developed in iterative stages that correspond to the company's state of readiness. There are four major deliverables:

1 **Business architecture blueprint:** This maps out the scope and reach of the delivery solution – including business architecture, performance, capabilities, and integration level required.

2 **Operating strategy:** This is a set of assumptions about how the future service arrangement will function. This deliverable should delineate alliance arrangements with third parties, resourcing arrangements, and knowledge transfer plans.

3 **Service operations blueprint:** This sets out the service definition – the nature and structure of the services provided – to set target performance, baseline volumes, operational and technical considerations. Service measurement and service charging are also included.

4 **Value realization plan:** This sets out the business case – how value is to be realized, and how risk and reward will be shared.

The integrated solution plan takes advantage of both current best practices and new knowledge acquired by the outsource supplier through other implementations. It also includes data about a client's current and future business needs. Equipped with all this information, the company and its provider can negotiate a sound outsourcing contract and proceed to the transition phase with confidence.

Don't spend too long on the discovery phase. Try to get the ratio right between due diligence and speed. Initial analysis will help with project scoping; however, don't expect to nail everything down. Collaboration over the first year of the contract will reveal inevitable detail changes required; structural shifts will surface as time goes on.

CFO INSIGHTS

- Outsourcing offers a true business transformation opportunity. Look beyond simple cost reduction.

- Opt for a change in location and the transformation of your processes in one go; research proves conclusively that this approach is best. Don't worry too much about where the service is going to be delivered from: Location is largely irrelevant if you are a part of a globally interconnected world.

- Don't invest in the creation of back-office service functions that are non-differential in terms of competitiveness. Why go to the trouble of investing all the time and effort into creating something that already exists and which you can immediately exploit? Take advantage of the outsource market which has in place the service capabilities you need.

- Develop a partnership arrangement that provides a *win-win* scenario. Strive for strategic long-term partnerships, not transaction-based commodity outsourcing.

- Decide on the balance between integration and best of breed. Consider the opportunity for technology investment and select the supplier with the best cultural fit and capabilities.

- Don't go slowly, proceed at a healthy speed. Develop a sense of urgency around a well-structured supplier procurement process and execution methodology.

FROM INSIGHT TO ACTION

OBTAIN CEO SPONSORSHIP FOR YOUR CHOSEN DELIVERY STRATEGY

CEOs have the broad vision to fully appreciate the benefits of transformational change. Raise the stakes in the game – focus on enterprise outcomes. Develop a bold strategic agenda and an innovative deal structure to fund the necessary investment. Motivate commitment by aligning goals, distributing risks, and promising rewards.

DEVELOP A SPIRIT OF PARTNERSHIP, TRUST, AND CONTINUOUS IMPROVEMENT

Once you've chosen your outsource provider, commit to a partnership mindset. Align your objectives. Manage partner relationships using four levers: contract negotiation, performance track record, governance, and personal relationships.

LOOK FOR A STRATEGIC ALLY, NOT A CONVENTIONAL OUTSOURCER

Align incentives and enterprise outcomes – make your agreements flexible, not airtight. Successful execution means clearly assigning leadership and control. Communicate, communicate, communicate!

PROCEED AT SPEED

Rapidly propel your outsourcing solution for business transformation from conception to execution. Prepare a robust value proposition; undertake thorough due diligence before deal closure. Start with a small team, ramp up resources later.

TRANSFORM CRITICAL PROCESSES FIRST, THEN LEVERAGE NEW CAPABILITIES

Set crystal clear expectations, embrace a team-based approach with your partner to find and unlock value. Take advantage of your business partner's partners.

DEMAND CONTINUING INNOVATION
Relentlessly drive performance improvements. Create an environment where your managers understand vision, are willing to improvise, and can drive implementation.

CREATE A BETTER EMPLOYMENT EXPERIENCE FOR BACK-OFFICE STAFF TO ENHANCE MORALE
Free up management, focus on core competencies. Leverage technology to increase self-service. Convey to employees the opportunities for growth that outsourcing can offer them.

ANNOUNCE THE DEAL TO THE OUTSIDE WORLD
Stimulate a positive reaction from financial markets by shedding non-core assets. Leverage your partner's brand. Manage the finance function as a business. Develop new revenue streams and provide flexibility for M&A, disposals, and launching new businesses.

THINK CORPORATE TRANSACTION
Don't treat outsourcing as an operational procurement. Be prepared to abandon your traditional 'RFP' based selection processes. Be clear – is your objective value creation or just cost reduction? Treat the supplier selection and negotiation process as you would an M&A deal.

REFERENCES

1 Accenture Institute for Strategic Change, *Business Process Outsourcing Big Bang: Creating value in an expanding universe*, 2002. www.accenture.com

2 Accenture and Montgomery Research, *Competitive Financial Operations: The CFO Project, Volume 1*, 2002. www.cfoproject.com

3 Gartner, BPO Validates: Verticalization and Aggregation Accelerate, *Market Trends*, February 2003.

4 Dr Wendell Jones and Stuart Kilmann, *Managing Outsourcing Relationships for Value Creation*, Michael F. Corbett & Associates Ltd, 2002.

5 IDC, Worldwide Business Process Outsourcing Forecast and Analysis, 2002.

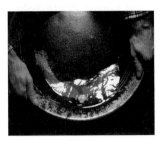

CHAPTER 4

Scoping: Deciding What to Outsource

DEVELOPING A HIGH-PERFORMANCE FINANCE FUNCTION WITH SUPERIOR ALIGNMENT TO THE COMPETITIVE IMPERATIVES OF THE BUSINESS

Michel-Marc Delcommune, CFO
MOL

MOL is one of a number of oil companies in Central Europe that have experienced a major structural shift in their environment in moving from a monopolistic, planned country-based economic system to the open market. Michel-Marc, the company's CFO, comments on the major company restructuring when MOL moved from the public to the private sector: 'Prior to privatization, not only were we an integrated oil company, but we also owned and managed a variety of activities not normally associated with the oil industry. For example, we owned a telecoms company using our gas pipes to run some 5,000 km of copper wire for data and voice transmission. We also owned a hotel and summer resort chain called MOL Hotels. We have since divested these businesses to focus on the oil business. As a result of the re-focusing process that we have gone through, we have gained considerable experience in deciding between what should be insourced and what should be outsourced.'

Michel-Marc started to evaluate finance outsourcing initiatives in 1999; this process was undertaken with considerable care and due diligence, and 13 months later the contract was signed with the service provider. He gained access to BP's finance outsourcing experience using this as a role model on which to base his own thinking: 'I had been watching with great interest what BP were doing since the early 1990s. John Browne, the BP CEO, had a vision, and a clear view of both the competencies the company should retain and develop to be competitive, and those processes and activities that could be delivered by a third party at superior levels of performance. At MOL I worked with our CEO to define what we believed were the distinctive industry core competencies that made a tangible difference to our ability to successfully compete, leaving the rest as candidates for outsourcing. For example, in our upstream business (exploration and production) we focus on technology, engineering, and geology. In the downstream business (refining and retailing), we focus on supply chain, wholesale pricing, and logistics.'

MOL discovered that a significant number of finance processes were better suited for the third-party service provider to perform. Michel-Marc says: 'Like BP, we found it difficult to offer accountants an attractive career path that was sufficiently fulfilling and motivating; after all, we are in the oil business, not the accounting business. We transferred more than two-thirds of our finance staff to the outsourcer. Soon our former accounting staff found their career fortunes had been transformed. Becoming part of an organization whose core competency and raison d'être was to provide high standards of service delivery in accounting and finance processing provided them with greater opportunities. They now have access to continuing education, training, and career development, and are able to exploit their skills on a wider range of work. This provides variability and is more interesting. When deciding what to outsource we drew the line to retain the competencies in finance that are directly connected to the oil industry – those that are differentiating and make a competitive difference.

MOL has outsourced the following transactional processes:

- **Payables** – *purchase invoice payment and matching routines are outsourced; purchasing and approvals are retained*
- **Receivables** – *in-country volume-based sales invoice processing (for Hungary and Slovakia) are outsourced; export invoicing, owing to its perceived complexity, is insourced*
- **Treasury** – *the back-office and bank reconciliation activities are outsourced; the decision-making and more risk-related activities associated with the front- and mid-offices, are retained internally*

- **General ledger** – *the integrated processing based on SAP is outsourced; original business journal entries are initiated by MOL employees. The service provider produces the profit and loss account and balance sheet reports that MOL signs-off and approves.*

Michel-Marc comments on those processes that were 'borderline': 'In retrospect we underestimated the complexities of an outsourcer taking on our local fiscal and regulatory requirements. We have as many as 1,300 different local tax payments to make every quarter, which means that MOL is better placed to manage this risk in-house. Conversely, with EU entry we could now outsource our export invoicing and receivables, as the service provider already has the requisite international capabilities and expertise.'

Today, MOL retains 250 staff dealing with planning, strategic treasury, tax, statutory, and international accounting requirements, investor relations, controlling, management information, and resource allocation. Michel-Marc is not in favor of outsourcing decision support at this stage in MOL's development as he believes his business analysis capabilities are a source of learning and people development inside the organization. He comments: 'As a newly privatized company, we have a special focus on shareholder value and in understanding the impact of the cost of capital on our various business units. Resource allocation, for us, is a critical process for evaluating investment returns and for monitoring performance. The MOL culture is becoming more and more entrepreneurial.'

When deciding where and when to cut the process for outsourcing, Michel-Marc believes that the issue of control and risk is most crucial. 'I strongly believe in the segregation of duties. The outsourcing of the back-office treasury management is a good example of where we have achieved improved control by transferring activity to a third party. Although cost savings are possible, particularly where high-volume batch procedures are involved, they should not be the overriding objective. MOL is expanding internationally. We recently expanded into Slovakia by acquiring Slovnaft; also by a strategic partnership with INA of Croatia. Undoubtedly we have needed the strong support of our outsourcing partner to accelerate the process of integration and to provide us with a platform for international growth.'

Michel-Marc examines the changing role of the CFO in relation to the role of the CEO at MOL and in the oil industry generally: 'I believe the CFO of the future will be more of an industry expert, and less focused on just accounting. The CFO is playing an increasing role in the evaluation and management of enterprise-level risk. In the oil industry recent events have shown that the CFO needs to be prominent in investor relations too. The investor community has become much tougher on management and less tolerant of mistakes in reporting. A best-practice finance function with clear lines of authority and standardization throughout the company is essential for fulfilling their demands.'

CFOs of companies such as MOL, tend to retain in-house strategic and analytical capabilities, or areas, such as tax where corporate reputation is at stake. They are committed to outsourcing parts of their business – such as IT, receivables management, and payroll – areas where outsource providers can transform processes at lower cost. Such companies do not want a 'commodity' service; they want a 'value-adding' process specialist. Other companies, like BP, Exel, and Thomas Cook, are also looking for transformational capability – but at an organization-wide level. The scope may vary from company to company, but the pivotal issue is the same – where should your company cut the process?

When deciding where to set scope – which functions to keep in-house and which to send out – some companies reverse the normal decision-making process. Initially, they put everything in the 'to be outsourced' box. Then if their managers want to retain something in-house, they have to provide a robust argument for retaining it. This rather atypical approach to scoping can give managers a better understanding of the benefits of outsourcing.

In this chapter, we profile F&A outsourcing experiences to show how far the CFO can go. In the course of our interviews with many experienced CFOs, a golden rule emerged. This is captured in the following quote from Alan Eilles, BP's global downstream vice president group financial infrastructure: 'Any F&A decisions involving *interpretation, policy* or *judgment* are retained inside. Anything else is a potential outsourcing candidate.'

As a general principle, finance processes where defined inputs have a defined outcome are good candidates for outsourcing. Processes requiring a degree of interpretation, analysis or creative insight are less appropriate. The commercial relationship between an outsource provider and its client requires a degree of predictability over outcomes so that service and quality can be measured.

Routine tasks associated with transaction processing are clear outsourcing candidates. Less clear-cut, but still common, outsourcing options are some of the more technically demanding finance and accounting activities associated with general ledger maintenance, consolidation, and statutory accounting. The key area of decision support is more difficult to delegate and is less commonly outsourced. In the cases of BP and Thomas Cook, routine, rule-based aspects of decision support are handled by their outsource providers. There are many examples where general ledger work, up to and including preparation of balance sheets for individual statutory entities, is outsourced.

Based on our research, the factors typically considered by CFOs in deciding which activities to include in an outsource shared service center are shown in Figure 4.1. The factors range from skills and ease of implementation to scale and complexity.

Our research also shows that the most common outsourced shared service functions, ranked by tier, are as follows:

- **Tier 1:** Accounts payable, accounts receivable, cash and banking, payroll, fixed assets, and general accounting

- **Tier 2:** T&E expenses, financial reporting, management reporting, credit & collections, HR, and treasury

- **Tier 3:** Planning and budgeting, benefits administration, and tax.

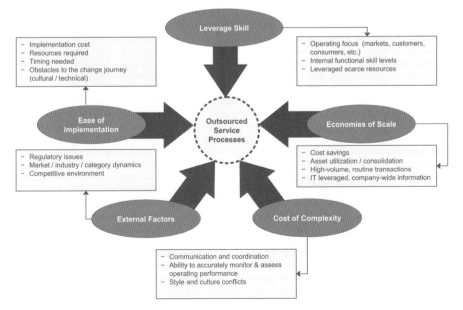

Figure 4.1   *Factors to consider when outsourcing F&A processes*

CFOs with considerable experience of outsourcing stress the importance of scoping the process *end-to-end*. This means, for example, not just payroll, but HR as well. Not just payables, but purchasing. Not just receivables, but credit management. Why? Because the value created is substantially greater, not just in cost savings, but also in dramatically improved service and quality by avoiding 'unnatural' breaks in the process. The point at which to cut the process is key; making the right decision ensures optimal 'hand-offs' between outsource provider and client.

WHERE TO CUT THE PROCESS

In Chapter 1, we reported the results of a CFO survey that explored what companies are outsourcing *now* and what they plan to outsource in the *future*. The survey showed that transaction processing is currently at the top of the outsourcing agenda (for example, payroll, receivables, payables, T&E processing, tax compliance, and general accounting). In the future, decision support (management reporting, analysis, risk, treasury, budgeting, and forecasting) will also be likely outsourcing candidates.

Figure 4.2 illustrates how some organizations have split activities that are outsourced from those they retain in-house.

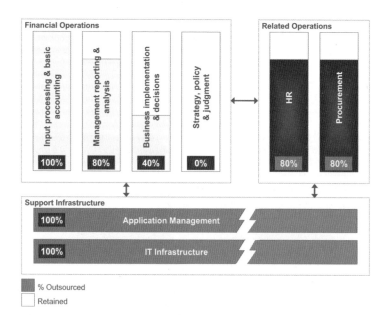

Figure 4.2 *Scoping back-office activities for outsourcing*

By outsourcing an entire process, including key related processes and supporting technology, you enable the outsource provider to take greater ownership and control over service outcomes. This requires a significant degree of confidence in, and partnership with, the outsource provider. This again points to the need for detailed service reporting, effective governance, and the selection of the right outsource provider.

Many CFOs interviewed for this book were concerned about deciding how and where they should cut the process. There are no hard and fast rules, but the issues most CEOs and CFOs should consider when making these decisions include:

- **Control and risk**

  Accountants have always been concerned about ensuring that processes are properly controlled, well documented, and auditable. Sarbanes-Oxley and the new international accounting standards and regulations have heightened this concern. Companies with strong experience in outsourcing say that it *increases* control, rather than *reducing* it. In a 2003 survey of 1,200 senior executives in manufacturing and consumer industries,[1] 86% of executives credited outsourcing with increasing their sense of control over business results.

  The research showed this increased control resulted from a combination of the commercial structures around service provision and the detailed documentation and service reporting that outsourcers provide. A professional outsource provider will use best practices, document the detailed processes involved, and comply with measurable control parameters as specified in its contracted service agreement. As a result, companies that have opted to outsource often see improvements in both their internal and external audit arrangements and relationships. However, overall responsibility for statutory compliance still lies with the CEO and CFO in the retained organization. For this reason, corporate executives must carefully consider their scope decisions in light of an outsource provider's capabilities. They must also accept responsibility for managing the outsource provider.

- **Scale and value**

  Some companies outsource their finance activities to gain greater economies of scale. In principle, outsource providers – and their clients – benefit from economies of scale in processing, management, skill and expertise, training and development, and recruitment. By managing a 'portfolio' of client service agreements, often from the same location, they also benefit from economies of scale in risk, not only in terms of disaster recovery and business continuity, but also in their ability to respond more flexibly to changes in their clients' business requirements by managing resources *across* deals. In addition, outsource providers can often secure favorable terms with third party 'best-of-breed' providers for services such as scanning or Optical Character Recognition (OCR) – benefits that might not have been available to individual client companies.

- **Best practice**
  F&A best practice requires injections of expertise and investment, which are difficult to sustain in-house. There are many examples of companies that have reaped significant benefits from the ongoing investment and expertise of their outsource service providers.

- **Customer contact**
  There are two current schools of thought among CFOs. One group believes that customer contact is a core, value-added activity and must remain in-house. The other group considers that there is a transactional and rules-based element to customer contact, and that, just like any other process, these aspects of customer contact may be better performed by an outsource provider. In this second group of companies, their value-added core activities often revolve around intellectual property and technical delivery rather than relationship management through customer contact. In addition, CFOs are beginning to see that a significant part of the receivables management process involves dealing with their customers' payables staff – and therefore is not actually key to customer contact or relationship management.

- **Process integration**
  Hand-offs – the points at which responsibility for a transaction are handed over from the retained organization to the outsourcer, or back again, are critical. For example, a purchase order has to be raised and handed over to the outsourcer by the retained organization for a purchase invoice to be approved and paid by that outsourcer. Connectivity points are not only process-related, they also rely heavily on human interaction and technology. Since these hand-offs define the interaction between the service provider and the retained organization (as well as the points at which service will be measured) it is important that they are carefully identified.

- **Complexity and expertise**

  Some finance executives believe that transactions or activities that demand deep technical knowledge and experience are best served by in-house resources. In some of the cases we examined, they were right! However, there are many examples where activities have been outsourced because a company sees that it does not have the necessary technical expertise or scale and is better served by external suppliers. Treasury and tax are common examples.

Where do you start with your decision about what should be outsourced – and what should be retained? First, baseline and benchmark your current competencies for each process area. There is extensive benchmarking material available from external specialists and advisors to provide you with an objective and realistic view of what can be achieved.

Consider the case of Kraft – the global food company.

 ## CASE STUDY

Approaching the scoping dilemma at Kraft

Kraft has grown via acquisitions, most notably, Nabisco. Its global portfolio of brands includes snacks, beverages, cheese, and grocery products. The company is focused on accelerating the growth in core brands and a drive towards world-class productivity, quality, and service. To maintain margin growth and to achieve the required return on the invested capital in acquisitions, Kraft, among other initiatives, has invested in shared services in North America.

James Dollive, EVP & CFO of Kraft, says: 'Our operational objectives are to:

- *Support and strengthen existing businesses*
- *Drive growth through acquisitions and new product development*
- *Aggressively manage costs down*
- *Build employee and organizational excellence.*

Our drive to improve earnings has led us to seek ways to reduce all costs. For example, we are leveraging the expertise of our procurement function across Kraft's global businesses to purchase the highest quality goods and services at the lowest imaginable costs.

'Process optimization is another important vehicle to drive productivity and improve ROI. We have a very successful shared services center in San Antonio,

Texas, which covers the F&A process for our North American operations. We are now evaluating opportunities to improve our SG&A costs in our international businesses.'

In Europe, Kraft is currently implementing SAP and standardizing processes across a number of countries. The objective is to improve consistency and management of data as well as drive synergies and efficiencies. Gary Chan, Kraft's European CFO, takes up the story:

'North America is a homogeneous market; implementing shared services there was relatively straightforward. In Europe, we operate in every major country, with all the inherent complexity this involves. Our customers differ from country to country and some of our brands are tailored to national tastes. Although we have achieved some significant improvements to our back-office, there are still opportunities we need to explore.'

Kraft International is currently considering the options of shared services or outsourcing its F&A processes. The successful outsource supplier will have to demonstrate a track record in implementing a trans-European shared service center. Gary goes on to say:

'The big question for us is where to cut the process. Currently, we believe that accounts payable, travel and entertainment expenses (T&E), general ledger, and fixed assets should be in scope for shared services or outsourcing. We may extend the accounts payable to include indirect purchasing. I am not sure about the order-to-cash process; we want to retain in-house our direct contact with our customer base in individual countries. I can see there might be a business case for outsourcing receivables, but we need to look more carefully at where and how the process is cut from a risk viewpoint. If an outsource provider could reduce the days sales outstanding from today's level, then there is a strong business case based on working capital reduction. However, we need to consider how our customer relationships would be managed.'

Companies like Kraft need to be convinced that an outsourcing provider can partner with them to manage the risks and relationships associated with suppliers, customers, and employees. They need clear evidence that, by outsourcing their F&A processes, they can achieve not only cost reduction, but also world-class service and quality.

In response to this need, this chapter now takes you through examples of best practice processes that have been outsourced: *purchase-to-pay; order-to-cash; credit and receivables management; general ledger; management accounting and reporting.*

PURCHASE-TO-PAY

The purchase-to-pay process encompasses making purchases, receiving goods and services, processing invoices and credit notes, creating and distributing payments through to maintaining the purchase ledger. Purchase-to-pay provides great opportunities for combining best practice processes, ERP, leading-edge technology, and shared services to achieve world-class performance.

CASE STUDY
Streamlining the purchase-to-pay cycle

The CFO of a major oil company was tasked with achieving an ambitious change agenda for his corporate finance function. The agenda called for improved:

- *Velocity: increasing the speed of finance processes*
- *Visibility: enhancing finance's ability to provide accurate information*
- *Value: achieving some quick wins.*

Detailed analysis of the company's purchase-to-pay cycle showed that the processing of invoices and credit notes offered the greatest potential for clerical cost reduction. An intelligent document management solution was chosen for integration with the company's e-Procurement and ERP systems. This enabled an electronic image of each invoice to accompany the three-way automatic match via ERP (the clearance of the invoice against order, price, and delivery). The intelligent document management software recognizes invoice data and processes it automatically using pre-set control parameters. Accuracy improved and is expected to increase, as the management system learns from its mistakes and control reports reject invoice data that falls outside pre-set guidelines. Overall, the benefits achieved through the purchase-to-pay process using intelligent document management proved significant:

- *A highly automated process was developed, with embedded business rules and logic*
- *A scalable solution was rolled out quickly across the enterprise*
- *Data entry was streamlined, with effort required only for exception management*
- *Transparent end-to-end processing identified and re-engineered bottlenecks*
- *Working capital and compliance costs fell through improved indirect tax reclaim.*

The business case provided a quick payback; transaction costs per invoice were cut from an average of $3.20 to 50 cents. The company processed approximately 2.5 million invoices a year and total savings amounted to $6.7 million.

The intelligent document management solutions referred to in Figure 4.3 support automated recognition, validation, and posting of manual invoices to the payables ledger.

This oil company believes that it has implemented best practice purchase-to-pay processes in its country-based shared service centers. It is now considering the next step – outsourcing. The outsource provider, based on past experience, has scoped the following split of activities between its outsourced European shared service center in Prague and the retained organization (see table opposite):

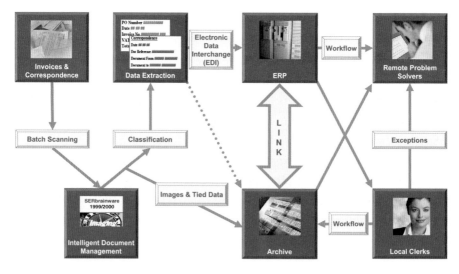

Source: "The CFO as Business Integrator", Cedric Read and the MySAP Financials Team, John Wiley & Sons, 2003

Figure 4.3   *Purchase-to-pay best practice*

Purchase-To-Pay:	
Transferred to Prague Delivery Center	Retained by Oil Company
Master Data	*Strategic Purchasing*
Manage and check vendor and employee master files	Define company procurement, T&E, and payment policies
Accounts Payable	*Purchase Requisition/Goods Receipt*
Process invoices and expense reports	Enter purchase requests and receive goods and services
Resolve any invoice queries (inc. vendor & employee inquiries)	*Payment Approval Processing*
Control coding and post adjustments to the system	Approve purchases, expense reports, and corrective actions
Reconcile suppliers statements to the AP ledger	Block payments as necessary
Payment Approval Processing	*Manage supplier disputes*
Generate payment list in accordance with business instructions	
Make payments to suppliers and employees	

By outsourcing, this company is able to standardize and consolidate purchase-to-pay processes across Europe. For example, the outsourcer maintains one standardized set of supplier master data, enabling the company to analyze vendor and purchase information across its operation. The outsourcer has provided a Web-based tool for this purpose. Improved analysis has led to substantial economies via consolidation of purchasing and reductions in the number of authorized suppliers.

ORDER-TO-CASH

Companies in every industry are pushing the technology envelope to achieve greater process efficiencies and cost savings:

- Using applications hosting, where possible
- Eliminating manual transaction processing and reducing order errors
- Hiring fewer, more skilled staff to investigate exceptions
- Implementing regional shared service centers
- Using browser-based applications to increase control and leverage scale.

Along with these broad benefits, there are some very specific advantages to fully automating and integrating key order-to-cash processes as follows:

Benefits of automating the **credit management** process

- Provides instant confirmation and faster decision-making
- Collects and processes data in order that staff can proceed *confidently* with transactions
- Frees up staff to focus on higher risk opportunities
- Consistent credit policy supports better risk assessment
- Increases sales by evaluating risk profiles with multiple finance partners
- Enhances ability to meet customer expectations quickly.

Benefits of automating **invoice generation** and **query handling** process

- Accelerates dispute resolution and reduces days sales outstanding (DSOs)
- Enables non-electronic data interchange (EDI) customers to trade electronically

- Integrates data into accounts receivable system; eliminates re-keying of information

- Offers online ability to review, modify, and approve invoice requests

- Facilitates cash forecasting and reporting

- Supports review, query, and request credit notes on outstanding invoices.

Benefits of automating the **collections** process

- Enables credit controllers to provide better, quicker service to customers

- Frees up staff to talk with clients, resolve problems, and reduce overdue accounts

- Reduces cost of administrative operations

- Puts accounts receivable data and payment trends at credit controllers' fingertips.

According to a recent Gartner study,[2] the number of companies sending out business invoices via the Internet nearly tripled by the end of 2002, from 9% to 26%. By the end of 2004, web-invoice delivery is expected to rise to 35%. Business-to-business electronic invoice presentment will dramatically reduce the current 41-day average payment cycle, allowing companies to cut debt and invest cash more quickly. Other major benefits of electronic billing presentment and payment (EBPP) include:

- Significantly reduced billing and payment transaction costs

- Improved cash-flow projections

- Simplified payment, settlement, and reconciliation processes

- Reduced float

- Cross-selling

- Better customer-relationship management

- Increased customer loyalty.

CASE STUDY
Building an integrated order-to-cash system

One global chemicals company headquartered in Europe had regional customer ser-vice hubs in Germany, the USA, and Singapore. Worldwide it had 3,000 customers. Each year, it processed approximately 100,000 customer orders and sales invoices. Sales executives in the field and customer relationship coordinators in each of the hub locations were the main contact points with customers.

The company's first-time order commitment was achieved in only 70% of all cases. To improve this track record, better stock availability and credit authorization processes were needed. Also, all invoices required some touching by hand, resulting in many invoicing errors. Benefits were sought in the following areas:

- *Pricing: provisional prices were often quoted and then had to be adjusted*
- *Rebates and commissions: adjustments to customer invoiced amounts were a constant problem*
- *Disputed items: communication between internal credit control, customer relationship coordinators, and sales executives was often poorly coordinated.*

In addition, the company was in the process of joining a new chemical indus-try exchange with a view to reducing costs and encouraging new business. This required linking up with 19 other industry partners. The company had also begun setting up its own private Website called the Customer Lounge. The site allowed customers to quickly see the status of their current orders, place new orders, share documentation or view their sales ledger account. ERP was connected to provide an integrated online system.

The next step was to further automate the order-to-cash process. This process encompassed qualification of the order, credit management, and agreement of terms through execution of the order, handling exceptions, managing returns and queries.

Improved billing and collection processes offered further improvement opportu-nities. The automation of the order-to-cash process resulted in the following:

- *Qualification and sales: online credit checking, factoring, and financing; use of mobile devices for transmission of orders and their validation; mobile access to relevant end-to-end account data*
- *Order fulfillment: automated data entry; customer self-service for order status.*

- *Returns and queries: automated routing of queries; self-service query support; reporting on returns and queries processing*
- *Billing: electronic presentment of invoices over the Internet; customer-managed billing; electronic customer payment facilities*
- *Collection: autoposting; customer viewing of sales ledger postings; online dispute resolution.*

The company also integrated its ERP resources with a number of best-of-breed systems, as shown in Figure 4.4.

The ERP system was supplemented with SAP Biller Direct (electronic billing presentment and payment) functionality. The Siebel package was used for customer relationship management (CRM) and was integrated with both SAP and specialist software for intelligent e-mail handling, credit checking, and accounts receivable. All information was collected for viewing through the company's portal.

Significant improvements were achieved in net cash flow, accounts receivable outstanding, and customer relations. Customers receive more responsive service

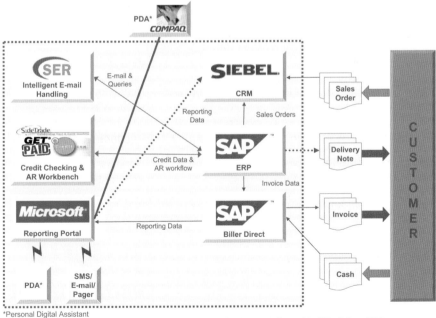

*Personal Digital Assistant
Source: "The CFO as Business Integrator", Cedric Read and the MySAP Financials Team, John Wiley & Sons, 2003

Figure 4.4 *One supplier's best practice order-to-cash integration solution*

through mobile access, more accurate invoices, and faster information access via the
Customer Lounge. Real-time cash flow forecasting on a global basis is now a reality.

Achieving best-practice processes, such as the order-to-cash system described by Figure 4.4, requires a mix of capabilities – ranging from the more strategic, such as customer relationship management and credit management, to the more routine associated with billing, accounts receivable, and cash collection. When moving to an outsourced shared service center, a standard order-to-cash process split is as follows:

Order-To-Cash	
Transferred to Outsourced Center	Retained by Company
Billing	*Order Entry*
Generate and send manual invoices and statements, rebates and credit note requests	Receive orders and maintain standard prices
Collections	*Billing*
Approve and action the plans to resolve collection issues	Define company procedures and pricing policies
Chase receipts and identify reasons for late payments	
	Collections
Agree on corrective action plan with appropriate resolver	Decide on provisions and write-offs
Cash Application	*Credit Management*
Lodge, match, and post payments to customer accounts	Approve new customers and credit terms
Investigate and report on any unmatched or part paid receipts	Provide credit status check reports
Issue resolution	*Pricing and special discount decisions*
General Ledger Accounting – Reconcile customer accounts to G/L	*Refund decisions*
Management Reporting Preparation – Produce appropriate management reports	

Some companies cut the order-to cash process between insource and outsource at the point of customer interface. For other companies, *everything* to do with the customer is treated as a source of competitive advantage and a value-creating core activity. For still others, the position is less clear. Ownership of the customer relationship is vital, but parts of the customer interface are more transaction based – and therefore lend themselves to specialist outsourcing.

Streamlined, coordinated financial information flows make it easier for CFOs to track customer profitability and credit issues – and gain a better understanding of their company's cost base. More efficient, cost-effective supply chains enable sales, marketing, and finance executives to make better-informed decisions about both customers and the bottom line.

CREDIT AND RECEIVABLES MANAGEMENT

One major company has recently outsourced its credit and receivables management. The company's business model has undergone dramatic changes over the past two decades. First, deregulation removed the company's monopoly. Second, it faced considerable new competition in the marketplace. Today, the company competes for customers; it faces risks it never had to deal with before. One of the most significant is consumer credit risk.

 CASE STUDY
Electronic billing presentment and payment (EBPP)

Electronic bill presentment and payment is also a growing trend. According to a recent Gartner[3] study, by 2007, 65 million US adults will view their bills online. This overcomes the previously leading hurdle: slow customer adoption. EBPP offers a host of business process advantages that promise to dramatically reshape billing and payment processes. Companies are now considering using an outsource provider with an existing EBPP capability to avoid sizable process transformation projects, yet get the benefits. Key advantages of EBPP include:

- *Improved payment services – automatic application of payments to accounts receivable, online payment guarantees, and multi-currency payment capacity.*

- *Reduced billing costs – lower cost of producing an invoice due to reduced labor, postage, paper, and equipment costs. Cheaper dispute resolution when a dispute is handled electronically.*
- *Links with shipping and logistical systems – linking EBPP with logistical systems can automatically trigger payment once buyers receive their goods.*
- *Improved financing services – when financing sales using the open account method, automation increases ability to leverage trading partner relationships.*
- *Document exchange and reconciliation – enables the exchange of documents and easy tracking. Review and reconciliation is also facilitated. This reduces disputes as sellers can be paid more quickly.*

A fully integrated and automated supply chain maximizes business returns. However, EBPP is being adopted slowly. Not all CFOs are keen to invest in building, testing, and implementing their own EBPP capability and risk a service interruption during transition. The benefit of outsourcing to a service provider is that their EBPP processes will already be in place. The upfront financial investment has been made, and the outsource service provider will be responsible for developing and innovating systems and processes.

Many businesses with high customer volumes, such as utilities, telecommunications, and financial services want to improve customer contact by offering benefits such as electronic bill display – and an external partner can provide speed to market. EBPP providers vary from comprehensive business process outsource (BPO) service providers to niche specialists called 'consolidators,' who can be used who can be used to aggregate bills from different suppliers for a single customer.

As figure 4.5 indicates there are several different ways in which EBPP systems can be modeled for optimal efficiency and speed.

A 'thick consolidator' model provides the greatest scope of service, with all bill information sent to the consolidator. In the 'thin consolidator' model the consolidator receives only the final amount (subject to tax on sales/purchases). The customer is then re-directed to the company website for detailed bill data.

As industries evolve, consumers demand increased levels of customer service and access to service-related information. The biller-direct method is key to successful customer-based initiatives,[4] as illustrated in the following case study.

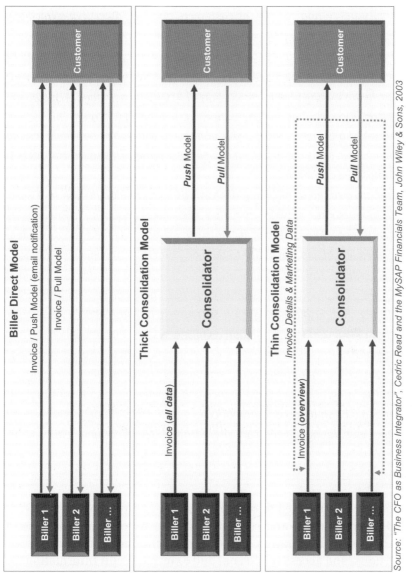

Source: "The CFO as Business Integrator", Cedric Read and the MySAP Financials Team, John Wiley & Sons, 2003

Figure 4.5 *Electronic bill presentment and payment models*

CASE STUDY
Outsourced EBPP in the utilities industry

One electricity utility had millions of customers and was diversifying into new market segments such as gas. Opportunities existed for cross-selling and up-selling using the customer accounting databases. Also, there were opportunities to streamline work order management processes – supported by the engineers – with those in the finance department. The strategy of becoming a multi-utility was fast becoming a reality.

Electricity and gas meter readers were connected using their handheld remote meter reading devices to the mainframe over the Internet. This saved transaction costs and improved cash flow.

The company wanted to move rapidly towards its technology vision so it partnered with an outsource provider to build a biller-direct capability to enhance its customer interface. New customer billing systems were required to consolidate billing facilities – enabling the utility to tie many orders to one invoice. Additionally, the call centers – the first point of oral contact with the consumers – provided a one-stop shop for processing customer enquiries. These call centers were linked using customer relationship management software to a customer data warehouse, that was not only linked to the outsourced billing system, but also incoming and outgoing email. The outsource provider's workflow processes were used to manage the credit control – coordinating dispute management and providing online dispute resolution. The integration between finance and engineering also meant that the call center could bring together automatically a truly cross-functional service for the customer, eliminating unnecessary internal and external communications traffic.

An outsourcer can be used to centralize credit control, providing effective credit management and reducing arrears. A company-wide credit policy requires the integration of distribution channels, automated real-time decisions, and access to internal and external credit information for all employees. Credit risk assessment, is another area in which external expertise can add value.

GENERAL ACCOUNTING, REPORTING, AND DECISION SUPPORT

Typically, in an outsourced shared service center environment, general ledger and the accounts closing process (in line with corporate policy, timetable and accounting manual) is included in scope. The client retains ownership of the balance sheet and financial results, undertakes interpretive financial analysis, and authorizes journal adjustments and non-standard provisions. The outsourced shared service center undertakes general accounting activities, such as standard provisioning, general ledger posting, *run netting* and interface reconciliation, cost allocation routines, and generates the financial and management reporting packs. From a consolidation point of view, it is common for the outsource provider to handle the trial balances of all the relevant legal entities before retained finance performs the technical consolidation and any group reporting. Normally, the outsourcer carries out more than 80% of the general accounting process. In one outsourced scenario, the scope unfolded as shown in the table overleaf.

The outsourcer is typically responsible for ensuring that the shared service center operates in compliance with tax rules from a transactional standpoint. The client company retains responsibility for ensuring that accounting practices adhere to tax regulations. Independent advisors provide tax advice and interpretation of tax legislation.

Normally, an outsourcing provider prepares the monthly group reporting pack, collates data for benchmarking purposes, and calculates and reports on routine metrics. The *outsourcer* typically also inputs the annual budget entries to accounting systems, provides ad hoc information requested by users, and maintains reporting tools. The *client company* specifies operational data and business parameters, timetables, and the data format required for analysis.

Activities retained *in-house* include most of the strategic aspects of budgeting, forecasting, and long-term planning. Analysis of trends and comparisons between accounting periods and with budget are normally also retained by client companies.

The cost of providing data and routine analytics for decision support is often difficult to quantify and can spiral out of control if demand for management information grows unchecked. The old adage of 'I know that half of the management information I produce is of no use – I just don't know which half!' applies. Few companies prepare a proper business case for the provision of management information, and yet significant in-house resources are tied up in technology, processing, and delivering information.

General Ledger Accounting, Consolidation, and Inter-Company	
Transferred to Outsourced Center	**Retained by Company**
General Ledger Accounting	*General Ledger Accounting*
Maintain Chart of Accounts (mechanical maintenance, not the controllership)	Define and maintain controllership of Chart of Accounts
Monthly/Quarterly Close	*Monthly/Quarterly Close*
Manage the closing process	Define the closing process
General Ledger Accounting	*General Ledger Accounting*
Prepare and post non-judgmental accruals and prepayments	Prepare and post business judgmental accruals and prepayments
Financial Reconciliation	*Financial Reconciliation*
Prepare, review, and reconcile the Trial Balance	Review and approve the Trial Balance
Inter-company	*Inter-company*
Prepare, issue, book, and process inter-company invoices	Prepare, approve, and input all inter-company purchase orders
Resolve day-to-day inter-company issues, agree inter-company balances, and resolution of disputed accounts	Resolve escalated inter-company disputed accounts and approve/return non-matching invoices
Consolidation	*Consolidation*
Consolidating of regional results and preparation of supporting schedules	Respond to questions and ad hoc queries
Prepare change analysis and *flash* results	Prepare accounts commentaries and non-financial data for reporting
Prepare financial/statistical data	
Reconcile intra-group balances	

For these reasons, companies are beginning to consider seriously the idea of outsourcing the provision of management information. A number of global companies are well along this path and their experiences will provide useful signposts for the future. The demand for outsource services for decision support is vast, and CFOs who have had a successful experience with outsourcing F&A are now looking to outsource this area too. Most CFOs, however, still need to be convinced that proprietary, commercially sensitive data will be kept secure and confidential before making such a move.

THE INTEGRATED F&A OUTSOURCE PROPOSITION

Today, the CFO stands at the center of a complex web of internal and external relationships, all of which must be astutely orchestrated and integrated. As integrator, the CFO must manage all aspects of financial operations. This encompasses all the processes and transactions directly affecting cash flow and working capital. Financial operations begin with supplier/buyer selection and extend through the payment process, information reporting and analysis, and cash flow forecasting.

Figure 4.6 shows how an outsourcing provider performs most of the activities in buying (purchase-to-pay), selling (order-to-cash), and accounting/reporting.

As shown in Figure 4.6, technology is used to link customers, suppliers, and a partner bank; the outsourcer does the rest. This approach enables the client to gain full advantage of advanced technology, shared services, and outsourcing resources in achieving its process vision.[5] By outsourcing major parts of financial operations, processes can be managed to positively influence receivables (DSO), financial forecasting, and working capital. Benefits include:

- Improved inventory control and cash management
- Significant reductions in working capital
- Lower financing cost on invested capital
- Fewer labor-intensive processes
- More efficient automated financial systems.

To the CFO, a strong, integrated finance operating solution offers an exciting new set of problem-solving capabilities. Specifically, it enables:

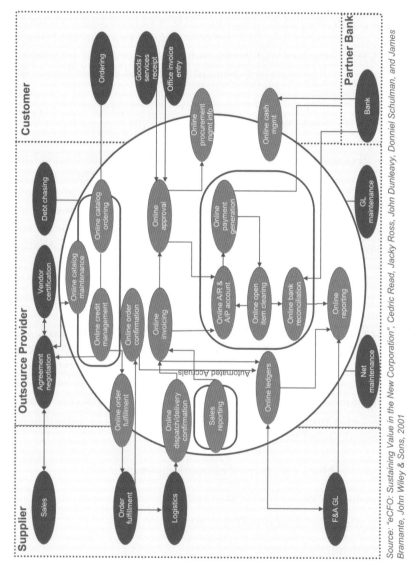

Source: "eCFO: Sustaining Value in the New Corporation", Cedric Read, Jacky Ross, John Dunleavy, Donniel Schulman, and James Bramante, John Wiley & Sons, 2001

Figure 4.6 *Vision of online, outsourced accounting service provision*

- More timely or precise data on receivables

- More accurate forecasting, based on more reliable receivables input

- A reduction in costly working capital float

- More detailed financial information

- More rapid resolution of payment issues

- A more holistic view of activities with trading partners

- More efficient capital allocation to higher ROI projects.

Exciting opportunities[6] exist for reaping cost savings and process improvements from outsourcing financial operations. Figure 4.7 illustrates the interactions between buyers and sellers – and the role that intermediaries can play in improving financial services.

Outsourcing offers attractive benefits in such circumstances, including:

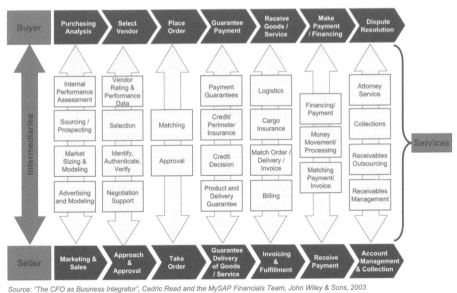

Source: "The CFO as Business Integrator", Cedric Read and the MySAP Financials Team, John Wiley & Sons, 2003

Figure 4.7   *The role of intermediaries in financial operations*

- **Upgraded operational efficiency:** all trading partners within supply chain networks can use advanced systems to trace delays, correct mistakes, and make preventive process improvements.

- **Support for sales, marketing & logistics:** a strong financial supply chain offers powerful analytic tools for sales (analyzing customer buying patterns and credit profiles, for example), supplier management, and related process areas.

- **Improved customer service:** by ensuring smooth, harmonious payment negotiations between buyers and sellers – and by generating timely data to resolve customer service disputes.

These outsourced financial operations can free your retained employees to focus on relationship building rather than on bookkeeping and basic accounting transaction issues.

CFO INSIGHTS

- For the best results, consider outsourcing the full scope of the extended process 'end-to-end.' Successful outsourcing strategies require a full vision of your target business process environment. Use business process best practices to stretch the imagination.

- When considering the business case for outsourcing of F&A, look at integrating every aspect of *financial operations* – from supplier through to customer.

- Most CFOs feel uncomfortable outsourcing those F&A processes involving direct customer contact. In reality, this is not such a big risk, unless there is considerable relationship complexity.

- The biggest untapped source of potential benefit from outsourcing lies in decision support. Few companies prepare a proper business case for improving decision support and yet major resources are tied up internally in providing information – representing poor value for money – not a cost-effective situation!

FROM INSIGHT TO ACTION

DEVELOP A VISION FOR YOUR F&A PROCESSES OF THE FUTURE

Take full advantage of what best-practice research, benchmarking studies, new technology, shared services, and outsourcing have to offer. Go for *lights-out* processing. Use the Internet to link customers, suppliers, and your partner bank – let the outsourcer do the rest!

MAP FINANCIAL OPERATIONS TO THE ENTERPRISE

Baseline metrics for DSO, vendor payment, working capital, and velocity through the physical supply chain. Set stretch targets – make your financial operations strategy the centerpiece of your F&A outsourcing value proposition.

UNDERSTAND WHAT IS GENUINELY A 'CORE PROCESS'

Which processes are really providing a competitive advantage? Try starting from the assumption that all processes are candidates for outsourcing – and work back from there.

KNOW YOUR OUTSOURCE PROVIDER'S STRENGTHS & WEAKNESSES

In which processes does your provider truly offer a competitive advantage? What are its key operating assets? Which processes offer economies of scale and risk mitigation?

GO END-TO-END IN YOUR PROCESS SCOPING

Full transformational benefits and value lie in linking purchasing with payables, sales order management with receivables, HR with payroll. Don't limit the results you achieve by creating unnatural breaks in the process.

DESIGN THE RETAINED ORGANIZATION

When you *cut* the process, only retain activities that require your judgment, interpretation, and policy. Then re-define your retained organization for its new role!

CONSIDER CONTROLS AND RISK

You are outsourcing many of your controls – but none of your responsibility – to a third party. But remember, many say that outsourcing has *improved* service quality and compliance.

THINK CAREFULLY ABOUT YOUR CUSTOMER RELATIONSHIPS

Keep in-house those customer-related activities that require your company's unique skill and capabilities. Consider the benefits of outsourcing credit and receivables management.

DEFINE THE HAND-OFF POINTS IN THE PROCESS BETWEEN THE OUTSOURCER AND WHAT YOU RETAIN IN-HOUSE

Hand-off points are not only process-related, they rely heavily on human interaction and technology as well. Do the hard work to define these in detail. Measure hand-off performance – for both sides of the fence – in service level agreements (SLAs).

'GO ALL THE WAY!'...TO TRIAL BALANCE, P&L, AND BALANCE SHEET

However, responsibility for accounting principles, practices, and external published information must remain with the CFO. Retain in-house ownership of the results, strategic financial analysis, and non-financial adjustments. Consider outsourcing general ledger maintenance, the '*fast close*' and routine journal adjustments.

PREPARE A BUSINESS CASE FOR DECISION SUPPORT

Test the developing market for outsourcing best practice, technology, and applications for your desired integrated decision-support architecture. Include in scope your budgeting, forecasting, scorecard, and routine management reporting.

REFERENCES

1 Linder, Sawyer and Goodman, *Control, Getting it and Keeping it,* Accenture Institute for Strategic Change, 2003. www.accenture.com

2 Gartner, BPO Validates: Verticalization and Aggregation Accelerate, *Market Trends*, February 2003.

3 Avivah Litan and Mike Cruz, Gartner, *EBPP Future Blends Direct and Bank Aggregation Models*, January 2004. www.gartner.com

4 Cynthia Moore & Avivah Litan, Gartner, *The State of E-Billing in the Utilities Industry*, October 2002.

5 Cedric Read and the PwC financial management consulting team, *eCFO: Sustaining Value in the New Corporation*, Wiley, 2001.

6 Cedric Read, Hans Dieter Scheuermann and the mySAP Financials Team, *The CFO as Business Integrator*, Wiley, 2003.

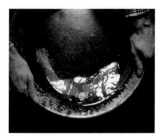

CHAPTER 5

Global Sourcing of Service Delivery

MIGRATING TO A GLOBAL DELIVERY NETWORK

Lim How Teck, CFO
Neptune Orient Lines

Neptune Orient Lines (NOL) is a global transportation and logistics company. NOL recently signed an eight-year agreement for the outsourcing of its transaction-based finance functions. The agreement covers activities in NOL corporate, its container transportation arm, American President Lines (APL), and APL's logistics business. NOL's CFO, Lim How Teck, says:

'This is a significant step in the group's ongoing drive to streamline finance and accounting processes around the world. Our core business is transportation and logistics, not financial processing. It makes good commercial sense to leverage the assets of our outsource provider, which has an excellent track record in offering this service to clients globally. This allows us to focus our own finance function on core activities that create value for the NOL Group.'

The company was looking for an external service provider with an international network in order to gain greater variability in its cost structure and increase scalability to accommodate changes in business volume. The overall outsourcing challenge was to support NOL in improving its competitive position and building core capabilities. Outsourcing would free NOL's finance team to provide enhanced decision support, globally centralized accounting, and to secure greater corporate control and transparency.

Assuming responsibility for accounts payable, accounts receivable, and accounts reconciliations, Accenture provides 24/7 coverage for the NOL Group's global operations in four continental theaters (Americas, Europe, Middle East, and Asia). Today, services are provided from a center in Shanghai, China, staffed with approximately 200 people. Twenty-three countries are supported, ranging from the United States, to France and Germany in Europe, to Saudi Arabia and United Arab Emirates (UAE) in the Middle East, to Thailand, Malaysia, Indonesia, Korea, and Japan in Asia.

Figure 5.1 shows the NOL service locations around the world that were transferred into the global outsourcing delivery center in Shanghai.

In addition to the main delivery center in Shanghai, the outsourcing provider also has customer service leads based in the United States, Europe, and Asia who work directly with NOL's management in each region. This innovative shared service initiative provides incentives for both NOL and its outsource partner. Opportunities for reward are shared based on the savings and benefits achieved.

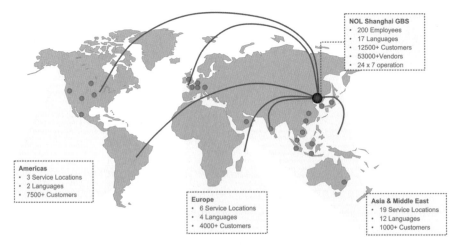

Figure 5.1 *NOL's global business services (GBS) delivery network*

The outsourcer decided that Shanghai was the best place to base NOL's service center for the following reasons:

- *Large skilled and educated labor pool (population: over 20 million)*
- *Western finance and accounting skills (over 20,000 multinationals from 100+ countries)*
- *Global language availability (17 languages supported in Shanghai center)*
- *Desirable location for skilled resources in China*
- *Modern infrastructure.*

Not only is Shanghai a gateway to China's massive domestic market of 1.5 billion people, it is also home to more than half the world's top companies. These companies are drawn by its favorable business climate: Shanghai's modern infrastructure, cosmopolitan character, and multilingual capability make it very attractive. In NOL's shared service center alone, employees speak 17 languages: Arabic, Bahasa (Indonesia and Malaysia), Cantonese, Dutch, English, French, German, Hindi, Japanese, Khmer (Cambodia), Korean, Mandarin, Spanish, Tagalog (Philippines), Thai, Urdu, and Vietnamese!

When visiting the Shanghai delivery center, potential multinational customers have been pleasantly surprised at the deep skills of Accenture's staff – not only in finance and accounting, but also linguistically. These skills have been enhanced by close contact with client employees. For example, the center' s new staff shadowed their experienced counterparts in NOL during the transition period, facilitating real-time knowledge transfer. Web-based training further enriched the Shanghai staff's business process expertise. The diversity of the outsourcer's management team – drawn from its pool of global experts – was also vital to the success of the transition.

NOL also has access to its provider's global delivery network for risk mitigation and contingency planning. The CFO concludes: 'In essence, we benefit from the opportunity to scale quickly and be responsive to changes in our market. We have greater transparency and better controls. Above all, we share a common view of NOL's strategic vision. I can say that we see the Shanghai delivery center as a very important node in our global infrastructure.'

The success of this global outsourcing arrangement depends on both partners being open and fair with one another – and their willingness to share both risks and *benefits. With its Shanghai center running efficiently and cost-effectively, NOL's finance team can focus on its primary strategic goal: adding value to its customer services.*

Companies today are intensely interested in setting up regional shared service delivery centers and locating them in countries around the world. Choosing where to go was once a very daunting proposition, especially when the question involved in-house shared services and the decision rested with a company's CFO and executive team. Increasingly, however, location issues are handled by outsource providers. As their global networking capabilities have grown, so has their expertise in this area.

As a result, the chief question that today's CFOs must wrestle with is not *where to go*, but *who to outsource F&A services to*. In choosing to outsource, they are striving to buy established services that deliver high-quality, well-defined business outcomes at a predetermined price. Many early outsourcing adopters used a dedicated center that serviced only their needs. Increasingly, however, companies are turning to multiclient service delivery centers. These offer standardized IT platforms, economies of scale, and the chance to leverage outsourcers' ongoing technology investments.

Where do you start in making a decision to globally source your company's F&A services? How do you rationalize seemingly conflicting issues? How do you weigh likely benefits and risks? This chapter provides answers to the big questions that executives routinely ask about how and where to locate outsourced services. It offers advice from outsourcing veterans and takes you down what is now a well-traveled path to making successful global delivery decisions.

THREE WAYS TO SOURCE GLOBALLY

- **Option #1:** Some large global corporations such as HSBC, British Airways, and GE have retained key F&A activities in-house but relocated their back-office operations to low-cost locations such as China and India. These are what we call 'captured in-sourced shared service solutions.'

- **Option #2:** Other companies have shifted their back-office processes to one of the many niche business process outsourcing (BPO) service providers. These are generally native operators based in low-cost countries such as India. Historically, this strategy has been used most often for IT outsourcing.

- **Option #3:** Buyers who select this approach utilize the global delivery networks of mega-service providers who operate from multiple locations around the world. By leveraging their outsourcers' resources, these companies shift back-office work to the geographic-and-skill mix that best fits their requirements.

Increasingly, industry analysts are forecasting that the third option will be the dominant strategy for multinational corporations. At its best, global sourcing brings together the right blend of people, skills, and capabilities to provide clients with price-competitive and cost-effective solutions. It also offers other powerful advantages, including high quality, reduced risk, and speed to market. Today's mega-service providers have global networks that offer clients the flexibility of multiple facilities along with 24/7 coverage. The result? Seamless service delivery – an important advantage in today's business environment.

The global sourcing proposition: beyond low cost

Corporations around the world are responding to the enormous pressure to realize savings by transferring major portions of their back-office operations to locales such as Bangalore or Shanghai. Executives are attracted largely by labor arbitrage savings: offshore labor rates of $20 to $30 per hour vs. $50 to $60 per hour in their domestic markets. To win new business, some service providers have discounted prices even further. For many companies, price points of 20% to 50% below in-house cost are too compelling to ignore.

Global sourcing of BPO allows service providers to drive down costs – and enables their clients to outsource many business processes that they previously couldn't touch – either because the economics did not work or technology wasn't available. Executives have repeatedly asked us: 'How long will this economic advantage be maintained?' Our research suggests that industry leaders will enjoy this 'edge' for at least 15 years – and perhaps beyond – as they reap the fruits of their investment in successive waves of technology innovation. We explore the issue of advancing technology in Chapter 11.

In more and more cases, service providers offer a 'prescribed' approach to meeting clients' F&A requirements based on sophisticated, highly 'engineered' delivery processes. This strategy is reinforced by high quality standards, certification from key institutions, and disciplined execution methodology. The result: Steadily improving business processes. As processes such as order-to-cash transactions become fully digitized, the benefits of outsourcing will far outweigh the advantages of simple labor arbitrage.

Ultimately, accelerated order-to-cash processing will cut completion time for the end-to-end process cycle. As a result, clients will have less cash tied up in working capital – a major financial gain. End-to-end automation will allow outsourcers to encourage clients to move beyond cost reduction and create new sources of economic value. This more holistic view – supplemented by new, insightful data on demand/supply patterns and customer profitability – will support superior decision-making.[1]

Outsource industry leaders are focusing on improving customer support by reducing delivery costs while expanding their global reach and services. We call this an 'extension of the footprint of finance across the business.' Examples include payment settlement services and business analytics. New capabilities like these can link CRM processes directly with back-office transactions such as cash collection. Integrating these functions will enable CFOs to deploy working capital more effectively and obtain better pricing.

The current finance BPO model can improve economic performance using legacy systems as the basis for service design. However, the new frontier is the availability of a global sourcing option that frees clients from this constraint by leveraging more standardized ways of working. This, in turn, enables service providers to benefit from scale in the same way that BP has in its UK North Sea operations.

Over the past two years, the global reach of the leading service providers has grown dramatically, fuelling competition in the BPO supply market and pitting country against country for the prize of being the location of first choice. To win a piece of the action, countries are racing to enact legal, regulatory, and infrastructure reforms. China, for example, is seeking to attract BPO activity through environmental enhancements ranging from intellectual property reforms to tax breaks for foreign direct investment. But why exactly is outsourcing growing in locations such as India, China, Eastern Europe, and the Philippines? Among the most critical factors are:

- **Skilled manpower availability:** India, for example, has the second largest English speaking workforce and the largest higher education system in the world (250 universities and 10,500 colleges).

- **Multilingual proficiency:** NOL's service center in Shanghai, for example, offers 17 languages – and this number is increasing.

- **Highly motivated employees:** Labor arbitrage, surging productivity, and higher quality levels are all having a profound impact on BPO operations. Centers are attracting better-educated, strongly motivated employees who see outsourcing as a career path.

- **Favorable government policies:** Tax concessions, telecom deregulation, patent protection, and better policing of software and intellectual property piracy.

- **Improvements in telecom infrastructure:** Costs continue to plummet in this area (for example, a 45% drop in India in 2002); bandwidth is improving; and cheaper, more efficient Internet technologies are easily available.

We see growing confidence among both domestic and multinational corporations about tapping into these new outsourcing locales. Clearly, the frontiers of globalization cannot be rolled back. To remain competitive, the vast majority of companies will need to consider global BPO sourcing at some stage in the next few years.[2] The implications for corporate resource deployment are huge. Companies once moved people to where the work was. Now, they are moving their work to where the people and assets are.

The power of BPO is based on accessing the skills of large concentrations of highly capable workers across the globe.[3] However, it requires more than offshore facilities to generate value; it requires the seamless integration of processes on a global scale. Leading outsource providers have adopted multiprocess, multiclient shared service center solutions to meet the aspirations of client executives like Allan Eilles at BP, which requires its outsource providers to 'follow the sun' through their service delivery locations in order to continually drive down costs.

So, should you globally source?
To clarify your outsourcing goals, ask yourself the following questions:

1 How much effort is needed to simplify and standardize processes?

2 Are the benefits of scale being reaped; if so, can you get more?

3 Have you taken advantage of labor-cost arbitrage?

4 If you are already in a low-cost location, could costs be reduced still further?

5 Should your outsource goals broaden beyond simple cost reduction?

6 Is there more to be gained from further investment in technology and would it be more efficient if someone else absorbed those costs?

Use the checklist in Figure 5.2 to pinpoint where you are on the development continuum.

Our research into service delivery location has uncovered some insights that, at first glance, appear counterintuitive. Among our findings:

- Choosing where to source service delivery is a *global* decision; at any point in time, however, some countries are viewed by corporate decision-makers as 'hot' places to go – and may rank inordinately high on their 'site' lists

- Executives frequently view site selection as a control and risk-reduction issue; in fact, they can place unnecessary limits on performance and benefits when they dictate service delivery location options to a service provider.

As most seasoned corporate executives have learned, it is more effective to leverage their providers' existing network of service delivery centers than to be overly prescriptive about how and where outsource assets should be deployed.

F&A Transformation Checklist

Benefits Realized	Not Started / Failing	Making Progress	Succeeded
High Performing Business Transformation			
Low Cost Location Adopted			
Shared Services Implemented			
Business Process Standardization (ERP)			
Business Process Simplification			

Capability Continuum

Figure 5.2 *Evaluating your ability to transform your F&A function*

Some companies, however, have both sufficient scale and the internal resources to set up offshore shared services centers on their own, using a standardized process model. Consider the following example.

 ### CASE STUDY
Offshoring higher value-added F&A functions

This industrial multinational has operations across the globe, with major resources in three markets: Asia-Pacific, the US, and the UK. The CFO responsible for the company's global service center is based at its corporate headquarters in London. She comments:

'We constantly strive to improve our back-office processes, increase efficiency, and secure the benefits of labor-cost arbitrage by exploiting our geographic reach.'

The company has been using offshore shared service centers for nearly five years now. Recently, many of its London-based operations were relocated to India. It now has more than 2,500 staff there handling operational and F&A processes. To quote the CFO:

'We operate in an uncertain world. We are trying to spread our geographic risk – and hedge our political, financial, and operational exposure. The group has set up an entirely separate internal organization, which runs shared services on a stand-alone commercial footing. Its criteria for selecting shared service locations include language capability, wage arbitrage, political risk, and fiscal exposure (tax advantage is a significant driver). 'Traditionally, we transferred offshore relatively low value-added processes with limited direct customer interface, such as retrospective transactions and account maintenance,' says the CFO. More recently, the company has begun offshoring complex, higher value-added transactions. The unit lead comments:

'Certainly, companies have successfully moved offshore the more routine elements of the finance function, such as purchase invoice payment. But there is less evidence for more sophisticated functions, such as general ledger or activities requiring direct customer interface, such as credit vetting and debt collection. We are looking at who is doing what in offshoring and in outsourcing higher value-added finance activities.' The CFO describes her next round of research:

'I am in touch with tax authorities in both the United Kingdom and India; our pricing approach for shared services has to satisfy the tax authorities from both a

direct tax and a VAT perspective. Our success in the past can be traced, in part, to our due diligence on such issues. However, it comes back to change management basics – detailed process mapping, rigorous training, buy-in from business users, and exhaustive migration planning.' The story does not end there. The company is constantly on the lookout for where the next attractive location to open a new shared service center might be. New lower cost alternatives will always be on the horizon.

This company is unusual in having made such significant progress in offshoring. To date, it has orchestrated the single largest transfer of finance operations to India.

MAPPING THE OFFSHORE LANDSCAPE

To meet the demand for offshoring, developing countries have emerged as havens for sophisticated providers ready and able to deliver superior outsource services. Many companies in these countries offer both high quality and competitive pricing. When it comes to offshoring, a country can offer a unique combination of benefits. Critical factors in determining suitability for offshoring are contrasted in Figure 5.3 for countries ranging from India to Ireland.

While characteristics vary from country to country, the most important selection criteria fall into one of two categories. The first category defines factors that service providers can do little to influence or mitigate.

Criteria	India	Philippines	China	Russia	Canada	Ireland
Fiscal Advantage	High	Medium	Low	Low	Medium	High
Skilled Labor Availability	High	Medium	Low	Low	Medium	Low
Infrastructure	Medium	High	Medium	Low	High	High
Educational System	High	Medium	High	High	High	High
Cost Advantage	High	High	High	High	Medium	Low
Service Quality	High	High	Low	Low	High	High
Cultural Compatibility	Medium	High	Low	Low	High	High
Time / Distance Advantage	Low	Low	Low	Medium	High	High
English Proficiency	High	High	Low	Low	High	High

Legend: Low, Medium, High

Figure 5.3 *Comparison of outsourcing criteria by offshoring country*

The second set of factors can be influenced by company location and implementation strategy.[4]

External factors that providers can do little to mitigate in relation to service delivery	External factors that providers can (at least partly) influence
Socio-geopolitical risks	Prevailing labor costs
Ecosystem & trade options	Communications
Business environment	Culture and behavior
	Infrastructure
	Prevalence of distinctive competencies
	Physical & time zone displacement
	Asset capability enhancement

Let's examine some of these factors in more detail.

Prevailing labor costs
Countries differ fundamentally in their economic structures, gross national products, trade balances, monetary and fiscal policies – and in other factors that affect labor pricing and availability. As cost saving is generally the major driver for offshoring, the opportunity for labor arbitrage is a key consideration.

Socio-geopolitical risk
Countries differ in their inherent stability: Social and geopolitical factors can quickly lead to unrest and disrupted business operations. Venezuela, for example, was gaining favor as a viable offshore location. However, various problems have, over the near term, diminished the ability of its service providers to attract both outside investment and international customers. In contrast, India once appeared on the brink of a nuclear conflict with Pakistan; today, it is a prime offshore choice.

Physical and time zone displacement
Technology has caused *'the death of time and distance'*. Physical distance is no longer a barrier to high standards of service delivery – and no longer

a crucial issue in offshore site selection. Internet technologies enable accounting operations to be carried out any time, anywhere – providing instant, online access via corporate intranets to data, such as financial statements, cash flows, and line-item transactional status. Regardless of locale, the CFO can access key information with a few key strokes; turn-around time is no longer a concern. Web-based innovation is making out-sourcing an attractive proposition for both small and large corporations.

Business environment

Countries differ in the 'friendliness' of their business environments. Friendliness factors include taxes, ease of dispute resolution through the legal system, ease of starting a business, and intellectual property pro-tection. The presence of such factors can diminish concerns and risks for companies seeking offshore sites. NASSCOM, a trade association in India, for example, has been instrumental in propelling the Indian software and outsource industries forward. India also recently reached new trade agreements with the United States, which promise to eliminate previous business constraints.

Language

Communication is not just about linguistic skill; it also encompasses accents, colloquialisms, and even body language. In voice-based out-sourcing (customer contact, employee support, telemarketing, collec-tions, financial services, etc.) speaking the same language is a key requirement. Outsource providers can positively influence language issues through employee training. When a mix of onshore 'high-touch' customer contacting is essential, network-based service delivery can fill the bill while also delivering routine operations for which language is not an issue.

Culture

Cultural affinity enhances communication and the growth of strong personal relationships. Consequently, when a high degree of value-added customer interaction is called for, cultural nuances can be critical. Invest-ment in employee training (including immersion in popular culture) can help bridge the cultural gap.

The results of a survey[5] showing sample countries' relative location attractiveness against local cost and capabilities are highlighted in Figure 5.4. As results indicate, India's abundant skilled manpower is making it increasingly attractive as a target destination for many multinationals.

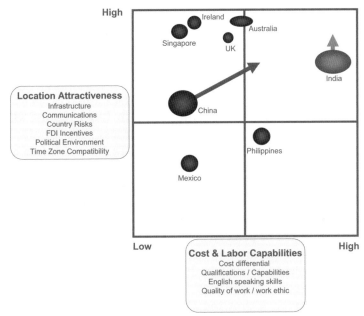

Source: Nasscom McKinsey & Co, adapted by Accenture

Figure 5.4   *Country attractiveness matrix*

A cautionary note: Care should always be exercised when evaluating location studies, given the rapidly evolving outsourcing landscape. In any
location analysis, certain criteria must be fully evaluated. These include:

Infrastructure
Communications infrastructure is a major factor in outsourcing/
offshoring choices – especially in the high-speed digital arena. Equally
important, though often taken for granted, is a clean, continuous supply
of electrical power. India, for example, has a relatively weak infrastructure. Many outsource providers based there have responded by equipping
their facilities to operate on a stand-alone basis.

Distinctive competencies
Countries differ significantly in the competencies they offer. Such
strengths are derived from national educational systems and industrial
conurbations that provide fertile training grounds and labor pools with
specialized skills.

USING GEOGRAPHY TO MITIGATE RISK

Correctly assessing risks and benefits has always been critical in offshore outsourcing.[6] The trick of course, is to mitigate the former while maximizing the latter. In an unstable world, executives quite rightly feel vulnerable. Given global tensions, they ask, does it makes sense to have mission-critical operations humming away in India, China, and elsewhere? Is the risk of going offshore greater or less than the alternative? These are tough questions. There is no such thing as a risk-free option.

In the best of times, outsourcing is a tough sell to business executives wary of foreign entanglements. Immediately following 9/11, many companies banned senior business executives from all non-essential foreign travel. Some businesses also backed away from global sourcing deals due to tightened budgets or perceived security risks. Today, amid economic cycles and terrorist warfare, anxiety persists about handing off critical back-office projects to vendors in distant locales such as India, Pakistan or the Philippines.

Recently, however, a growing chorus of executive testimonials has eased concerns about offshore security. Despite the occasional panic, executives with significant global experience say that global outsourcing remains viable. Today's unstable environment simply means that companies and their partners must develop better contingency plans in case of business disruption. Security remains a pivotal issue, no matter where you outsource – even in your home country. *The message: Executives need to adapt their sourcing strategy to an insecure world at home and abroad.*

Here is some advice from offshore outsourcing veterans:

- **Minimize foreign travel:** Once initial negotiations are over and your outsource operation has been up and running for 12 months, globally sourced deals require very little travel. Home-based project managers can manage contracts quite successfully and a service provider's account team, which frequently is split between the delivery locations and the customer's headquarters. In-house staff can interact with a service unit team via videoconferencing, which is far more cost-efficient than foreign travel.

- **Keep the code at home:** Software piracy has always been a concern when doing business globally. Most globally sourced projects are no longer completed at the vendor's remote site or on the vendor's systems (which may be corrupt or insecure). Typically, offshore delivery centers communicate via the Internet off their clients' systems, applications, and data – all of which are housed at secure sites or service networks. Core assets – business and code knowledge – should mainly remain in the client organization and its home country.

- **Have a back-up plan:** Aside from international travel, the biggest concern many people have about outsourcing is service disruption: What happens if communications and/or electricity are cut off? The leading outsource providers all have back-up communications systems (including satellite and fiber-optic capabilities). Mega-providers also have personnel deployed in the home countries of their clients, as well as overseas, to monitor systems. Emergency programs are supplemented by back-up plans that provide interoperability among multiple delivery centers in different geographies.

SOURCING CHOICES

Executives new to outsourcing are understandably concerned about location decisions and the risks they involve. Our advice: be open and flexible. Don't limit your choices up front and needlessly constrain your outsourcer's capabilities. Exploit your provider's experience and expertise in this area! Working together, you can carefully evaluate factors such as political stability, depth and availability of talent, cultural fit, and fiscal policy.

The bottom line? 'It's just not a good idea to have all of your eggs in one basket anymore,' says Marty McCaffrey, executive director of Salinas, California-based Software Outsourcing Research.[7] Bearing this in mind, here are brief profiles of some major global outsourcing locations:

India
The well-established leader in offshore IT outsourcing, India has a $4bn IT services export industry, a decade of experience over most other countries, and more than 80% of the offshore IT market. India continues to aggressively market its well-educated, skilled labor pool as a prime outsourcing asset.

China
With a population 1.3 billion strong, a solid educational system that emphasizes technology, and an average programmer salary of less than

$9,000 a year, it is not surprising that China is a key contender in the outsourcing world. What *may* be surprising is that the Chinese government, after years of trade policies that hampered IT development efforts, is setting up software parks and offering tax breaks to fertilize its growing IT services sector.

Russia

This country boasts a large supply of talented technology professionals (including rocket scientists laid off by the government) working for annual salaries of $5,000 to $7,500. Russia's IT services market (centered around Moscow, St. Petersburg, and Novosibirsk) has been growing from 40% to 60% per year. Like India, Russia has established an agency, the National Software Development Association, to foster continued growth. Gartner[8] estimates that by 2007, Russia will have captured a 5% market share of offshore services revenue from North America and Western Europe.

The Philippines

Under US rule for nearly 50 years, the Philippines is the destination most culturally compatible with America. English fluency is key to the Philippines' popularity as a site for call center operations. The country has a strong, 20-year base in programming skills and a solid IT infrastructure (established by the US military).

'I'm a huge fan of the Philippines,' says William Lewis, senior international liaison at LexisNexis, a Dayton, Ohio-based company. 'There are great values to be had there and growing offerings in software services. Its highly Westernized culture makes it very attractive to those with little offshore experience.' Rounding off our review, we offer basic information on three other popular outsourcing destinations.

Czech Republic

- **Geopolitical risk:** Low

- **Infrastructure/Communications:** Good. Solid investment in IT and communications infrastructure

- **English proficiency:** Good

- **Labor cost advantage/average IT programmer salary:** $4,800–$8,000/year; minimum wage similar to Hungary and Poland ($1,132–$1,584/year)

- **Pros:** The Czech Republic churns out 5,000 technical graduates every year. The IT services market experienced double-digit growth at a time when the global IT services market grew just 6%

- **Cons:** Low pay scales may give talent little reason to stay

- **Cultural compatibility:** Fair

- **Government support/laws:** Fair

- **Quality initiatives:** 334 ISO 9000 certifications

- **Major providers:** Deltax (www.deltax.cz); ICZ (www.i.cz); ISS (www.iss.cz); Minerva Czech Republic (www.minerva-is.cz); Prago-data (www.pragodata.cz); Accenture (www.accenture.com)

- **Major customers:** NA

- **Cities/Centers of outsourcing:** Prague

- **National IT organization:** NA

- **Size of industry:** $689.2 million

- **Total labor force:** 5.1 million

Venezuela

- **Geopolitical risk:** High

- **Infrastructure/Communications:** Fair. Modern, growing telecom and IT infrastructure

- **English proficiency:** Poor

- **Labor cost advantage/average IT programmer salary:** NA. Minimum wage is $2,556/year

- **Pros:** The government says it wants to support growth in its IT sector to reduce the country's dependence on the oil industry ...

- **Cons:** ... but hasn't done much yet. The government is in a state of flux

- **Cultural compatibility:** Poor

- **Government support/laws:** Poor

- Quality initiatives: 373 ISO 9000 certifications
- Major providers: Accenture (www.accenture.com)
- Major customers: NA
- Cities/Centers of outsourcing: Caracas
- National IT organization: Venezuelan Chamber of IT Companies (www.cavedatos.org.ve)
- Size of industry: NA
- Total labor force: 10.2 million

Brazil

- **Geopolitical risk:** Moderate
- **Infrastructure/Communications:** Good
- **English proficiency:** Poor
- **Labor cost advantage/average IT programmer salary:** NA. Minimum wage is $1,308/year (less than Chile, Argentina and more than India, Russia)
- **Pros:** Local companies are beginning to develop their own IT services delivery capability
- **Cons:** Until recently, IT activity in Brazil was limited to multinational companies
- **Cultural compatibility:** Good
- **Government support/laws:** Fair
- **Quality initiatives:** 9,489 ISO 9000 certifications
- Major providers: CPM Systemas (www.cpm.com.br); G&P Projectos e Systemas (www.gpnet.com.br); Proceda (www.proceda.com.br); Vetta Technologies (www.vettatech.com); Accenture (www.accenture.com)
- Major customers: GE Engine Services; Goodyear; Xerox; Coca-Cola
- Cities/Centers of outsourcing: Rio de Janeiro; Sao Paulo
- National IT organization: Sociedade de Usuários de Informática e Telecomunicaçaoes (www.sucesusp.org.br)

- **Size of industry:** NA

- **Total labor force:** 79.3 million

Additional factors to be considered when transferring F&A processes to offshore locations include:

- Finance qualifications and skills

- Tax incentives and accounting regulations

- Legal, data protection and intellectual property.

Figure 5.5 offers a comparative cost impact evaluation of 16 different European countries and their legal requirements for accounting records, invoice preparation, contract documentation, and credit checks.

A study of relevant country laws is essential for avoiding unwelcome complications in the use of foreign country resources. Most offshore providers will claim to have expertise in whatever service a customer needs. However, the sophisticated outsourcing buyer will see beyond marketing – and focus on the real capabilities and processes required.

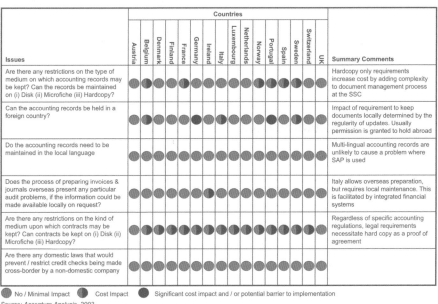

Figure 5.5 *European comparative cost impact evaluation*

Offshoring invariably involves sharing proprietary information with a service provider. While contract terms bind the provider and provide protection, we have found that data and intellectual property protection practices often fall short of clients' expectations. Stipulations up front about proprietary information and its use can help prevent later misunderstandings.

OUTSOURCING DUE DILIGENCE

It takes a deep knowledge of the global sourcing lifecycle to avoid mistakes in identifying appropriate sites, screening candidates, and selecting the best provider fit. Inadequate planning and insufficient due diligence can expose a global sourcing initiative to a variety of operational risks. CFOs must evaluate outsource providers using criteria such as process knowledge, infrastructure, quality management, risk mitigation, delivery capability, and financial stability.

Consider the due diligence programs conducted in these two case studies[9] by companies interested in offshoring their operations:

 ## CASE STUDY 1

A Fortune 500 healthcare services company needed to reduce costs and change its cost structure from a fixed to a variable cost model. Its solution: Outsourcing the applications management of important, but non-core functions, such as hospital management, patient care, and billing management. The company decided to look at offshore and nearshore sourcing solutions, specifically India and Canada. Initial research showed that Canada offered a low-cost solution with minimal risk. India offered even greater cost advantage, but the company was hesitant about the risks involved. While detailed due diligence had been performed, the company's CFO was still not sure that the quality of the proposed service and pricing levels could be sustained.

Subsequently, the CFO commissioned an independent third-party specialist advisor to undertake a thorough capabilities assessment. This provided the additional due diligence needed to accurately measure delivery capabilities. The CFO obtained detailed data points comparing country infrastructure and stability, as well as pro-

vider capability. As a result, he was satisfied that the providers on his short list would be able to produce the results promised in their contractual documentation. The CFO made an obvious choice – in this case, the lowest-cost Indian provider – and used the assessment results to negotiate better service-level agreements and pricing.

 ## CASE STUDY 2

A global technology services company wanted to offshore major portions of its call center operations. Key business requirements included significantly reducing cost – by as much as 50% – while finding a provider with a highly educated workforce and a strong telecommunications infrastructure. Providers bidding on the project needed reference accounts, proven track records, and the ability to handle a high volume of calls per day. Providers had to meet current call volume, but have the capacity to adjust to forecasted growth patterns. During due diligence, the CFO needed validation of a low-risk, cost-savings scenario for choosing an offshore provider as a partner.

The CFO's procurement department reviewed the standard industry certifications for process quality. However, these third-party certifications provided only process data. The CFO responded: 'Yes, the outsourcing providers have a process in place to answer calls in 5 seconds or less. But I have questions about their linguistic capabilities. What about appropriate cultural training? And do they have the necessary resources and infrastructure if we have a growth spurt?'

The CFO expanded his due diligence to pinpoint potential provider weaknesses. He became proactive: asking questions, probing relevant issues, and confirming that satisfactory solutions would be in place. Armed with ample data from this analysis, the company ultimately chose an outsource provider from a short list of three. The provider selected had not been the CFO's initial first choice – in fact, early on, the successful contender had been regarded as an 'also ran!'

Global sourcing offers immediate cost savings, but without proper precautions, long-term risks can lead to higher, rather than lower, costs. Consequently, due diligence audits, which can be conducted by independent third-party specialists, are vital for qualifying provider performance capabilities – and reducing risks over the offshore outsourcing lifecycle. We discuss the role of third-party outsourcing advisors in Chapter 7.

EMERGING GLOBAL SHARED SERVICE CENTER NETWORKS

At the beginning of this chapter, the CFO of NOL made the case for migrating to an outsource provider's global network of service centers. The interview that follows elaborates on NOL's decision. Viewing the partnership from the service provider's perspective, Accenture describes its strategy and investment in global outsourcing assets.

CASE STUDY
Accenture's delivery center network

The Accenture delivery center network has more than 50 integrated facilities around the world. This network drives the company's technology and outsourcing solution delivery capability. To quote Harry You, the CFO of Accenture: 'We emphasize these benefits to our clients: quality solutions, reduced risk, speed to market, and certainty of outcome.'

The centers offer the following:

1. *Software development, Web services, business process and IT outsourcing, and application management*
2. *An end-to-end lifecycle delivery approach, from design to execution to solution management*
3. *A flexible, technically skilled labor pool trained in Accenture's proven solution delivery approach*
4. *An anytime, anywhere development environment available to clients globally, ensuring speed of delivery*
5. *An integrated suite of assets, methods, tools, and techniques.*

Harry goes on to say:

'We are a big provider in the F&A market. For example, we process more than 9 million purchase invoices a year through our centers and collect more than $34bn a

year in cash! This scale provides a huge cost advantage to our clients. We also have practical, hands-on experience in implementing and managing world-class finance processes. For example, we reduced one client's working capital by $90m in just four months. For another client, we reduced purchasing spend by $25m through the diligence of our purchase contracts compliance team.'

The Accenture delivery center network benefits from interoperability. The location of these integrated facilities – including the 22 that provide F&A outsourcing services – are pinpointed in Figure 5.6.

Here are some examples of the process coverage and the business benefits achieved by two delivery centers within Accenture's international service-delivery network:

1   Houston: *This center was established in 1995 to manage F&A outsourcing services for BP. The center now provides F&A and application outsourcing services to other clients in the energy industry. It has grown four-fold since its inception and the number of companies it supports has increased significantly. Today, the center employs 600 F&A and IT professionals. Languages spoken: English and Spanish. Countries supported include the US, Canada, Venezuela, and parts of the Caribbean.*

Map is representative of the growing number of finance and accounting centers open in 2003
Source: Accenture, 2003,

Figure 5.6   *Accenture's finance and accounting delivery center network*

2 Prague: *This center was established in 2001, initially to cover 60 locations across Europe for Rhodia. Six months after its launch, the center began work for a second client – a multinational automotive parts manufacturer. A number of other companies are now being served from, or in transition to, the center. Currently, more than 700 employees with extensive F&A expertise staff the center, together with an expatriate management team. Languages spoken include Czech, English, Dutch, Flemish, French, German, Italian, Polish, Portuguese, Romanian, Spanish, and Slovak.*

Assets such as Prague and Houston are now being networked together to provide clients with the benefits of geographic integration, global process standardization, time-zone coverage, mutual workload support, flexibility, and back-up.

TECHNOLOGY SHAPES THE FUTURE

Arguments for and against relocating to either a nearshore or offshore location are often predicated on technology. On the one hand, technology supports long-distance communication. On the other, it could ultimately eliminate the need for physical jobs altogether. During research for this book, many CFOs requested views on the impact of future technology on their location decisions.

New technologies are constantly emerging – and standards are evolving. For example, extended mark-up language (XML) technology and its relationship with its predecessor EDI is a big issue for the CFO because it is the medium through which financial information is transported online. Systems development, trading relationships, accounting transparency, and security – as well as reporting – are all affected.

Also, delivery center management tools are often forgotten in making outsourcing service provisions. Automated service management reporting, for example, will help with managing service level agreements (SLAs) and reporting on shared service center performance. A virtual help desk service can track and respond to queries raised by business users, as well as third parties, such as providers and customers. It can also automate query resolution. Technology can also facilitate self-help – for example, enabling vendors to deal with their own invoice payment queries.

Shared service centers that exploit leading-edge technology do not just achieve cost reduction; they add still greater value by improving man-

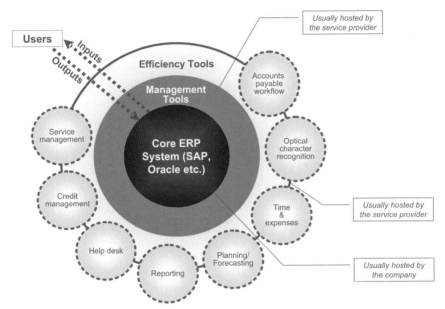

Figure 5.7 *Three layers of technology for outsourced service delivery centers*

agement control and business performance. In Figure 5.7, we illustrate the approach that one service provider used in structuring its technology assets.

Leading-edge service delivery networks today benefit from:

1 **Management tools:** for help desks, delivery centers and service management reporting

2 **Efficiency tools:** for automated credit and collections, and accounts payable workflow

3 **ERP:** for transaction processing and desktop procedures.

While no new wave of technology is poised to completely revolutionize business, existing technologies will continue to develop, making it easier to gather, communicate, and process information whenever and wherever it is needed. Wireless technology, Web services, and *silent commerce* all offer exciting opportunities for improvement and innovation (we discuss this further in Chapter 11). The question for the CFO is whether to make these technology investments in-house or to leverage the substantial ongoing investments already being made by service providers.

CFO INSIGHTS

- The debate on which single country to locate a regional shared service center in, has turned into a debate on which combination of processes should be delivered from a mix of globally interconnected service centers.

- Moving to a new location allows a new service-oriented culture to be created, one that is separate and distinct from the parent company's heritage. New employees are not entrenched in old patterns of behavior.

- Consider the range of geographies potentially available. If you focus on one location, you may place unnecessary constraints on the performance results that an outsource solution can deliver.

- Options range from the simple to the complex, including highly customized solutions in which a combination of onshore, offshore, and nearshore locations delivers a unique mix of processes.

- Technology has caused 'the death of time and distance.' Physical distance is no longer a barrier to high standards of service delivery – and no longer a crucial issue in offshore site selection. Increasingly, companies are turning to the networks of multiclient service delivery centers run by outsourcing providers.

FROM INSIGHT TO ACTION

DECIDE WHERE YOU ARE ON THE DEVELOPMENT CONTINUUM
Do you have more to do to simplify and standardize your processes? Could you benefit further from economies of scale? Be honest! Evaluate your capabilities to transform. Can you benefit from investments in technology by mega-service providers?

DETERMINE YOUR SHARED SERVICE CENTER LOCATION STRATEGY
Offshore, near-shore or in-country? Evaluate your choice of location against cost and capability criteria. Consider languages, cultural fit, local infrastructure, and skills required. Rank and weight your priorities. When you outsource, this becomes an 'input' rather than an 'output'.

CLARIFY YOUR LOCATION OBJECTIVES FROM THE OUTSET

Are you looking for labor-cost arbitrage or do you want something more? Be clear. Your strategic options range from a pure play, global full-service provider with transformational process and ERP capability to local offshore lowest-cost outsourcers. Do you want to share a service provider with other clients or follow the one-to-one service model? Be flexible: Do not dictate the choice of location to your service provider.

PERFORM DUE DILIGENCE

Carefully evaluate outsourcing providers' capabilities: process knowledge, infrastructure, quality, and risk management – *as well as their financial stability and ability to offer a 'structured control environment.'* If global sourcing, it may be wise to engage a specialist third party advisor for an independent provider qualification.

CONSIDER INTERNATIONAL REGULATORY, LEGAL, AND FIDUCIARY CONSTRAINTS

Different countries have different tax structures, legal accounting requirements, industry regulatory controls, labor laws, and contracting practices. These can change over time and you will need to keep abreast.

EVALUATE LOCATION RISKS

Low-cost countries initially seem attractive. However, political and socioeconomic conditions can change unexpectedly. Prepare contingency plans for natural disasters – flooding, earthquakes, and wars. Remember: Your corporate reputation could be at stake.

CAPITALIZE ON YOUR SHARED SERVICE CENTER NETWORK AS A GLOBAL ASSET

Benefit from your outsource provider's investments. Take advantage of geographic spread – *interoperability* between centers offers workload management, resilience, and disaster recovery. Encourage your outsource provider to grow its capabilities. You'll benefit from lower unit-cost levels as more companies join with you in leveraging scale.

REFERENCES

1 Peter Bendor-Samuel, CFO, *Outsourcing in 2003: How Offshoring is Changing the Industry*, Everest Group, January 2004. www.outsourcing-journal.com

2 Stephen Dunn and Todd Furniss, COO, *Offshore Comes of Age in 2003. New Players Enter the Field to Service Buyer's Competitive Needs*, Everest Group, January 2004. www.outsourcing-journal.com

3 Beth Ellyn Rosenthal, Editor, Finance and Accounting BPO Adds Up to Business Transformation, *CFO Magazine*, January 2003.

4 neoIT, *Mapping Offshore Markets*, April 2003.

5 Nasscom McKinsey & Company, *Survey on Offshore Outsourcing in India*, Ernst & Young, 2003. www.ey.com/india

6 Laton McCartney, A Shore Thing? *CFO Magazine*, March 2003.

7 Stephanie Overby, Passages Beyond India, *CIO Magazine*, January 2003.

8 *Gartner presentation at Gartner's symposium*, 2004.

9 neoIT, Offshore Sourcing Supplier Due Diligence: Services Assurance for Buyers, *The Outsourcing Journal*, December 2002. www.outsourcing-journal.com

CHAPTER 6

Pricing and Shaping Your Deal

SHAPING THE DEAL FOR A CO-SOURCING

Ian Ailles, Managing Director of Specialist Businesses
Thomas Cook UK

Thomas Cook UK (part of Thomas Cook AG which is jointly owned by Lufthansa and Karlstadtquelle), is a leading European travel company with one of the most widely recognized and respected travel brands in the world. More than 14,500 employees work in its collection of travel agencies, tour operations, airlines, and hotels. In 2001, Thomas Cook UK needed to turn around its business performance to ensure survival. Ian Ailles, who was group finance director at the time, comments:

   'The UK business was losing over £50m per year. Our shareholders were not going to provide more investment so we needed a partner who could help us consolidate and transform. Our operations were based on inefficient business processes, we were spread over too many diverse geographic locations, and our organization was not sufficiently profit focused. We launched our business transformation program with the objective of substantially reducing our cost base, increasing margins, and changing towards a more profit-based culture.'

   The company appointed a new management team to lead this transformation program and the results have been impressive. Head-office operations have been relocated from London to Peterborough UK; new brands targeting specific customer segments have enhanced the performance of tour operations; cost savings have been achieved through the closing of offices, consolidation of operational bases for the airline, and through a program of centralization and management streamlining. Ian goes on to say:

'Our initial focus for the transformation of our business was to aggressively reduce the cost base while maintaining the appropriate level of investment. We have eliminated unprofitable flying routes and reduced excess tour operator capacity. At the same time, we have invested in re-branding existing businesses and creating new ones such as BlueSky, a direct business, and Beach Plus, an activity brand. Importantly, we engaged in a strategic sourcing exercise to create a new shared service center in conjunction with an outside partner. We needed a partner who would share the financial and operational risk – initially not only to make savings, but also to invest. In deciding upon the deal shape, we studied other business models, but focused on what was important to us and our business. This tailoring was crucial to the success of the arrangement. Key suppliers are providing us with a service that is core to their business.

'We have retained control of investment, policy, procurement and strategy, but the deal shape has the structure and the funding necessary to drive additional transformation. We built a commitment to continuous improvement into the arrangement, but have constructed it flexibly, so that charges can be adjusted if there is a business need to change the scope of the service.

'We decided to go for a fixed price based on the business case for the transformation. The service arrangement is 'open book' to provide transparency, and has an in-built risk and reward mechanism fed by a balanced scorecard. This risk element of the fee is subject to the attainment of a range of quantitative metrics based on defined service level agreements, and there is a process for assessing and establishing payment.

The business case for the new, shared service center involved closing 13 out of 22 offices and focusing on the new center in Peterborough. As a result, staff costs were substantially lowered, procurement activities were centralized, third-party contracts re-negotiated, and system development projects were reduced by more than 80%. Ian Ailles explains:

'We decided to base our new center in Peterborough since we already had operations there and we had so much to do. We had to move from legacy systems to SAP *and to consolidate disparate working practices into a single location. When these new arrangements are bedded down we shall be looking further afield for greater economies. A number of outside suppliers helped us set up the external support center. One maintained our legacy systems, while another helped us implement our new SAP enterprise resource management system. We chose Accenture to out-source many of our business processes ranging from finance (finance, purchases, payroll to general ledger, HR administration, and IT support) as well as our applications and operations management and IT infrastructure. Logistically, this could have been a nightmare, but we coordinated our outsourcing suppliers successfully using a rigorous governance framework. We hold a strategic meeting with our partners every two months at the Finance Director, HR, and IT/Business Transformation Director levels; detailed operational meetings are held weekly with our partner counterparts.'*

The people working directly for Thomas Cook are now better focused on the core travel business and are no longer distracted with the administrative back end. By entering into a strategic long-term partnership, the company enjoys shared respon-sibilities and goals, as well as shared financial returns. Thomas Cook retains control of investment, policy, procurement, and strategy. But it has now found a partner that is committed to business process innovation and has the necessary outsource contract structure to drive and fund additional transformation. Ian Ailles says:

'Our outsource contract started with a very wide scope and we have held to it; in finance we only retain our analytics and commercial advisory functions. We have the flexibility to change the services outsourced as our business changes direction and now have the ability to finance investment. Our choice of partner was crucial – it had to understand the business and encourage innovation, and where we didn't have this capability in our support functions, we now do. This new innovation disci-pline is energizing us to continually seek performance improvement.'

The company has been able to start investing in integrated management infor-mation. It has implemented value-based management targeted at improving shareholder value and this has now become a common language inside the busi-ness. And all this has been achieved with a headcount reduction within finance of 35%. Employees affected by the outsourced contract have reacted positively to the creation of the shared service center and to their transfer to Accenture. Ian Ailles goes on to say:

'Our people have moved from a back-office to a service-oriented culture. There is a much more structured approach to the operation of IT. We are using formal service management metrics and living a best practice delivery culture. Of course, there are still issues to resolve, but today Accenture and Thomas Cook work together to get things done. A true test of partnership.

'Go beyond the bounds that feel safe for the accountant – initially, our stake-holders in the business were timid, but their confidence grew as the rationale for the change was explained and the experience of the outsourcer came across. You need to constantly seek ideas from the consumer of the service – start with what they are looking for, measure it, and then ensure they get what they need. Keep this service model under review. The key enablers for transformation have been "speed to delivery" and consistent, open, and honest communications with staff. We had one voice across our three business units and we framed all our messages under the transformation strategies: "fixing the old" and "creating the new". Be open to new business models and innovative financial arrangements – the deal has got to work for both you and your outsourcer. Expand your own business capability and improve through strategic sourcing.'

In Figure 6.1 the journey that Thomas Cook UK undertook is illustrated.

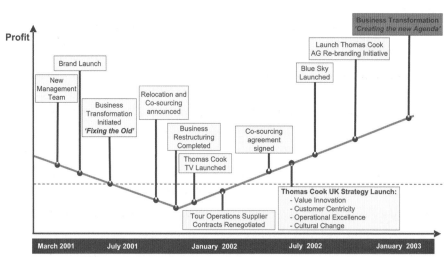

Source: Adapted from Thomas Cook Presentation, 2003

Figure 6.1   *The Thomas Cook transformation*

Few companies have achieved such major transformation in so little time, although many might wish to. Yet we have discovered that Thomas Cook's experience is not unique. Combining its cost-reduction program with a far-reaching business transformation means making some tough decisions internally. It also means choosing and working with business partners who could help make it happen.

As the Thomas Cook experience illustrates, the choice of an outsourcing partner comes down to one broad challenge: finding the right strategic fit between corporate goals and the capabilities, reach, track record, and commitment of the outsourcer. When there is a good strategic match, all the other pieces of the arrangement – projected benefits, responsibilities, and deal structure – can be negotiated with an eye toward flexibility and shared gain.

PULLING THE LEVERS OF SHAREHOLDER VALUE

In *The CFO: Architect of the Corporation's Future*,[1] a strong case was made for redefining shareholder value. The book examined the move from earnings to cash, and from an accounting-based earnings approach to economic value added (EVA), and other cash-based valuation methods. The best outsourcing arrangements that we have examined tightly bind these same metrics to deal structure.

Figure 6.2 illustrates the relationships of earnings, cash, and capital investment.

So, what are the implications of stakeholder value in practice? We reviewed the outsourcing business case for a $6bn division of a major US-based foods company, whose CFO was seeking to use the contract to drive value into the organization by:

1 Reducing F&A headcount in the outsourced areas thereby cutting sales, general, and administrative (SG&A) costs and improving margins

2 Reducing debt by working with the outsourcer to cut days sales outstanding (DSO) and improve working capital efficiency

3 Making procurement savings by implementing the outsourcer's best-practice processes and management disciplines

4 Using a new, regional operating model to increase tax efficiencies and boost post-tax earnings

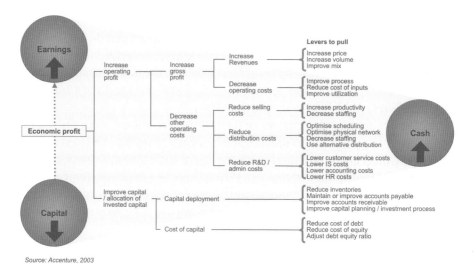

Source: Accenture, 2003

Figure 6.2 *Pulling the levers of shareholder value*

5 Financing investment via an outsourcer willing to fund the restructuring program – reducing the capital investment required through re-use of the outsourcer's assets.

The solution outlined above generated $99m annually in cost savings, released $128m in working capital back into the business, and constituted a net present value of $1.3bn. In addition, the change program was designed to be earnings accretive in the first year of the contract arrangement. The message? Outsourcing can be truly transformational, provided that scope and outcomes are clearly defined.

CFOs and outsourcing partners tell us that they pay painstaking attention to co-developing change initiatives that will generate early payback and strong returns. In many cases, the financial benefits embedded in an outsourcing contract are front-end loaded for the client company. This means that initial one-off investments to eliminate redundancy and spur process transformation are absorbed within the financing structure of the deal.

Do not fool yourself into a false sense of security, though. There is a delicate balancing act between managing risk and reward for both parties and satisfying transparency requirements for statutory accounting standards. Outsourcing transactions affect the P&L and balance sheets of both clients and service providers in different ways. For example, a *cost-*

reduction recognition issue for the client company becomes a *revenue* recognition issue for the outsourcer. Post Sarbanes-Oxley, both partners must be acutely aware of how cost, revenues, and capital flows are recognized and understood from a statutory accounting viewpoint.

SHAPING THE CONTRACTUAL RELATIONSHIP

The contract sealing a deal must clearly recognize each party's contribution to the arrangement. The real challenge is to match the incentives and rewards detailed in a contract to the business outcomes that are being sought. Figure 6.3 charts various available pricing mechanisms against the varying degrees of financial risk and reward the parties are prepared to accept.

The primary consideration in the commercial construct of the deal is the level of *risk* that the CFO is prepared to embed in the arrangement and the degree of certainty needed with respect to *business outcomes*. To build a productive relationship, CFOs should encourage transparency and the right partnering behaviors, define clear responsibilities, and differentiate between structural changes that are strategic in nature and the operational changes that are purely tactical. In terms of risk, they should feel confident that their business case is robust and deliverable. They should also feel a high level of certainty that new services will be delivered on time (without disruption), and that performance improvement will be sustained.

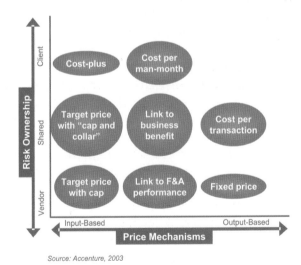

Source: Accenture, 2003

Figure 6.3 *Pricing mechanism comparisons*

CASE STUDY
The evolution of an outsourcing deal

A UK manufacturer of glass products for the automotive and building products industries decided to build a shared service capability with a twofold goal: improving value for money and reducing cost. After looking at an in-house program, it decided to review a proposal from an outsource provider. The provider and the company's management conducted a three-month feasibility study that found:

1 Additional operational savings and economies of scale could be achieved by using the outsourcer's existing low-cost facility where labor costs were approximately 30% of those in the United Kingdom.

2 Restructuring and transition costs could be reduced through rapid implementation, leveraging existing infrastructure, and the help of a project manager experienced in similar programs.

The outsourcer proposed using its transition migration methodology, which focused on:

- *identifying and containing risks*
- *maintaining service stability*
- *managing staff through intense periods of change*
- *establishing new commercial and service relationships*
- *structuring a new operating organization.*

A team of corporate and service provider employees would manage the transition. In-country company staff would maintain continuity of business operations and knowledge transfer until migration to the new center was complete. The company gained confidence in the outsource provider's ability to deliver the proposed benefits and was especially impressed by the outsourcer's willingness to share risk and reward. Operational scope was to include the following processes:

1 accounting operations – payables, receivables, general ledger, cash and banking

2 financial accounting – statutory accounting, tax compliance and reporting, aspects of sales and procurement administration

3 management accounting – routine budgeting and business performance reporting

4   *applications operations & maintenance.*

The scope was defined flexibly to satisfy changing circumstances. The company wanted to retain in-house strategic financial management activities, including cost analysis, tax planning, internal audit, and pricing.

Beyond consolidating existing activities, other potential outsourcing benefits included:

- *Management reporting tools for better decision support & financial analysis*
- *A Web-based portal offering one-stop reporting and remote accessibility*
- *A new ERP (SAP) solution to standardize best practice processes*
- *Continuous improvement via joint incentives, coaching, and quality management*
- *Scale opportunities through the development of multiclient service capability.*

The company evaluated a number of deal options ranging from cost plus only, to cost plus with balanced scorecard, to fixed price with a financing option. The company matched different pricing options against its appetite for risk sharing and accountability. Additional factors were also evaluated, including:

1   *Simplicity of contract and administration*
2   *Clarity and stability of scope*
3   *Degree of change required*
4   *Incentives for continuous improvement*
5   *The culture of both parties and the proposed level of partnership (mutual trust, risk sharing, and investment).*

The fixed-price option provided the company with the most benefits. The price was to be established up front and then adjusted, based on changing service volumes and levels. Control mechanisms would track service changes and price revisions. The outsourcing provider assumed the cost risk; the company could be certain of the price and the delivery of the services specified. There was an incentive for the outsourcer to improve service performance (tracked via a balanced scorecard). And finally, the company could take advantage of the outsourcer's financing structure to even out the initial heavy transition costs over the seven-year term of the deal.

As this case study suggests, a well-designed outsourcing deal is flexible enough to adapt to market circumstances – and robust enough to withstand technological and organizational change. Well-structured outsourcing relationships share four key attributes:

1 **Common purpose and alignment of interests:** While contracts are essential, they are not sufficient. Win-win relationships allow the customer and service provider to work together to improve the services provided. Financial incentives should be in place to reward better-than-expected results – or penalize poor performance. In a flawed outsourcing arrangement, economic results for both parties are not equitable (i.e. there is no common purpose). In the best deals, the business case is shaped by both parties from a broad and holistic point of view. The scope of the deal encompasses not only costs directly influenced by the transfer of services to the outsource provider, but also those indirectly affected by the arrangement. Our research reveals that the most popular pricing mechanism is fixed price. This is because it provides the company with a defined service benefit for a set cost and incentivizes the service provider to continually innovate – driving down operating costs and further improving margins.

2 **Transparency:** Outsourcing relationships can be complex. Due to their length, most contracts require built-in flexibility. Transparency reduces risk for both partners and provides the basis for adding and/or adapting services over time.

3 **Strong governance:** There are two often-neglected aspects of governance. The first is *disciplined adherence* to the service model. Buyers must manage metrics, close performance gaps, and rigorously monitor the outsourcing relationship. The second governance area that many firms fail to handle effectively is *identifying additional opportunities* to create value in parts of the business that lie directly outside of the outsourced processes. How far a company goes in capturing these broader business benefits depends upon the level of confidence it has in its outsource service provider.

4 **Understanding the sources of leverage:** When a buyer and service provider *jointly shape* a solution based on mutually understood goals and strengths, they set common objectives and expectations – and have a well-defined plan for achieving them. Under these circumstances

both parties know whether they are entering into a contract with a focus on either a *pure F&A service* or on *improving the performance of the enterprise* – a much bolder proposition. It is surprising how often objectives are not clearly stated during a deal's planning stage – and remain ambiguous until later stages of the contract process.

PRICING OPTIONS

Pricing options fall into three categories ranging from the simple to the sophisticated: *traditional pricing* – such as unit cost per transaction processed; *fixed fees* for a defined scope, level, and quality of service; and, *value-based risk/reward structures*. The best choice for your company depends on:

- The type of service your company needs

- Your outsourcing objectives

- The relationship that you want with your outsource provider.

Where outsourcing is well established – for example, in payroll processing – the goal is usually to achieve cost savings through scale and efficiency. In such cases, a transactional pricing model works well. In contrast, the market for high value-add outsourcing services is driven by process improvement goals – not just cost reduction. Quality and business impact are as significant as the unit cost of the service. In such cases, companies are not so much outsourcing parts of their F&A function as they are purchasing a guaranteed F&A service outcome, as well as a defined business result.

Why consider alternative pricing options? The answer is to offer *incentives* that are likely to deliver *high-impact business improvements* and encourage *innovation*. A number of early outsourcing adopters are on this path. Their goal; to push beyond efficiency improvements in F&A and achieve enterprise-wide transformation.

Figure 6.4 illustrates various mechanisms that can be used to motivate your outsource partner and encourage partnering behaviors that best meet your needs – balanced against the risks you are prepared to take. These and other potential financial arrangements are outlined here:

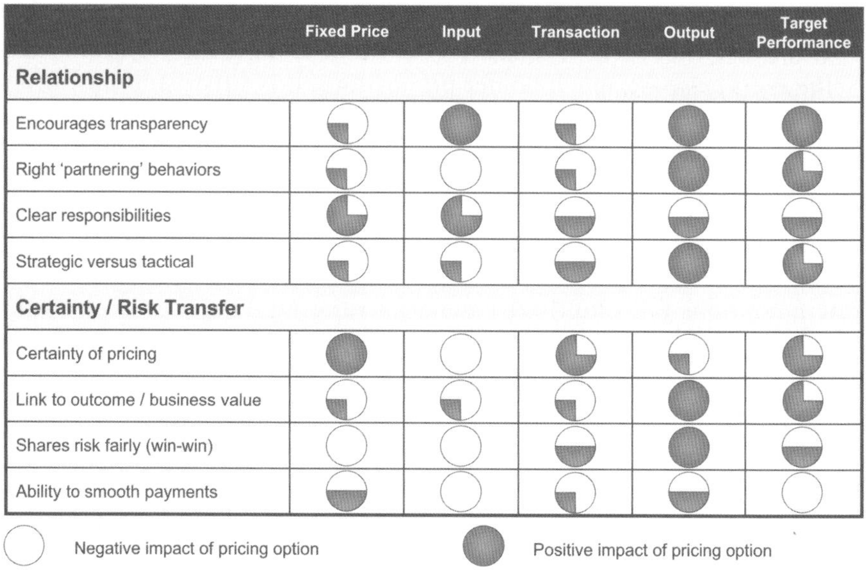

	Fixed Price	Input	Transaction	Output	Target Performance
Relationship					
Encourages transparency	◑	●	◑	●	●
Right 'partnering' behaviors	◕	○	◔	●	◔
Clear responsibilities	◕	◕	◒	◒	◒
Strategic versus tactical	◑	◔	◒	●	◕
Certainty / Risk Transfer					
Certainty of pricing	●	○	◕	◑	◕
Link to outcome / business value	◑	◑	◑	●	◕
Shares risk fairly (win-win)	○	○	◒	●	◒
Ability to smooth payments	◒	○	◑	◒	○

○ Negative impact of pricing option   ● Positive impact of pricing option

Source: *Accenture, 2003*

Figure 6.4   *Pricing options: balancing relationship and risk*

1 **Fixed Fee:** includes all costs of delivery and profit margin for the life-cycle of the engagement, usually divided into quarterly installments. It is by far the simplest of all the options available and is the one usually favored by most CFOs and service providers.

2 **Per-transaction fees:** a set price per transaction, multiplied by the number of transactions during any given period.

3 **Input-based fee + per-transaction fee:** a base fee covers the cost of discrete, project-based services (consulting, integration) while operation of the process is priced per transaction.

4 **Input-based fee + per seat fee:** the base fee covers the cost of discrete project-based services; operation of the process is priced per *user*.

5 **Shared risk/shared reward:** a variation of fixed fee pricing and/or per transaction pricing. The provider gets a bonus for *over*-performance according to a defined set of metrics with corresponding penalties for *under*-performance.

6 **Business benefit based:** the provider receives a proportion of the business value created by the project or service, such as a percentage of increased profit or decreased cost.

7 **Open-book pricing:** based on the exact cost of service delivery plus a pre-negotiated profit margin. Both client and vendor agree to full financial disclosure.

8 **Joint venture investment:** the client and service provider form a new company to deliver services. This too, is an equity-based relationship. Equity investments by JV partners may take the form of capital, people, expertise or other assets. This is the least popular of all the options available.

The results of a Gartner survey on the adoption of different pricing models for process outsourcing are shown in Figure 6.5.

As Figure 6.5 shows, the three most common pricing models are fixed fee, transaction based, or a combination of the two. However, we've seen a steady increase in external financing on larger outsourcing contracts, sometimes in the form of equity participation. In some countries, both client companies and the outsourcers are using third-party financing houses for engagement funding. These new contact-pricing vehicles may be risky if undertaken in an immature country market.

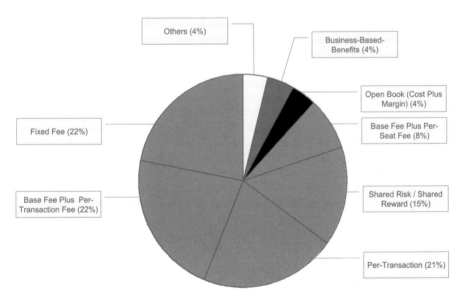

Source: BPO Validated: Verticalization and Aggregation Accelerate, Market Trends, Gartner, February 2003

Figure 6.5 *Survey of pricing methodologies for BPO contracts*

Pricing should be structured to allow for flexibility and review during the contract lifecycle. Figure 6.6 illustrates how a UK-based company used the *fixed price plus gain share* mechanism for its F&A outsourcing. This outsourcing arrangement is expected to deliver £8.4m in cost reductions over a seven-year period.

The scope of service in this case covers a small cluster of the company's business operations, including accounts receivable (AR), accounts payable (AP), general and fixed asset accounting. By year seven, as shown in Figure 6.6, this will represent an annual recurring cost saving of 45%. This pilot program proved so successful in its first six months that the outsourcing arrangement was expanded to include other geographic and business units.

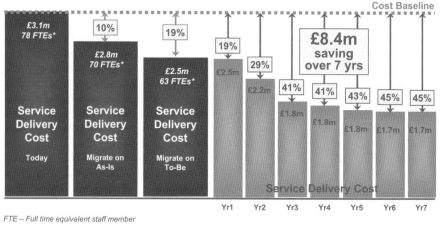

FTE – Full time equivalent staff member

Source: Accenture, 2003

Figure 6.6   *Example of the profile of annual service charges*

PRICING AND CONTRACTING PRINCIPLES

Few CFOs realize the potential impact that business evolution can have on their outsourcing relationships. In reality, a host of far-reaching, but often unpredictable, factors can affect the scope and nature of the services required. Outsourcing agreements can be affected by changes in:

- Corporate structure, product lines or market focus

- Consumer demand

- Technology or business processes

- Regulatory environment
- Service delivery models.

The strategic variables above influence the structural shape of service delivery. In addition, the economics of an outsourcing deal and its pricing are significantly affected by tactical and operational factors. These include:

- The responsibilities of both parties
- Scope: process and geographic
- Commercial provisions for increases/decreases in scope
- Baseline performance metrics for financial operations, such as accounts receivable, (metric availability accuracy, and validity, etc.)
- Gain-sharing principles, mechanics, and payment
- Choice of pricing mechanisms (e.g. fixed vs. transaction vs. target pricing)
- Financing structure
- Accurate interpretation of the commercial construct of the proposal
- Service center delivery locations and process distribution across the network
- Employee and staffing arrangements
- Transition costs
- Investment in new assets and technologies
- Sarbanes-Oxley/International Financial Reporting Standards (IFRS) in Europe compliance requirements
- Change control principles
- Contract terms, including: length; start and end date; billing arrangements; inclusions and exclusions; termination/exit arrangements; foreign exchange; inflation adjustments; service levels metrics, standards and expectations.

Many of the companies we have interviewed told us that *price* was rarely the determining factor in the final economics of their outsourcing deals.

The reason: It is simply not possible to be that precise about the economics up-front because there are so many detailed variables to work with both during and after the contracting process. The desire for clear and detailed numbers should be balanced against the need for speed. The granularity achieved around the finer economic points should only be detailed enough to generate an *accurate* high-level strategic picture.

All of the factors listed above influence the economics of an outsourcing engagement. As a result, a well-structured deal is based on six broad principles[2] for managing costs and benefits when change occurs:

Principle 1: Don't get bogged down in the detail too early

Resist the natural tendency to hammer out every detail from the outset. Experience shows that material factors and variables are relevant, not the detail. Develop a level of confidence in your outsource provider. This will enable you to agree on the factors that are central to the business solution you want to achieve. Support these central points with contract management principles that provide flexibility for both parties. Then progressively work out the fine details of an agreement based on your experience by working together.

Principle 2: Do not accept additional charges for non-material changes

No matter what the cause, non-material changes to the services should not give rise to additional charges, a reduction in charges, or a renegotiation of charges. There are several reasons for adopting this principle. Primarily, it is debilitating for the relationship if partners have to negotiate every change, no matter how insignificant. Moreover, if the customer was managing the program in-house, it could implement non-material changes using existing resources. This would obviate the need for additional costs for personnel or other resources. From the company's perspective, an outsourcing arrangement should be no less favorable.

Principle 3: Determine price increases on a 'net' basis

Additional provider charges should be determined on a 'net' basis. In other words, any price increase should reflect the additional costs incurred by the provider, 'net' of any costs the provider may reasonably be able to eliminate by virtue of the change. For example, if the provision of a new function renders an existing function unnecessary, then the provider should reduce the additional charges to reflect the costs eliminated. For a long-term relationship to survive, each party must believe that the other is acting fairly and equitably. If the provider is earning a windfall, the company is unlikely to view it as fair and equitable.

Principle 4: Price adjustments, not price increases
Adjustments to pricing should not be a 'one-way street.' If a change results in a reduction in the provider's costs, a reduction in the provider's charges may be appropriate, depending on the pricing structure. In other words, price adjustments may be in either the provider's or the company's favor.

Principle 5: Develop consumption-based unit pricing
The parties should develop and agree upon pricing algorithms that will accommodate changes in the volume of services consumed by the customer.

Principle 6: Provide for significant one-time events
In the case of a significant non-recurring event, the parties should review and, if appropriate, adjust pricing. For this purpose, the term 'significant non-recurring event' refers to an occurrence that is not part of the ordinary course of the company's business (e.g., an acquisition or disposition of a major line of business). A major internal event can give rise to a significant (more than 10%) and permanent change in the volume of services consumed. In some circumstances, it may be necessary to review an outsourcing arrangement rationale and business case to realign service with the new imperatives of the business.

TAX CONSIDERATIONS

The creation of a shared service center – be it insourced or outsourced – sometimes gives rise to tax issues that must be managed carefully to maximize value – and minimize risk and liabilities. Early involvement by the CFO of the in-house tax group and external tax advisors should mitigate any unbudgeted costs and potential risks.

Many countries, states, provinces – and even cities – provide tax and financial incentives to attract shared service centers. These incentives typically take the form of:

- Reduced corporate tax rate
- Tax credits

- Indirect tax concessions

- Financial cash grants or subsidies

Tax and financial incentives need to be considered hand in hand with profit repatriation and financing strategies. These incentives must be reviewed in conjunction with relevant labor, technology, and infrastructure availability. Examples of potential tax and financial incentives are listed in Figure 6.7.

Many countries require you to obtain clearance from a tax or incentive viewpoint before moving your F&A functions offshore.

The SSC can be a critical component of a regional (or even global) tax-efficient operating model. It is one of many operations that can be centralized and benefit from a favorable tax rate. If you are implementing a SSC and/or considering outsourcing as an option, this is a prime opportunity to review the tax efficiency of your overall operating model. A tax-advantaged European business model has the potential to enhance post-tax profitability, as illustrated in Figure 6.8.

Consider the case of a UK-headquartered global engineering company with operations in the United States, Australia, and many countries across Europe. The challenge faced – to set up a tax-efficient European operating structure in conjunction with its move to an outsourced shared service operation for F&A.

CASE STUDY
Adopting a new asset ownership model

This European engineering company had enjoyed modest revenue growth, but found itself under severe profitability pressure. The CFO identified significant opportunities for simplifying the business, reducing costs, and maximizing revenue. To quote the CFO:

'Our basic finance and accounting (F&A) processes were broken, we were using non-standardized data, and we had a serious skills shortfall. Customers complained in significant numbers about the quality of our invoices and expressed doubts over the quality of the information we provided to help them manage their inventories. Across Europe, we had diverse working practices that were inconsistent with our global model. We needed better information on performance. We needed to migrate from country-based reporting to pan-European reporting. We also needed

Location	Standard Corporate Income Tax Rate	Potential Tax and Financial Incentives*
Czech Republic	28% (2004)	- Subsidies are available for strategic services for investments which: are greater than CZK50M (of which 25% must be equity), create 50 new jobs, and where at least 50% of services are to be exported - The subsidy is for up to 10 years and is up to 20-50% of either salaries or fixed assets, depending on location.
Hong Kong	17.5% (2004)	- No specific shared service center incentive, but low rate.
Hungary	18% + 2% max Budapest Local Business Tax (2004)	- Tax incentives are granted by the government for a 5-year period as a corporate income tax credit for investments greater than HUF10B/HUF3B, depending on location. - Amongst other requirements, qualifying investments must result in the creation or extension of facilities and 500/300 new jobs within 4 years, or 50% of supplies must be from small to medium sized enterprises.
India	35% + 2.5% surcharge (2004)	- Tax holidays for up to 10 years are available for qualifying undertakings activities exported from a Special Economic Zone or for 100% export orientated Undertakings.
Ireland	12.5% for trading or 25% for passive (2004)	- No specific shared service center incentive, but low rate for trading income.
Malaysia	28% (2004)	- Operational Headquarters (OHQ) are taxed at 10% for up to 10 years on income derived from the provision of qualifying services to the OHQ's offices or related companies outside Malaysia
Singapore	22% (2004)	- There are many tax incentives available, each will need to be approved by the relevant Ministries and government agencies. Examples of incentives potentially applicable to SSC include Business Headquarters (BHQ), Operational Headquarters (OHQ) and Export of Services. - Most incentives offer up to 100% tax exemption for up to 5-10 years.
Switzerland	8.5% federal + 15-30% cantonal (taxes deductible) (2004)	- Some of the cantons which are currently quite favorable towards shared service centers include Zug and Schaffhausen.

*Source: Accenture, February 2004; * See note at end of Chapter*

Figure 6.7 *Comparison of tax rates by country*

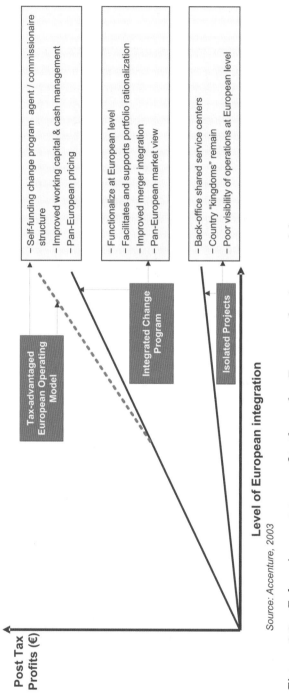

Figure 6.8 *Enhancing post-tax profits through a European business model*

to unblock the constraint to growth in new territories, such as Central and Eastern Europe.'

The company proposed a self-funding transformation program to regain financial control and discipline. Working with an outsource provider, it developed a centralized asset ownership model with the following objectives:

1 Simplifying cross-border transactions and streamlining management accounting
2 Reducing the volume of inter-company transactions
3 Eliminating 'dispute resolution' problems arising from inter-company charges
4 Achieving direct cost savings from transaction processing
5 Reinforcing the vision of a single pan-European business.

A new Irish entity was proposed, wholly owned by the UK-listed parent. This Irish entity would be the central asset owner and would benefit from the low-tax regime in Ireland. Initially, the following business processes were to be outsourced:

Management accounting
- period close
- management reporting
- budgeting and forecasting
- financial accounting

Customer administration management
- customer transaction processing
- accounts receivable

The company's finance function worked with its outsource partner to shape a value proposition to meet business and financial needs. This is shown in Figure 6.9.

The value proposition was to be self-funding. The service charge in the first year was leveled to equate with the service charges in subsequent years, so the outsource partner absorbed the initial up-front investment charge for restructuring costs. The savings were shared between the two parties on a risk-reward basis and a multi-year strategic partnership was defined in the contract.

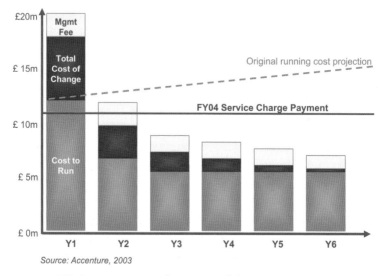

Figure 6.9 *F&A outsource value proposition*

The proposed solution also incorporated some tax-efficiencies, leveraging the availability of the Irish tax rate of 12.5% compared to an average tax rate of 35%. How much the Irish tax rate could be utilized depends on a host of factors: business operating model design, transfer of head personnel, risks and activities, direct and indirect tax costs, and the degree of change the company and its outsourcer were prepared to undertake.

This company is not alone. World-class leaders like Microsoft, Procter & Gamble, Frito-Lay, and Xerox have set up pan-European operating models that provide a broader range of economic benefits in terms of post-tax results. Such models enhance organizational flexibility and can respond at speed to new markets, new opportunities, and new sales channels. They also allow forward-looking companies to increase control by embracing local preferences while supporting a coordinated European sales strategy, supply chain rationalization, and renewal of their procurement and sourcing capabilities.

THE NEGOTIATION LIFECYCLE

Consider first the relationship that you want to have with your outsourcing provider. When initiating discussions, focus more on developing rapport and less on details. To achieve early alignment, outline high-level expectations of both parties; the scope of service, target economics and other relevant strategic information. Otherwise, you and your outsource provider may fall into the trap of becoming overwhelmed by the myriad challenges and low-level details you will encounter in getting a deal off the ground. Start with the quality of your working relationship: Build trust and mutual respect before you tackle substantive aspects of your arrangement, namely ensuring that the terms of the contract make sense and that service-level performance metrics are tight.

Industry leaders like BP focus on maximizing the value of their outsource relationships over the longer term by building and implementing what we call the *relationship management infrastructure*. This infrastructure includes:

- **Internal alignment processes:** Appoint a relationship manager. Over the entire lifecycle, ensure that this executive communicates decisions to all parties involved – providing rationales and supporting evidence.

- **Relationship due diligence:** Identify the management issues most likely to occur with an outsource supplier, pinpoint potential relationship risks, and carefully assess the likelihood that you and your outsourcing provider can overcome these risks.

- **Negotiation preparation and launch:** Preparation is key to effective negotiation. Clarify your company's position, priorities, and potential trade-offs. Be clear on your team roles and responsibilities. Agree on a process for negotiations and managing execution.

- **Conflict management:** A good working relationship does not mean the absence of conflict. No matter how effective the planning, conflicts will inevitably happen. Develop a conflict management process that enables both parties to work together to diagnose what is wrong and search for a solution. Should agreement not be reached, look for a constructive, collaborative resolution that does not damage the long-term relationship.

Build on the idea that this relationship can be developed, *with insight and creativity,* to generate *value*. Explore common goals and mutually beneficial deal terms. Finally, recognize and agree on what is fair and appropriate. Do not attempt to coerce or override your partner's strategic intent – it would be better to walk away!

Outsourcing arrangements are generally long-term; they involve multimillion, or in some cases, even multibillion-dollar decisions. Since outsourcing is critical to a company's future, only the most trusted executives should be in a position to sign off on such far-reaching agreements. Advisers can lead and guide you through the process, but responsibility for the deal cannot be delegated to them.

CFO INSIGHTS

- We have found that well-structured outsourcing relationships have four key attributes: understanding sources of leverage, strong governance, transparency, and alignment of interests.

- Share both risk and reward with your chosen outsource provider. Structure a deal flexible enough to allow for short-term volume fluctuations and the ever-changing nature of your business.

- A number of early adopters are on a path that goes beyond just efficiency improvements in F&A to wholesale transformation. They consider the full array of alternative pricing options. The options chosen tend to offer the incentives most likely to deliver high-impact business improvements and encourage innovation.

- Leading multinational companies have set up European operating models that provide a broad range of post-tax economic benefits. Such models enhance organizational flexibility and can respond at speed to new markets, new opportunities, and new sales channels.

- Major, unexpected one-time events have to be anticipated and, ultimately, accommodated in the deal structure. They can give rise to significant and permanent change in the volume of services consumed by the customer.

FROM INSIGHT TO ACTION

BUILD A LONG-TERM RELATIONSHIP WITH YOUR OUTSOURCE
PROVIDER
Understand the sources of leverage between you and your potential partner – and shape a solution based on your relative goals and strengths. Ensure the financials of the deal are transparent – this reduces risk for both sides.

REVIEW THE PRICING OPTIONS AVAILABLE TO YOU
Consider the type of service provider, your company's goals, and the degree of sophistication you want in your outsourcing relationship.

FOLLOW BEST-PRACTICE PRICING PRINCIPLES
Think ahead to likely changes in your customers, products, technology, and your general business environment. Identify areas of changes in the contract that are likely to be non-material and material.

SHAPE THE VALUE PROPOSITION
The deal should recognize each party's contribution in delivering sustained value creation. Share benefits promptly when business objectives are achieved.

PULL ALL THE LEVERS OF STAKEHOLDER VALUE
Don't underestimate the potential impact of capital efficiency and the outsourcer's capacity for funding capital investment. Outsourcing offers far more than operational cost savings.

DESIGN A REGIONALLY EFFICIENT OPERATING MODEL
The creation of a shared service center sometimes gives rise to tax issues that must be managed to maximize value and minimize both risks and liabilities. Such models may also assist in improving sales, manufacturing efficiency, and procurement. Differentiate between those operations that are core, those that add value, and those that address risk.

CONSIDER ALL STAGES IN THE DEAL LIFECYCLE
Work with your outsource provider initially in value targeting. Obtain CEO sign-off. Develop a set of business principles – keep these separate from the contract and *socialize* them with board of directors and key stakeholders. Include your company's *leaders of the future* in your deal evaluation team.

REFERENCES

1   Cedric Read and the PwC financial management consulting team, *CFO: Architect of the Corporation's Future*, Wiley, 1999

2   Adapted from: Allen Keith, Latham & Watkins, Contracting for Change, *The Outsourcing Journal*, 2004. www.outsourcing-journal.com

NOTE

Almost all incentives referenced are subject to the approval of authorities. This summary is only intended to provide a high-level illustrative insight into the tax landscape. Accenture does not provide tax advice, and the information herein should not be construed as such. For further information refer to your corporate tax specialist.

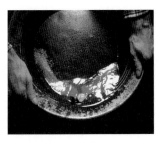

CHAPTER 7

Stakeholders: Achieving Buy-In

REACHING STAKEHOLDERS THROUGH OPEN AND HONEST COMMUNICATIONS

David Harrison, Vice-Chairman
Accenture Business Services of British Columbia

BC Hydro, power generator and distributor, serves more than 1.8 million customers across the province of British Columbia (BC), Canada. The government-owned utility is the third largest in Canada, with an $11bn asset base, $6bn in annual revenues, and 6,000 employees. British Columbia is currently self-sufficient in electricity, but by 2007, the province will be forced to buy electricity at volatile market prices unless additional capacity is added. This investment will require cash injection, and therefore, initiatives to improve the company's economic performance are being encouraged.

BC Hydro and Accenture recently joined forces to create an outsource entity – Accenture Business Services of British Columbia (ABS-BC), which employs 1,600 people in the areas of customer service, IT, HR, F&A, and purchasing. David Harrison, previously CFO of BC Hydro – and now vice-chairman of ABS-BC – picks up the story from the beginning:

'BC Hydro is one of the largest organizations in BC, but we couldn't get the advantages of scale and cost savings that we wanted on our own. This is a publicly owned utility, but the local government – though not keen on privatization of core assets (such as dams and transmission lines) – did have a desire to see what the private sector could do in the services part of the business.'

A 10-year, $1.45bn (CDN) agreement was signed in early 2003. Over the life of the deal, it will provide significant savings to BC Hydro's customers. The agreement gave ABS-BC a platform on which to expand its offer for customer relationship management, IT, HR, finance, and procurement. Coupled with the signing of outsourcing arrangements with a number of other major utilities, Accenture Business Services for Utilities was subsequently formed and now serves 6 million customers, more than any utility in North America. David Harrison and his colleagues had started to look at the feasibility of this venture some 18 months earlier. David notes:

'We started to prepare a request for proposal (RFP) to test the market for such a service. This had to be a public document, which of course employees would read. So we needed to communicate with our employee groups very early on and keep them in the picture. There was also public opinion to consider: our customers, politicians, and regulators. Press coverage was another factor we had to contend with.'

David's leadership role in communicating with the BC Hydro employees affected – and in transitioning the services to the new outsource entity – has been crucial. This was an unusual situation for David, whose career at BC Hydro spanned 24 years, culminating in his position as executive vice-president and CFO. As the senior officer originally responsible for evaluating and initiating the outsourcing process, he moved from BC Hydro to the outsource provider to help with the transition and subsequently bed it down. He says:

'We had many meetings with all of the original 2,000 employees affected. I met them in large groups of 100 to 200 and in small groups of 30 to 40. This involved a lot of travel around the province since our operations are widely dispersed. I was deeply involved in our employees' situation from a personal point of view. I had known many of them for years and was a familiar face to them. The staff trusted my judgment. When they learned that I was going too, I believe it helped them make the transition to the new company.'

From the very beginning, communication was open and honest. David and his team reinforced face-to-face meetings with regular staff newsletters and the use of a dedicated website to provide updates. To monitor employee reactions, regular opinion surveys were carried out. BC Hydro was seen as an attractive and solid employer; initially, the reaction of staff was mixed. While most people were positive about moving to the new service entity, others were neutral – and a small number clearly didn't want to change their situation.

Ultimately, more than 1,600 BC Hydro staff transferred to the new outsourced entity. The last opinion survey carried out before the move showed that more than 70% were looking forward to it. A great success! The internal HR group handled most of the communications and change management activities; many of its members were also in the services affected and transferred to ABS-BC. The operational organization – the internal customers of the services to be outsourced – also had to be satisfied that outsourcing internal services would not lead to a loss of control and would make their lives easier.

BC Hydro's CEO, once he was convinced that it was the right move, helped drive the change program. As CFO, David worked very closely with the EVP for Operations, with whom he had a strong relationship. To quote Larry Bell, chairman and CEO at the time the deal was publicly confirmed:

'This agreement makes it possible for BC Hydro to continue delivering the world-class customer care our ratepayers expect, while at the same time significantly reducing our costs and dramatically increasing our operational efficiency. With the contractual obligation to deliver at least the same, or even better, customer service – and to achieve cost savings of $250m over 10 years, this is a terrific opportunity for the British Columbia economy, consumers, employees, and both companies.'

The BC Hydro employees who moved to ABS-BC took with them valuable knowledge and skills in all areas of the service provided. They have greatly expanded their career opportunities; they are now part of a world-class business services company with attractive opportunities for market growth. ABS-BC is committed to delivering innovation and creating tangible value through its ability to mobilize the right people, skills, alliances, and technologies. David Harrison comments:

'We received 19 different proposals from potential suppliers. BC Hydro chose Accenture as its outsource partner because it had worldwide credentials and experience, proposed the most advantageous economic terms, and offered our staff the best prospects. The staff transferred with compensation packages similar to their previous ones and a three-year union agreement gave them continuity. Clearly, changes in business process and working practices were necessary. But, throughout the change program our approach to stakeholder management was built on mutual trust and high integrity.'

The outsourcing initiative became a bit of a political 'hot potato' in the province. BC Hydro had presented the proposal in its early stages to the Provincial Govern-

ment, which supported the change and modified legislation to approve it. The move sparked significant press and media coverage – and efforts were made to sensationalize the event. But the government, BC Hydro, and the selected outsource provider worked together to make it happen. BC Hydro's electricity consumers, the ultimate stakeholder, have not seen much change. Service levels have been maintained, costs are being held down, and corporate reputation has been sustained.

Not many organizations have been as fortunate as BC Hydro in having a CFO, like David Harrison, actually transfer as part of an outsourcing arrangement and help make it a reality. It was only late in the day, in fact, that David approached BC Hydro to say that he was willing to make the move.

The BC Hydro case study shows that an organization can successfully outsource a very large part of its infrastructure without a loss of service. It also shows the importance of exceptional CEO and CFO leadership. Sensitively managing stakeholder needs and expectations is key to a smooth, productive transfer. In a publicly owned entity such as BC Hydro, stakeholder issues can be especially complex.

Time and again, we have found strong evidence to support the connection between a carefully planned communications strategy and a successful transition. Well-defined stakeholder management processes were also in place wherever and whenever an outsourcing journey led to a truly successful outcome.

This chapter is devoted to stakeholders – their fears, their needs, and the management techniques that have been developed to ensure success when outsourcing.

LEAD FROM THE TOP: THE CEO AND CFO WORKING TOGETHER

The CFO and CEO are nearly always involved in a major outsourcing transformation. The process cannot be delegated or handed off to a project-management committee. F&A outsourcing must bear the CFO's personal stamp, not just his or her authorization. It is accomplished most efficiently by following a number of principles:

1 **Strong leadership, commitment, and a sense of priority must be evident:** Persuade by example, do not delegate, and be careful not to involve too many people in the up-front decision. Treat this as an

M&A transaction. Only when an irrevocable decision has been made to proceed should the communication process be broadened. The natural tendency of senior management to delegate accountability for the process to lower levels within the organization often spells trouble.

2 **Impose rigor on the process:** In most cases, it is probably best to keep organizational issues in the background, although people will keep trying to drag them in for discussion. An outsourcing program is normally a subset of a far broader change plan. Keep the spotlight on behavior and process; organization issues come later. Set clear reference points for the deal team using time frames and milestones so that the process can be tightly managed.

3 **Accept ambiguity:** Remain open minded and flexible. Be prepared to commit to outcomes without necessarily knowing in advance the road to be traveled. Improvise from time to time. If you try to nail down every detail and milestone up front you will (a) be forced to bring more people than necessary into the inner circle, and (b) struggle to make meaningful progress. We found numerous examples during our research of well-intentioned initiatives that simply failed to get off the ground despite endless months of effort.

4 **Patience is important, but so is pace:** Once a decision is made, move at speed to complete the transaction, communicate fully and openly, and then shift rapidly into transition planning.

The executive team leading an outsourcing initiative must be bound together in secrecy. Confidentiality is of paramount importance up to the point at which a deal is announced. The behavioral style of management is an important consideration as well, since this often dictates how decisions are made, contract negotiations are handled, and change management is executed.

In Figure 7.1, we illustrate a range of management styles that need to be recognized and debated openly between the leadership teams of the company executive and the service provider. By doing so, conflict and miscommunications between styles can be minimized.

We have found some common traits among the CEOs and CFOs interviewed for this book – boldness, a willingness to move at pace, the ability to accept ambiguity, and a collaborative mindset which views the outsourcing partner as a trusted advisor.

Ultimately, outsourcing is a corporate transaction. As such, it is similar, in many ways, to a merger and acquisition (M&A). Like M&A deals,

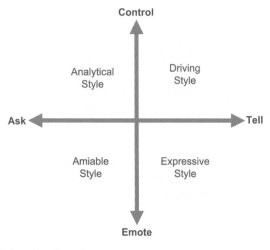

Figure 7.1 *Behavioral styles*

initial outsource plans do not need to specify up-front new organization structure, new processes or detailed systems requirements. Despite this, we discovered plentiful evidence of promising outsourcing proposals that were derailed by a prematurely deep dive into the details of how an arrangement was going to work. In these situations, matters quickly became confused. Strategic imperatives lost momentum.

Outsourcing programs and in-house change projects require different mindsets. With internal change projects, it is essential to evaluate how all the facets will come together and how they will be implemented to achieve a total solution. The opposite approach is required in an outsourcing arrangement: A CFO is buying a set of outcomes and transferring responsibility for solution design and implementation to the service provider. Akin to post-M&A integration, planning takes place *after* the deal has been consummated. Post-deal activities include anticipating and jointly planning for challenges, establishing decision-making and escalation procedures, and defining shared performance targets and metrics.

When shaping an outsourcing arrangement, our research points to a clear set of conditions required for success:

1 Avoid getting bogged down in detail early in the decision process

2 Lead from the front and top; don't rely on consensus, you won't get it!

3　Preserve confidentiality and secrecy in the early stages at all costs

4　Form a high-powered deal team; don't drive the process by committee

5　Adopt a corporate M&A transaction posture

6　After the green light is given, quickly move to solution design and transition planning.

Once a CEO approves the business case for proceeding, the final go/no go decision to outsource is usually made by a small inner core of executives with broader management support. The CEO and his or her immediate advisors focus on issues of materiality – questions relating to 'what and why' rather than 'how.' Once these are agreed on, second-tier execution concerns can be handled at regular management team meetings.

YOUR NEW STAKEHOLDER: YOUR OUTSOURCE PARTNER

The key to outsourcing success: Creating and maintaining a healthy and enduring partnership with your service provider. Supported by a proven track record, your provider should quickly assume the role of a trusted advisor. Longevity is important because exiting an outsourcing arrangement early is not just painful, it can also be expensive, emotionally and financially. Both the service provider and the company invest in the outsourcing process and become dependent on each other. As a result, bringing services back in-house or switching to an alternative service provider can be prohibitively expensive. Often a service provider makes substantial investments in improving processes and technology. If an arrangement breaks down, they may face considerable hardship.[1]

For these reasons, both parties need to work together and lay out a roadmap – negotiating in a way that sets good precedents for how the relationship will work after the deal is signed. The outsourcing deal shape process resembles a merger or acquisition transaction, yet it has one big difference: During the post-deal phase, the service provider has a big stake in delivering expected synergies. Mutual respect, commonality of purpose, a commitment to working through difficult challenges, and trust in each other's intentions are essential if an outsource partnership is to succeed.

Negotiation and solution development should cement the bond between supplier and buyer. Using an 'interest-based' approach to negotiating helps focus the relationship on important principles and common interests – and increases the likelihood that a relationship will endure over time. In contrast, a positional-based 'spec and bid' process tends to highlight differences, focus on detail and distracts from the overall purpose.

In a successful outsourcing partnership, a 'degree of intimacy' develops, transcending the traditional, arms-length customer-supplier relationship. At its most effective, a continuing collaboration occurs, rather than a one-time transfer of people and processes. Remember that, as one seasoned corporate executive observed: *'Outsourcing is like chess. If you only play your own pieces, you usually lose. You have to play the other guy's pieces too.'*

Communication and negotiation between companies and their outsourced service providers has proven so central to success that a new role for third-party advisors has emerged.

THIRD-PARTY ADVISORS

Early in their decision-making process, companies must determine whether or not to use an outsourcing advisory firm experienced in designing, structuring, and negotiating contracts. Such firms can help guide the CFO through uncharted territory, giving impartial advice that can sometimes be invaluable. The role of third-party intermediaries in both sole and multiple provider sourcing approaches can vary from project to project. It ranges from providing support during the initial selection of a service provider through participating in contract negotiations and management.

Advisors who are former employees of service providers sometimes describe themselves as 'poachers turned gamekeepers.' Tim Lloyd, Director of ALS Consulting, a third-party advisor based in the UK, notes that, 'the support we provide is mutually beneficial to both client executive and service provider. We are able to neutralize the adversarial nature of the process – a factor that can sometimes creep in. We help ensure that the client secures the best possible deal while balancing this goal with the understanding that the service provider also has a sustainable value proposition in the long term.' Supplier negotiations are managed as a collaborative process; the focus is on maximizing value for both sides, while avoiding coercive tactics aimed at 'squeezing the last dollar' out of suppliers.

Negotiation should be used as an opportunity to build a strong foundation for a good working relationship. Focus as much on setting the stage for working together effectively once a deal is signed as on arriving at specific contract terms.[2] Both sides have to make concessions for the arrangement to work.

Some executives object to the idea of retaining a third party advisor because they see it as an additional cost and/or feel that this strategy simply prolongs the agreement process. Kathy Goolsby, a senior writer for The Outsourcing Journal comments that, *'Outsourcing advisory services frequently end up on the chopping block. Such thinking results from the traditional mentality of "buy the pencil at the lowest cost." That is an ill-fated approach, since an outsourcing arrangement can provide advice and deep insight as well as cost reduction'.*[3]

Figure 7.2 shows the results of a poll about the extent to which third-party advisors are used.

There is a clear correlation between the success of an outsourcing transition and the use of advisors. They can help ensure that your objectives are wedded to the strengths of the service provider.

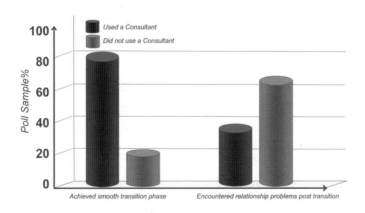

Source: "Cost vs.Value of Using an Outsourcing Consultant", Kathleen Goolsby, The Outsourcing Journal, 2003
www.outsourcing-journal.com

Figure 7.2 *Impact of consultant use on the success of outsourcing transition*

EMPLOYEES: TREATING THEM WITH CARE AND INTEGRITY

Employee groups usually come first to mind when thinking of stakeholders in a broad-based outsourcing initiative. As soon as a change program becomes tangible, executives find themselves asking questions like: Will our operations staff go along with this? How will headquarters respond to their concerns? Understandably, many managers also start speculating about specific individuals: How will they react? Will they see this as a threat? How can we persuade them that this is a real opportunity to change things for the better? One executive divided the employee population into three major stakeholder categories:[4] those transferring to the service provider, those who would lose their jobs, and everyone else affected by the initiative. He then crafted different transition strategies for each group, with incentives for those moving to the outsourcing service provider and generous benefit extensions to those who were not. The company ended up keeping 90% of the employees it wanted to retain.

From an employee's point of view, a certain degree of anger is unavoidable and should be expected. Anger can also serve a useful purpose, especially in large, bureaucratic organizations. One executive we spoke to said that his paternalistic corporation's outsourcing decision sent a dramatic message: Management was deadly serious about turning the company around. The resistance to re-engineering dropped dramatically.

An organization's culture and behavioral dynamics are often more powerful than any particular business process. If executives focus on process to the exclusion of culture, desired performance improvements – and even an outsourcing transformation itself – may never be realized.

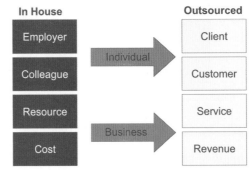

Source: Accenture, 2003

Figure 7.3 *Transition to client relationships*

Figure 7.3 shows that when employees transfer to an outsource service provider, their relationship to their previous company changes drastically; former colleagues suddenly become customers. In their former company, employees managed a finite set of internal resources. As part of an outsourced operation, however, they play *the role of service providers* who must meet clearly defined and measured targets. Financial focus shifts as well, from that of a cost center and overhead function to a revenue-generating operation. This total redefinition of relationships can be disorienting for some individuals and must be managed with discipline.

Making such transitions involves a profound change in organization culture and individual mindset. Generally, as illustrated in Figure 7.4, there are multiple stages in the 'journey'.

A dedicated relationship manager should be appointed early in the change process. This manager can play an invaluable role by acting as an internal advocate for the service provider, serving as a resource and sounding board, and coordinating the different internal groups that interact with the outsourcing company.

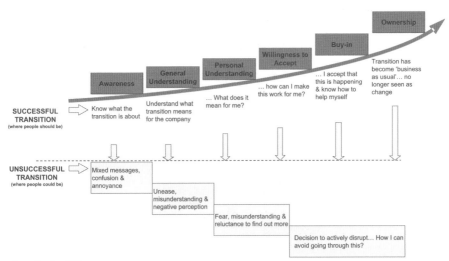

Source: Accenture, 2003

Figure 7.4 *The emotional change journey*

All employees affected by an outsource engagement will experience a readjustment period, regardless of whether they see the change as positive or negative. To ease this inevitable process, consider the following:

- Acknowledge and attend to employees' fears; focus on how to handle resistance to change

- Provide opportunities for employees to discuss their emotions in *safe* settings (one-on-one, team meetings, management briefings)

- Reassure employees who are staying that the people who are leaving will be treated fairly and receive adequate severance benefits

- Communicate clearly what you expect from employees at every stage.

The key goal in taking these steps is to manage the 'people' aspect of an outsource transition in ways that avoid significant dips in morale and productivity. Figure 7.5 illustrates typical employee reactions that a company faces during an outsource program.

Successfully managing emotive issues is best achieved through an early and open dialogue with the service provider. This dialogue will help ensure that employee concerns are based on fact rather than misperception. Involve employees by encouraging candid discussions and fostering ownership. Once you have determined which communication channels work best for your organization, map out a phase-by-phase communication plan.

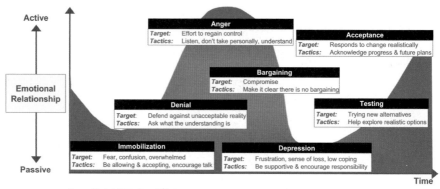

Source: Elizabeth Kubler Ross, ODR, Inc.

Figure 7.5 *Typical employee reactions to organizational transformation*

THE ROLE OF HR IN OUTSOURCING

Outsourcing is ultimately about people – shifting support functions to others who are better able to handle them and then focusing retained employees on the value-creating core of the business. It is no surprise, then, that some of the most important issues in an outsourcing transaction are human resource (HR) issues. A transaction can rest on a brilliant business structure and be captured in a finely articulated contract; but if careful thought is not given to the concerns and the motivation of the people involved, the undertaking is not likely to achieve its full potential – or it may flounder altogether. A comprehensive HR framework, as illustrated in Figure 7.6, needs to be deployed flawlessly if outsourcing is to succeed.

HR managers should be well versed about the impact of employment law on the outsource transition process. Such legal requirements can differ dramatically from country to country. HR professionals, supported by the service provider, should work with government agencies, unions, works councils (in the case of Europe), and other constituencies to satisfy national, regional, and local labor requirements.

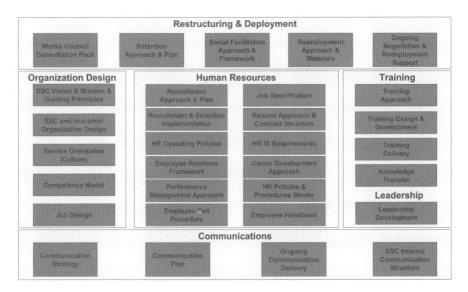

Figure 7.6 *HR components supporting outsourcing*

CASE STUDY
MOL, the Hungarian Oil and Gas Company[5]

Michel-Marc Delcommune, the CFO of MOL, put together an outsourcing plan for its entire transactional processing team. Over 400 staff were to work in a new shared service center run by a third-party specialist. Though the potential efficiency gains were clear, the plan he was proposing was totally new to Central and Eastern Europe. As a result, it could fall foul of Hungary's various social provisions and statutes.

Even before the delivery center could open, MOL faced a mountain of work to get its legal and regulatory infrastructure in place. Nevertheless, as CFO of the country's largest employer, Michel-Marc forged ahead. Seven months after he first proposed the plan, 406 staff left MOL to become the first employees of the delivery center, which now takes care of MOL's accounts payable, accounts receivable, cash accounting, general ledger, external reporting, and tax processing. Only a handful of finance staff remains at MOL to oversee such areas as strategic cost analysis, internal audit, and tax planning.

Michel-Marc recalls the challenge: 'I wanted to cut the finance department's annual operating costs by 25%. The finance department would set a good example for the rest of the company: centralizing and standardizing MOL's accounting processes into an SSC is central to our efficiency drive.' The only way the CFO could move the project forward was to win the stamp of approval from various unions. Union officials homed in on management and HR issues – and pored over the new contractual arrangements and transition procedures. The unions also wanted to be involved in the communications program. Delcommune comments: 'The staff affected by the outsourcing program were nearly all female with an average age of 42 years. Most had been with MOL all their working lives. They felt that they were being left out in the cold and thought that outsourcing would be used as a way to treat them unfairly. Everybody was getting very nervous, wanting to know what would happen to them individually.'

So, mimicking the investor roadshows he had recently undertaken, Delcommune embarked on an ambitious communications program similar to the one followed by David Harrison at BC Hydro. He toured MOL's 14 sites explaining the project. Along with a website providing regular updates on the project's progress, members of his team held one-to-one sessions with each employee who was moving to the delivery center. Michel-Marc goes on to say: 'As soon as we started communicating, we could feel the levels of nervousness going down. If anything, the meetings drove home the importance of choosing the right outsourcing partner to run the delivery center. We could not afford to fail and/or go with a partner who would be experimenting to our detriment.'

Michel-Marc Delcommune's sensitive approach to confronting employee concerns, communicating clearly and often, and gaining the support of key stakeholders, such as union executives, helped make MOL's outsource transition a resounding success. So much so that his company's efforts were recognized throughout Europe when in 2002, MOL won *CFO-Europe* magazine's Best-Practices Award for Internal Efficiencies

MOL's experience underscores the vital importance of robust, disciplined communication in ensuring a successful outsourcing program. It is essential that you clearly articulate the purpose, objectives, rationale, and impact of the program in a relevant, accurate, timely, and consistent manner – to all the stakeholders.

COMMUNICATIONS STRATEGY

The communications strategy provides a framework for directing and coordinating communications during the lifecycle of an outsourcing initiative. It creates a platform for transferring information to in-scope employees about changes to their working arrangements.

A typical program supporting a communications strategy is illustrated in Figure 7.7.

More than just being a morale booster, the communication process supports legal requirements across multiple geographies and enhances interaction with service providers. It is essential to success that you communicate effectively, not just with employees, but with all stakeholder groups, including:

- **Customers:** We think about customers in two ways. First, we view them as external consumers that we do business with. For them, the decision to source F&A activities differently has minimal impact, although they are likely to experience more prompt billing and cash collection! Second, we think about customers in terms of the support that local operating entities will need from the retained finance organization. For this second reason, it is important to articulate both the newly defined role that finance will play within the business and how it will interact with internal and external customer groups.

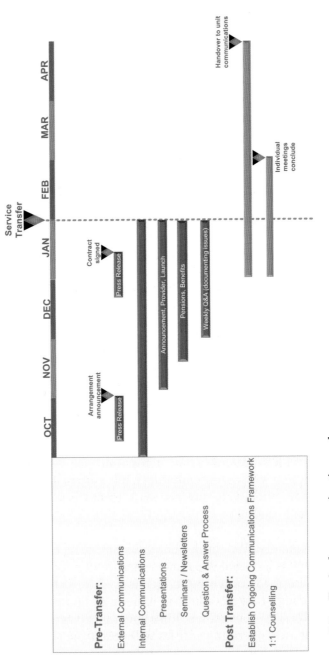

Figure 7.7 *Typical communications plan*

- **Non-executive directors:** Companies have different internal governance guidelines for reporting on programs of particular sizes, scope, or impact. Depending on the size and impact of the transaction, the board of directors sometimes needs to be educated about an outsourcing initiative to understand, and, if necessary, sign off on the decision. Preferably, board involvement will occur during the early stages of the outsource process. Both corporate and provider executives will likely need to invest substantial time and effort in board-level communication. Many companies are increasingly concerned about reassuring their boards that compliance with Sarbanes-Oxley legislation will be fully satisfied by a proposed outsourced services arrangement – and that it offers adequate control, resilience, and transparency.

- **Suppliers:** Several of the examples we have researched involved structural changes in the procure-to-pay or source-to-settlement processes. Suppliers can be affected by the centralization of accounts payable processing. They can also be affected because the scope of an outsourcing effort may include procurement cost reduction, and could therefore require supplier rationalization.

- **Finance service providers:** Changes affecting this group typically involve banking and treasury operations. During an outsource program, a new set of relationships emerges between a company, its banks, and outsource service providers. Since most outsource delivery centers use electronic funds settlement, the change often simply involves setting up new processes and reporting mechanisms with the outsource service provider.

- **Regulators:** Employment, legal, and statutory financial regulations raise a number of sensitive issues which have varying degrees of impact in different territories. These requirements are discussed in Chapter 9.

The table in Figure 7.8 illustrates the change in the regulatory environment over the last couple of decades.

In many cases, senior executives such as David Harrison, former CFO of BC Hydro, are affected personally by an outsource initiative. Their involvement raises personal, career, and corporate issues. It is vital for a company's CEO and CFO to understand how their outsource agenda affects the behavior and development of their top management team. This impact must be given due consideration in the decision-making process.

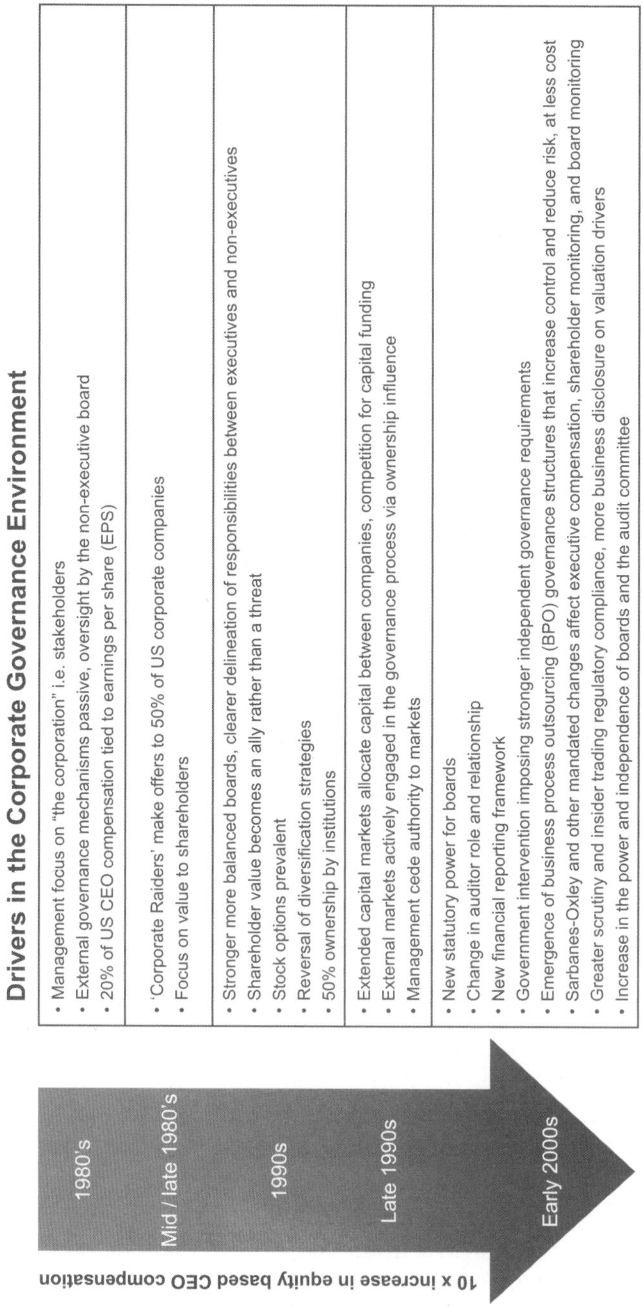

Drivers in the Corporate Governance Environment

1980's
- Management focus on "the corporation" i.e. stakeholders
- External governance mechanisms passive, oversight by the non-executive board
- 20% of US CEO compensation tied to earnings per share (EPS)

Mid / late 1980's
- 'Corporate Raiders' make offers to 50% of US corporate companies
- Focus on value to shareholders

1990s
- Stronger more balanced boards, clearer delineation of responsibilities between executives and non-executives
- Shareholder value becomes an ally rather than a threat
- Stock options prevalent
- Reversal of diversification strategies
- 50% ownership by institutions

Late 1990s
- Extended capital markets allocate capital between companies, competition for capital funding
- External markets actively engaged in the governance process via ownership influence
- Management cede authority to markets

Early 2000s
- New statutory power for boards
- Change in auditor role and relationship
- New financial reporting framework
- Government intervention imposing stronger independent governance requirements
- Emergence of business process outsourcing (BPO) governance structures that increase control and reduce risk, at less cost
- Sarbanes-Oxley and other mandated changes affect executive compensation, shareholder monitoring, and board monitoring
- Greater scrutiny and insider trading regulatory compliance, more business disclosure on valuation drivers
- Increase in the power and independence of boards and the audit committee

10 x increase in equity based CEO compensation

Source: Adapted from "Corporate Governance, Ethics, and Organizational Architecture", James A. Brickley and Clifford W. Smith, Jr. Jr., Journal of Applied Corporate Finance, Vol. 15, No. 3, Spring 2003

Figure 7.8 *Changing drivers in the corporate environment*

So what are the fears expressed by executive stakeholders? Among the most prevalent:

- 'Loss of control' and autonomy by independent business units
- 'Loss of flexibility' to meet changing market and business information needs
- Conflicting priorities that will sap internal project resources and investment
- History repeating itself of another failed change program
- 'Loss of institutional knowledge' of customers, products, and markets
- Becoming overwhelmed by the magnitude of the change required
- Flaws in the business case
- Lackluster executive sponsorship.

CFO INSIGHTS

- Lead from the front and top. Preserve confidentiality and secrecy in the early stages at all costs. Avoid getting bogged down in detail early in the deal. Form a high-powered deal team and don't drive the process by committee. Adopt a corporate M&A transaction posture towards outsourcing.

- CEO and CFO commitment to an outsourcing project is vital – and their sense of urgency must be communicated to all stakeholders very early on. They are the visionaries, initiators, and to a very large extent, the orchestrators of any enterprise-wide initiative.

- View the outsourcing partner as a trusted advisor from the outset. Service providers generally make considerable up-front capital investments to improve processes, so if an arrangement breaks down they face considerable hardship.

- Managing all stakeholders is essential for success. You will need to spend a lot of time eliciting views and drawing stakeholders into agreement. The effort pays – it will allay doubts and anxiety. The stakeholder landscape is dynamic and positions change. Remember: Former colleagues may now be your new customers!

- Confront the reality faced by your employees – and be bold. Outsourcing is ultimately about people; shifting support functions to others who are better able to handle them, while focusing on retained employees and the value-creating core of your business.

FROM INSIGHT TO ACTION

IDENTIFY YOUR STAKEHOLDERS

They will affect and be affected by what is happening. Stakeholders range from shareholders, the government, and regulators to internal and external customers (suppliers and employees). As CFO, don't forget your own team – members may be committed now, but their loyalties can change.

KNOW YOUR STAKEHOLDERS

Different stakeholders will perceive the same changes in very different ways. Stakeholders can change their minds. Take their pulse as events unfold. Identify where your employees are on the change curve.

ADOPT TRUSTED ADVISOR BEHAVIOR

Take this posture from the outset and use the negotiation process as a means of creating an enduring relationship. Lay out a joint road map in a manner that sets out precedents for how both parties will work together when challenges are encountered and things go wrong.

INVOLVE HR EARLY

It's all about people. If careful thought is not given to the concerns and motivations of the *people* involved, your outsourcing undertaking is unlikely to achieve its full potential.

COMMUNICATE AT THE RIGHT TIME TO THE RIGHT PEOPLE

Take advice from your service provider and design a precise timetable that defines what to communicate, to whom, and when.

REFERENCES

1   Peter Bendor-Samuel, *Build Relationships Around Service Provider Strengths*, Everest Group, May 2002.

2   Jonathan Hughes *et al.*, *20 Best Practices for Negotiating and Managing Key Supplier Relationships*, Vantage Partners, 2003.

3   Kathleen Goolsby, Cost vs. Value of Using an Outsourcing Consultant, *The Outsourcing Journal*, 2003. www.outsourcing-journal.com

4   Thomas Healy and Jane Linder, *Outsourcing In US State and Local Government: Value In Leadership*, Accenture, 2003. www.accenture.com

5   Ben McLannahan, *Best Practices Awards*: Michel-Marc Delcommune, CFO, MOL, *CFO Europe*, April 2003. www.cfoeurope.com

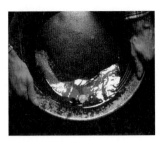

CHAPTER 8

Ensuring a Successful Transition

TRANSITIONING TO A EUROPEAN OUTSOURCED SHARED SERVICE CENTER

Pierre Prot, CFO & Paul Van Beveren, Finance Change Manager
Rhodia

Rhodia, once part of the Rhône-Poulenc Group, is one of the world's leaders in specialty chemicals. It employs 23,000 people worldwide and provides products to industries ranging from automotive manufacturing to healthcare and consumer goods.

Rhodia's management decided to outsource finance and accounting (F&A) operations after benchmarking revealed that its support functions were performing below industry average. Pierre Prot, the CFO of Rhodia, formulated the strategy to centralize and standardize processes that were scattered across many European production facilities. Pierre comments:

'Rhodia already had a successful US-based shared service center for our 30 plants throughout North America. So I believed we should adopt a similar shared service center approach for our 60 European facilities.'

In 2001, the company evaluated outsourcing options and sought a partner with the experience and capability to move Rhodia's European F&A activities into a single European location. Pierre goes on to say:

'Today, Rhodia has a shared service center in Prague. Thanks to our outsourcing service provider, we have transferred the bulk of our F&A processes to the Czech Republic – revolutionizing functions that had been spread across more than 60 locations in seven European countries. The multiclient service center built for us was one of the first in central Europe and, more significantly, the first to provide multi-country resources. Since the transition, our outsourcing arrangement has delivered substantial benefits – among them, a 30% reduction in costs.'

Paul Van Beveren, who was Rhodia's Finance Change Manager during the transition and has since joined Accenture, comments:

'We had to sell the whole idea of outsourcing to Rhodia's management since it was still a very new concept in mainland Europe. Many companies fear a loss of control. But we had the support of our chairman and CEO, who took the attitude "if we can improve profitability and guarantee that it will not affect quality adversely, then let's do it!" Prague was, in some respects, a natural choice since it had significantly lower labor costs than our other shortlisted countries, Poland and Slovakia, where we already had supply chain operations.'

The IT landscape at the time was a complex mix of 'systems spaghetti.' Going it alone without a professional systems partner would have been prohibitively expensive and fraught with risk. According to Paul:

'The transfer of the company's finance function to the shared service center was not only remarkably smooth, but also surprisingly swift. This is a tribute to the power of the partnership, which I liken to a marriage. If one of you makes a mistake, you can't sit back and tell the other to fix it – you have to jump in and help one another to solve the problem. You can't put that kind of a relationship into a contract. It has to be built on mutual trust.' Paul comments on the transition:

'Transferring the activities of 170 people from 60 locations to just one over an 18-month period was a major challenge. In France, for example, the proposed change was treated as a starting point for negotiations; people always wanted to discuss and argue about it. Valuable time could have been lost formulating and completing staffing agreements, with the risk of knowledge gaps arising if our retention strategy failed. But even in these difficult situations, we still had things under control.'

Transitioning to the delivery center in Prague was phased – starting with all the UK units and followed by waves of 30-to-50 people at a time. Knowledge transfer, a key element in the transition program, was treated as a priority. Since it was *assumed that few, if any, employees from the existing organization would want to leave their home countries, new personnel in Prague had to be recruited and trained. Paul reports:*

'Transferring the knowledge from existing UK staff progressed smoothly and took only 4 months; it took another 2 months to stabilize the process. Our success was partially due to a single-system, single-language move.' In contrast, there were some glitches and 'social' delays in the first wave of the transition from France to Prague. At one site, employees went on strike for a week. At another, there was already a parallel – potentially competitive – restructuring initiative under way. However, 90% of the transition was completed by the target date. Pierre comments,

'Our service provider's expertise in planning for the transition was invaluable; even with delays and plan changes, we stayed within budget. In fact, because the technology upgrades went so smoothly, we under-spent by 10%. We have contractual arrangements with our outsource provider based on what we call in France 'engagement on the result.' Essentially, this is a fixed price agreement, but if both companies underestimate the complexities, we both react flexibly and in partnership mode by adding additional resources to cope.' The manner in which the partnership is built is very important to Pierre. He goes on to say:

'It must go beyond the contract. Neither party has found it necessary to refer back to the contract during our first two years of working together. Where we need to adapt, we have done so. You do that when there is complete trust. Our relationship works very, very well.'

Pierre and Paul can certainly declare a victory. Their shared service operations are very visible in Europe: The Prague center regularly receives visits from other companies wishing to replicate Rhodia's success. As Paul sums up:

'Shared services – creating value and high performance at low cost – is much easier to do in the United States. Bringing this idea to Europe, and, in our case, to multicultural regions with up to 15 different languages and 10 different accounting projects, is quite another thing.' Rhodia believes this was the first such F&A outsourcing project in Europe developed by a non-Anglo-Saxon group and built in central Europe. Other companies now are starting to follow in its footsteps.

To reap the benefits of outsourcing, companies like Rhodia need to plan carefully and deploy resources properly. Making the transition requires substantial management time. The challenges of migrating entire processes to an outside provider and mastering staffing issues can be huge. Getting an outsourcing program up and running demands, not only a convincing business case, but also a mixture of conviction, skill, diplomacy, and persistence. This chapter explores the management issues faced during the transition of an outsourcing project, from planning to steady state operation. We consider the key elements of a transition, from developing an overall framework to implementation management. Then we look at people strategy, including communication and leadership, both of which are essential for success.

TRANSITION FRAMEWORK

A smooth, successful implementation requires a structured, disciplined framework – and a holistic view of change. Figure 8.1 outlines the principal steps involved.

In Chapters 6 and 7, we focused on the first three steps in the transition framework: deal shape, contract planning, and communications. Continuous improvement is dealt with in Chapter 10. This chapter covers implementing the transition. Implementation typically unfolds in four stages: planning, mobilization, stabilization, and integration.

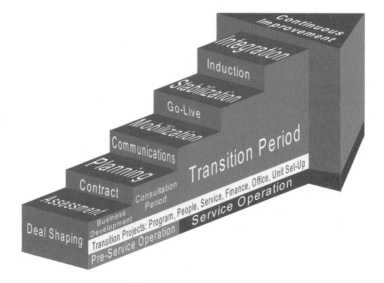

Source: Accenture, 2003

Figure 8.1 *Transition framework for outsourcing*

Here is some best-practice advice, drawn from practical experience, for successfully managing each of the four implementation stages:[1]

1 **Planning – 'Allow lots of time upfront'** Overall, when we asked what they would do differently in structuring their outsourcing relationships, both buyers and service providers said they would do more upfront planning during the transition stage preceding actual service transfer. Outsourcing is ultimately a big management time-saver. However, launching a program generally demands substantial effort from the executives driving the change – almost inevitably more than they bargained for. Navigating the approval process, particularly in decentralized organizations, can be a hurdle. Ingersoll-Rand's shared services group, for example, had to win approval from the presidents, CFOs, and CIOs of each of its four main product sectors before it could finalize a contract.

2 **Mobilization – 'Build a consensus'** Don't stop at the executive suite. Line managers often bridle at outsourcing because centralization threatens their power and authority. Ignoring this opposition is a mistake. Forcing outsourcing on an organization doesn't lead to a productive partnership relationship. Building a team is the better approach. **'You don't want to do this with just a small core of people,' says Colgate's VP of finance, Mr Pohlschroeder. 'You want everyone involved.'** Finding a few business-line champions who embrace the idea and lobby for adoption is one good idea. Another is to explain persuasively that outsourcing is not a loss of control but rather a form of enhanced control. 'The major issue for most companies considering outsourcing is the initial perception of a loss of control,' notes OneResource Group's chief operating officer, Mr Reilly. **'They need to understand that they are not really losing control, but changing the way in which they exercise it. Instead of controlling employees and every step of the process, they retain control by focusing on results and demanding that they be delivered.'**

3 **Stabilization – ' Measure performance'** Metrics not only measure the success of an arrangement, they also provide data to reinforce and protect programs. 'Benchmarks help us publicize our successes,' says Mark Abruzino, director of financial shared services at TRW Automotive, a leading maker of automotive safety systems. TRW measures 20 key items for its outsourced payroll and check-printing activities – and keeps a scorecard for each. 'We are concrete. We want no gray areas,'

says Abruzino. Quantitative measurements should be combined with qualitative feedback from internal customers. Consumer-satisfaction surveys can assess whether business units are getting the service and information they really need.

4 **Integration – 'Ensure proper oversight'** Outsourcing ultimately enables senior finance executives to focus on critical business issues. But that doesn't mean they can wash their hands of outsourcing once implementation is complete. Continuous supervision of the relationship is vital; usually this requires minding the broad strokes rather than monitoring the day-to-day detail. 'You have to stay with it through the whole life of the contract – forever – to make it work properly and get the benefits,' says one UK finance director. A company can never abdicate responsibility for the function.

TRANSITION MANAGEMENT

Outsourcing introduces new relationships and cultural pressures into an organization. No matter how hopeful and positive the parties feel at contract signing, unless strategic steps are taken at the outset to properly manage the agreement, *the challenges encountered during the first year – the transition year – become pitfalls that can destroy the relationship.* It happens little by little, as unexpected problems occur.

Relationships when outsourcing are both complex and challenging. The provider's marketing team nearly always paints a picture of a smooth and seamless transition to the buyer. But the reality is that most outsourcing transitions are bumpy. The idea of a trouble-free transition sets unrealistically high expectations.

Nevertheless, the bumps are controllable. Pre-engagement, any buyer should ensure that a potential service provider has pointed out any likely problems 'coming out of the gate.' The provider should also offer a viable set of remedies to overcome these obstacles and minimize the risks they reflect.

Best-practice remedies for the pitfalls often experienced during the transition are illustrated in Figure 8.2.

As Figure 8.2 shows, if best practices are not put in place, potential problems can lead to a troubled or even a failed relationship. Be careful when interpreting this simple illustration as some of the activities are

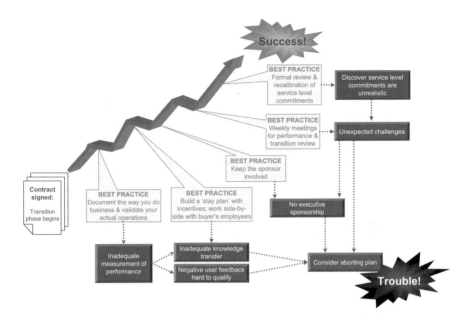

Figure 8.2 *Best practice remedies for transition pitfalls*

launched before the contract is signed, e.g. a staff retention plan is developed pre-contract.

Develop baseline metrics of performance

New process mechanics and business relationships can be uncomfortable. Inevitably, users are going say that 'things aren't working as well as they used to.' To minimize disruptions and risk, be sure to baseline performance pre-transfer. It goes without saying that service levels should not fall below this baseline during the transition year and you should use the first year to agree the specific service improvements that you expect.

Plan and document knowledge before transfer

Inevitably, an incoming service provider will not know all the intricacies and issues that have been absorbed by a company's staff over the course of many years. Unless knowledge transfer is extremely well planned, a drop-off in service levels is unavoidable the day that the provider takes over the process – even if it mechanically performs the work correctly and efficiently. Transition planning should go beyond official policy and procedures – and focus on the informal relationships and workflows that actually underlie processes and outcomes.

Keep the sponsor involved

Hold weekly performance and transition reviews throughout the first year of the arrangement. These reviews should include the highest-level sponsor of the outsourcing effort (for example, the CFO). This person – who may be the original outsourcing decision-maker – must stay involved. He or she must keep track of where everyone is in the cycle, monitoring milestones and next steps.

Accommodate the unexpected

There is no way to foresee every possible problem. Best practice is to assume early on that there will be substantial challenges. With this in mind, formulate realistic scenarios that anticipate and plan for unexpected events. For example, if extra resources are required, how will they be mobilized?

Remain flexible

At the onset, tremendous effort is typically put into constructing contracts and detailing service-level specifications. However, when the service provider takes over, it is not unusual to uncover unexpected glitches. Flexibility should be factored into the contract to avoid destructive pressures that can easily undermine the confidence of both parties. Best practice is to build in a formal review and tightening phase around contractual service-level agreements – say six months from the initial transfer date. If recalibration is needed, the contract can be refined by mutual agreement.

To summarize, transition management experience indicates that there are three essential ingredients for success:

1 A well-crafted strategic transition management framework

2 A detailed transition plan defining activities and milestones

3 A documented people strategy outlining the steps required to effect a skills transfer and sustain workforce motivation.

DETAILED IMPLEMENTATION PLANNING

An integrated outsource transition plan is illustrated in Figure 8.3. In this instance, F&A activities were to be transferred from existing locations in the United States, North Asia, South Asia, and the United Kingdom to the outsourcer's delivery center in India.

This transition was achieved via four implementation *releases.* Each geographic release included four transitional phases:

- **Phase A:** Commencement (assumption of service delivery by the provider)

- **Phase B:** Transfer preparation

- **Phase C:** Transfer execution

- **Phase D:** Management of the *steady state* operation.

The business processes (and the people affected) were grouped into three functional *towers* to segment the service transition into manageable projects. In addition, there was a component for cross-functional support services. Each functional *tower project* had three workstreams:

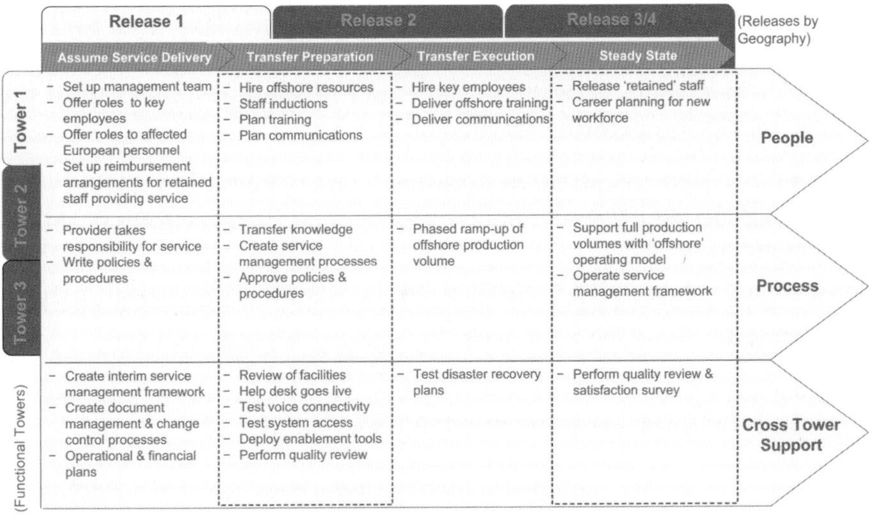

Source: Accenture, 2003

Figure 8.3   *Integrated transition plan for outsourcing*

1 **People deployment:** The transfer of personnel to the provider and recruiting of new resources in the offshore location, communication, and the resources required to enable employees to work in the new environment.

2 **Process implementation:** This establishes the new organizations required to provide outsource services and transfers process tasks and knowledge from exiting company personnel to the provider.

3 **Support delivery:** This implements technology changes and sets up new facilities to support the provision of service delivery via the new management and operational framework.

The transition plan sets out milestones and timelines for each geographic phase. As illustrated in Figure 8.4, each geographic release required 6 to 8 months to complete migration to the new offshore delivery center.

You should satisfy yourself that the outsource provider has deep expertise in the transfer of services and staff. Process and control frameworks are required for high-quality service delivery. Overall, the transition risks you must plan for include:

1 **Connectivity:** Technology (IT and telecommunications) connectivity plans should provide for end-to-end management and problem analysis. A key issue is the ability to switch over to back-up connectivity.

2 **Service impact during transition:** Key personnel may need to travel to the delivery location for post-transition support. There should be sufficient overlap between onshore and offshore resources until the new service is operating satisfactorily.

3 **Staff attrition:** As attrition occurs, the service provider should have the capacity to back-fill critical vacancies with appropriately skilled personnel.

4 **Overall business impact:** Stakeholders should be identified and kept informed.

PEOPLE STRATEGY

Companies typically underestimate the resources required to deliver a major workforce transition. Bearing in mind all the people-related issues that can occur during an outsourcing program, what steps can be taken to ensure a successful workforce transition?

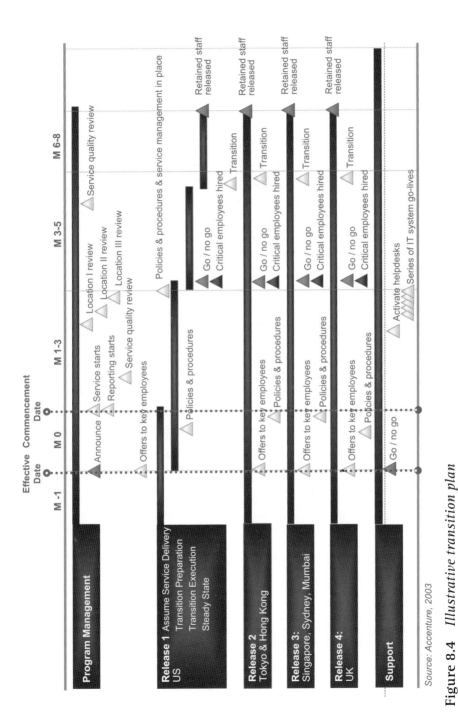

Source: Accenture, 2003

Figure 8.4   *Illustrative transition plan*

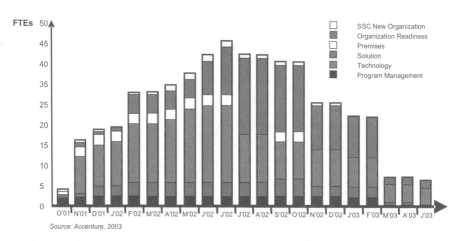

Source: Accenture, 2003

Figure 8.5 *Transformation team headcount profile*

As Figure 8.5 shows, a high proportion of a transformation team is devoted to change management tasks – such as organizational readiness – as opposed to purely technical tasks.

The following guidelines will help ensure a well-orchestrated workforce transition:

Design phase:

- Determine the job changes needed to deliver the new process design

- Establish resource baseline to enable accurate labor savings measurement after go-live

- Benchmark workforce reduction efforts and review best practices from other organizations

- Summarize the workforce transition plan impact on timing, contingency plans and implementation sequencing

- Ensure existing workforce reduction plans are compliant and define career options

- Obtain workforce transition plan approval from human resources and business units.

Build phase:

- Develop the communication plan to help local resource professionals manage the transition

- Review process design and workforce impacts with business units and gain buy-in

- Arrange for contingency staffing to minimize the risk of business disruption

- Arrange outplacement services for those employees who will not be offered new positions

- Communicate plans to employees.

Consider a global manufacturing company's experience in launching an outsourced shared service operation in a low-cost location. The roll-out program was split into a number of country-based efforts to reduce risk and to maintain service stability.

CASE STUDY
A well-crafted transition program

A $3bn turnover manufacturing company had more than 210,000 employees scattered across 150 countries. Its objective: To transfer most of its F&A and back-office processes to a European shared service center. The company set out a very detailed plan. It started by carefully selecting an outsourcing provider, then developed its value proposition and deal structure, and finally moved into the contract stage. Transition projects were started very early, covering such aspects as people, premises, service, and finance. During the initial planning phase, consultation and communications were highest on the agenda.

The outsourcing provider was chosen based on its extensive experience in transitioning such activities across Europe, and in particular, for its knowledge of European employment law. The outsourcing provider invested heavily in the transition, building an experienced team so that the company's management could focus on providing uninterrupted service delivery.

A joint solution team was mobilized, incorporating staff from both the company and the outsourcer. The first job was to validate work done to date on service scope, costs, headcount, and transition planning. In parallel, steps were taken to recon-

figure out-of-scope activities and management tasks into a retained organization structure. Following extensive due diligence, the transition program was broken down into the following implementation workstreams:

1 *People transfer/recruitment*
2 *Knowledge transfer*
3 *Service management*
4 *Finance management*
5 *Technology and work environment*
6 *Operation start-up*
7 *Transformation 'quick-starts'.*

The workstreams were integrated into a 15-month master plan that focused initially on mobilization. Workstreams were set up for transferring master data and to support new shared service center launch and stabilization. Subsequently, migration was split into geographic phases. Phase 1 involved the transfer of F&A activities from France/Spain/Germany; Phase 2, UK/Italy; Phase 3, Austria/Poland; Phase 4, Sweden/Finland. The go-live date for each phase occurred at three-month intervals. Underpinning these phases were communications and management programs.

Some final tips from past experience:

- Do not miss the opportunity to record accurately 'the way it was' – the performance of key processes and services prior to change. This establishes a baseline that goes beyond purely financial metrics.

- HR capabilities must be deployed **prior** to service takeover; otherwise staff will be preoccupied with personal issues and concerns.

COMMUNICATION STRATEGIES

- **Attend to morale:** Cost-cutting logic means that outsourcing almost always entails redundancies, particularly of finance and accounting staff who work at the 'coal-face.' Even when operations do not move globally and outright layoffs are avoided (in fact, even when finance personnel remain at the same desk in the same building), they generally face the uncertainties of a transfer onto the books and to the authority of a new employer. Morale tends to suffer, threatening day-to-day operations and the transfer of knowledge to the outsourcing provider (or shared service center). This poses challenges for the service provider, who must motivate disgruntled staff – and for the parent firm, which must keep operations running during the transition.

- **Communicate the upside:** As many companies have found, it is vital to convey that a shift to an outsourcing provider is not a dead end. Far from it! Such a move can offer transferred staff new career opportunities with a company whose core competency is, after all, finance and accounting. MOL, the Hungarian oil-and-gas company, moved 406 accountants to its outsourcing partner. 'Although there has been a headcount reduction,' reports CFO Michel-Marc Delcommune, 'former staff seem more motivated working for the outsourcer than as accountants at MOL.' Thomas Cook UK found that service center employees initially felt resentment, but soon saw a link between the transfer and their rising skills. This has made them convincing advocates of change for other transfer candidates.

- **Stick to specifics:** To ensure continuity, affected staff need concrete information about their fate as soon as possible. What really convinced MOL's staff was a side-by-side comparison of their pay stubs before the transfer with their salaries and benefits after it. Moods improved still further with the provision of a redundancy premium to compensate for lost vested rights. CFO Delcommune says that once employees saw that they were getting a fair deal, **'all the turmoil stopped and people concentrated on making the project itself a success.'** Where headcount is cut outright, as happens when finance operations move around the world, it's important to devise an incentive structure that encourages departing employees to train their successors effectively. One firm that shifted finance operations for six countries to a central European center, gave redundant staff nine months to conduct their job searches. Redundancy payments were only awarded only after relevant knowledge had been captured from departing staff.

As described in Chapter 7, all employees will experience a readjustment period. Once you have determined which channels work best for your organization, you should begin to flesh out a full-scale communications plan. HR benefits require especially clear communication. In outsourcing transfers, employees are usually assured that their new benefit package will be *comparable* to their current one. But they may not understand that

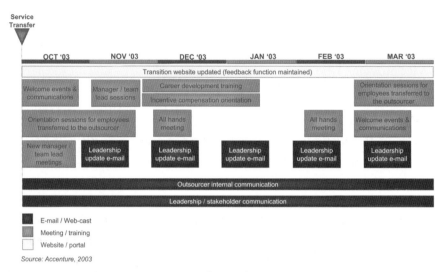

Figure 8.6   *Illustrative six-month employee communications plan*

comparable doesn't mean *identical*. Clearly, no two companies have absolutely the same benefit plans. Your HR professionals will determine what is needed in a benefits package to make it acceptable to all concerned – management, retained employees, and transitioning employees.

An example of a six-month employee communications plan is outlined in Figure 8.6.

An effective employee communications plan is key to reducing employee trauma. Strong communication can sustain productivity, maximize retention, and pave the way for a smooth transition. Consider the case of BP, which used finance outsourcing as a catalyst for change.

 CASE STUDY
Outsourcing as a catalyst for change

Alison MacKenzie, today a business support services director at the multiclient F&A delivery center in Aberdeen, Scotland, has been on both sides of the outsourcing table. Having moved from BP to its outsourcer, Accenture, her experience highlights the positive potential of outsourcing. She recalls the first day when BP announced that it would be outsourcing its finance department:

'A stunned silence followed the announcement. No one spoke, as the employees in the room tried to digest what they had just heard: Their department was being outsourced. Gradually, it dawned on them that their careers had just taken an unexpected turn. Soon people were in tears. Loyal BP employees felt like the company had let them down. They felt hurt and angry that they had no say in the matter.'

BP learned quickly from that initial experience – and developed a framework to speed up the transition process and ease the change for affected employees. MacKenzie recalls how helpful it was for her to air her concerns soon after the initial outsourcing announcement was made:

'We broke up into small groups later that afternoon and everyone got a chance to talk and ask questions. Open discussions such as this one are part of our transition framework's communication methodology. This included one-on-one meetings, question-and-answer sessions, a telephone hotline, Website and e-mail.'

In a professional life, an unexpected twist – such as outsourcing – can be unsettling. Almost everyone has a family to support, financial goals, career aspirations, and hopes for the future. MacKenzie, for example, wanted to be sure that the move to Accenture wouldn't affect any of her BP benefits. She was pleased that her new employer had put together a benefits package that was responsive to her needs and concerns.

The outsourcer's transition framework included a comprehensive analysis of client benefits and compensation aimed at crafting a workable and competitive hiring plan. Stock options, retirement plans, pension funds, and other benefits were analyzed to create fair and attractive offers. The intent was to quickly address employees' basic needs so that they could make informed career choices and the new team could begin working together with that of the old. MacKenzie summarizes her feelings:

'The outsourcing has turned out to be a blessing in disguise. BP is really interested in oil, not finance and accounting. By joining the outsource provider I'm part of a core competency instead of just a support function, which has proven great for my career!'

Alison MacKenzie's experience is one of many such stories. When employees learn that their company is considering outsourcing, they immediately feel concern and uncertainty. Outsourcing can be a frightening prospect for employees who, quite understandably, worry about their futures. Yet our research shows that the vast majority of employees find themselves much happier in their post-outsourcing environment.

LEADING THE TRANSITION

As the BP case demonstrates, strong leadership is essential from the very top of the organization, not only at the beginning, but throughout the lifecycle of an outsourcing arrangement. John Browne, the CEO of BP, has been behind the change from its very inception in 1991 to this day. His enthusiasm percolates down through the various layers of management on both sides of the outsourcing fence.

As a new outsourced service structure evolves, leadership challenges will evolve as well. Principles and practices that have worked historically may no longer apply. The leader of an outsourcing transition should be a well-respected senior executive known for being able to work across all business units. The leader must also be a vigorous champion of the outsource vision: higher service and performance with a superior set of economics.

Be sure to separate the role of the change project leader from that of the operational leader of the outsource center. The skills and focus of each of these two leaders are different. It is especially difficult for one individual to play both roles during roll-out, when time must be devoted to both the transition and to daily operational issues. Successful outsource programs use two distinct leaders, one for change management and one for operations:

- **Change leaders**: Employees have to be convinced that change is necessary. So steering committees should include top executives from both the corporate organization and the business units affected.

- **Operational leaders**: Strong day-to-day project managers are a must. They must be recognized for their commitment to delivering quality work within tight time frames. People will not follow their strategic direction if they are not viewed as credible and effective.

As the outsourcing arrangement develops, there will be increasing interaction between the change team and the new operations team. Some change team members are likely to migrate to the new shared service center.

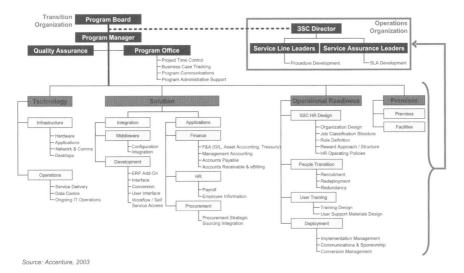

Source: Accenture, 2003

Figure 8.7 *Program development organization for F&A outsourcing*

Figure 8.7 shows an F&A transition organization with its links to the new shared service center organization.

The organization represented above illustrates both the temporary transition team and the parts of the shared service center involved in the migration. The engine room of the transition team comprises the three workgroups labeled – solution, technology and operational readiness; this is where most of the work takes place under the leadership of the program manager who liaises closely with the shared service center director. The outsource service provider is responsible for the planning, mobilization, service transition, people transfer, solution implementation, and managing the transition.

This chapter has been about ensuring a successful transition. Considering this, you may think it strange that it includes so little on **what** you are transitioning to. The outsource service provider will have an integrated service management framework or set of standardized management processes for integrating people, processes, and technology into their organization. This framework is discussed in Chapter 10, which focuses on 'keeping the deal working' through continuous improvement.

CFO INSIGHTS

- As CFO, you have to stick with it through the transition lifecycle. A smooth, successful implementation requires a structured, disciplined framework – and a holistic view of change.

- The idea of a trouble-free transition sets unrealistically high expectations. If the challenges encountered during the first year are not handled properly, they may become pitfalls that destroy a promising outsourcing relationship. It happens little by little, as unexpected problems occur. Nevertheless, the bumps are controllable – if you are prepared.

- Companies typically underestimate the resources required to deliver a major workforce transition. Surprisingly, a high proportion of a transformation team is devoted to change management – such as organizational readiness – as opposed to purely technical tasks.

- The vast majority of employees find themselves much happier in their post-outsourcing environment. However, the initial outsourcing news is almost always a shock. An effective employee communication program is key to reducing distress and paving the way for a smooth transition.

FROM INSIGHT TO ACTION

START TRANSITION ACTIVITIES EARLY
Allow lots of time. Getting an outsourcing program off the ground generally takes significantly more senior management effort than you imagine.

CRAFT A TRANSITION FRAMEWORK
The first 12 months – *the transition year* – is the most crucial. Put special effort into knowledge transfer and work shadowing prior to 'cut-over.' Segment design, build, and roll-out phases. Prepare scenarios to deal with unexpected events, such as high attrition.

EMPLOY THE RIGHT LEADERSHIP
Separate the new leadership roles of *change management* and *operations*; they require different skills. Win over the 'bosses.' Without senior level sponsorship, outsource projects are doomed to failure.

HAVE A PLAN AND MANAGE TO IT
Expected project outcomes should be communicated to everyone involved, internal and external. Phased release establishes interim goals and deadlines. Keep pace and intensity high throughout the outsourcing project lifecycle. Manage through regular status and issue resolution meetings.

DEFINE BOTH THE SERVICE LEVEL AGREEMENT (SLA) AND THE OPERATING LEVEL AGREEMENT (OLA)
The SLA defines the service levels of the outsourcing SSC. The OLA, on the other hand, defines what is required of the company as whole – including the retained organization.

COMMUNICATE! COMMUNICATE! COMMUNICATE!
Attend to employees' fears early. Prepare your managers to handle resistance to change. Communicate what you expect from people during the transition. Create baselines for current performance levels to demonstrate quick-wins. Make communication *two-way.*

REFERENCES

1 Accenture in cooperation with The Economist Intelligence Unit, *Outside Upside: Finding focus through finance outsourcing*, 2003. www.accenture.com/financesolutions

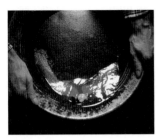

CHAPTER 9

Reducing
Risk with
Outsourcing

WEIGHING UP RISK AND OUTSOURCING

Thomas Buess, CFO
Zurich Financial Services

Zurich Financial Services, the Swiss-based insurance company, has offices in more than 60 countries, employs more than 60,000 people, and serves more than 38 million customers. Annual revenue is approximately $55bn. Thomas Buess, CFO, comments:

'The life insurance industry is suffering all over the world and Zurich is no exception. The year 2002 was very critical for us – we were in crisis. We were underperforming. We had to implement a special profit improvement program and raise extra capital to keep the business afloat. Thankfully this is now behind us.

'Our overall profitability has significantly improved and we can now move from a survival mode to investing in new business. Our non life insurance business has improved, but returns in our life business are still relatively low. We have made great strides in streamlining our fragmented organization. We can now focus on investment and creating value. We need to revisit our value drivers and identify where we can make money in the future.' Thomas comments on his next steps:

'We were considering outsourcing parts of our F&A function. We've launched a feasibility study, called Project Athena, to assess relative risks and benefits. We have two clear objectives: First, we must streamline our processes and standardize our systems based on SAP software. We need to consolidate geographically into possibly three shared service centers (Europe, the Americas, and Asia).

'Second, we need to reduce cost through labor cost arbitrage. We are considering offshoring with an outsource provider. We don't just want to cut costs, we want to improve our processes and benefit from innovation. We know that some outsource providers will inject capital to help with such a transformation – making the upfront investment and then recouping it through ongoing process efficiencies.'

The team at Zurich is weighing up several options. High on the agenda is working out the size of the prize. Thomas has received some wild estimates from potential suppliers, but is skeptical, since the scope of the planned F&A outsourcing is relatively narrow and involves approximately 500 people. However, his team is also looking at where to cut the process. If, for example, the scope of the outsourcing is broadened into the claims processing area, the potential benefits could be enormous. Thomas says:

'The scoping for outsourcing needs to consider not only the F&A process, but also our global IT function. The transformation program – if you combine the business process and IT investment required – may involve up to $0.5 billion in operational costs per year. But I believe there is significant low-hanging fruit. We also see opportunities to outsource our purchasing and logistics. We've had a positive experience in outsourcing these functions in the United States, but have not done so yet in Europe. Our team is weighing our strategic options, and most important, the risks.'

In making its move, ZFS is evaluating some difficult, risk-sensitive issues:

- Offshoring – should it streamline processes first and then go offshore, or go offshore first and then streamline?
- Shared services – should it set up a global shared service center internally first, secure the benefits and then outsource, or should it outsource first using an external provider's existing shared service assets?
- Transformation – should the company choose an outsource partner who can deliver just cost savings, or a partner willing to invest in and lead its transformation?

There is much due diligence ahead. For example, ZFS is studying the experience of banks that have located shared services centers in India, China, and Malaysia. The company is also studying outsourcing experiences in the insurance sector – not just in F&A, but in premium management and claims. Thomas notes:

'For us, the jury is still out. We need more evidence that there is a robust business case and that others have gone down this path and succeeded. We are using our own methodology – Total Risk Profiling – to assess our options by looking at:

- *Country risk: As an insurance company, we specialize in providing political risk cover. When looking at global sourcing options, we need to question political security. We are attracted to the idea of interoperability – spreading the risk of our shared services across multiple locations.*

- *Regulatory risk: The insurance industry faces demanding regulatory require-ments; these will affect our decision on what to outsource and how. Financial controls? Regulations differ country by country. Physical records, for example, need to be maintained in Germany, Belgium, and France. The regulatory envi-ronment is more volatile today than ever before. New rules and regulations are introduced rapidly in response to the latest crisis. This, in turn, changes the accounting processes involved (increasingly, at short notice), and will require a very responsive outsourcing environment.*

- *Operational risk: In the financial services industry, simple operations (such as investment accounting) have led to major operational breakdowns, causing not only financial risk, but damage to reputation and credibility. Technical risk or IT failure, for example, is also a major concern.*

- *Audit risk: We understand that it is possible to reduce external audit fees as a result of outsourcing! We feel quite comfortable with this risk, since we already outsource our internal audit and it works well. Getting our external auditor to check up on the performance of an outsourcer should not be an issue. We also understand that outsourcing F&A can actually improve dis-cipline and documentation quality, since increased precision is required to operate at higher service levels. As a result, we should have better transaction transparency.*

'We are not directly affected by the Sarbanes-Oxley regulations yet, but we are under pressure from members of our Audit Committee, who see this as best practice and require us to comply. We have a Chief Risk Officer (CRO) who reports directly to the CEO on this and other risk issues.' Does Thomas Buess and his team believe that ZFS is a suitable candidate for outsourcing? He answers:

'Clearly turkeys don't vote for Christmas! We need buy-in from our staff for this change. We need to realistically assess our finance function's capabilities against the outside market. We need to look at the trade-offs between short-term cost saving and longer term transformation, between doing things internally and an outsource solution.'

Outsourcing is like diving into a swimming pool. Once your feet leave the platform, you are committed. This is not the time to discover the water is only a few inches deep! That is particularly true for business process outsourcing – where entire business functions are offloaded, as opposed to single aspects of IT.

A growing number of organizations are taking the outsourcing 'plunge' and deciding that the advantages and business benefits outweigh the risks. However, before a CFO places key processes in the hands of another company, a certain level of confidence needs to be reached.

It's worth reflecting that the risks associated with the changes you want to make – ranging from process standardization (using SAP), to implementing shared service centers or even going offshore – will be present irrespective of whether you insource or whether you outsource. **In fact outsourcing, if implemented properly, should reduce the risks involved.** Think about the case of a European roll-out of a single shared service center for F&A covering twenty or so different countries. If you choose an outsource provider to carry out this task on your behalf, and that provider has done it before and already has a European SSC in place, then the risks have to be lower.

IDENTIFYING THE RISKS

For every outsourcing success story, there is a cautionary tale of outsourcing gone awry. The following quotes from some finance executives capture the central risks associated with outsourcing:

'I am a proponent of outsourcing – especially when you are planning on downsizing. But you have to understand that it will never work with a bad partner. You will inevitably hit issues that you never planned for or anticipated and that is when the spirit of partnership will save you.'

'The number one mistake many companies make is not knowing why they want to outsource. You need to have a clear picture of what you want to achieve. There are numerous reasons to outsource – do you want to reduce costs? Do you want to increase service levels? Do you have a talent shortage? Do you want to integrate new technology?'

'Not performing proper due diligence can lead to disaster. The three most important criteria to look for in a supplier are; a proven track record, technical excellence, and the ability to deliver.'

'Satisfaction levels are lowest in the first year of outsourcing. Hopefully they improve in the second year and improve again in the third year. But the transition period is where most of the pain points are.'

Nevertheless, there are significant risks that relate specifically to outsourcing for you to consider at the outset:

- Deciding whether there really is a deal to be done
- Selecting the right business partner
- Securing commitment at CEO level, and all the way down
- Maintaining momentum
- Baselining and establishing performance measurement
- Operational risk
- Transformational risk.

Risk exists whatever you do. The art is to manage and mitigate it. When outsourcing, the key strategies include:

- Formulating an appropriate contract that incentivizes the right behaviors

- Setting up a suitably sensitive and flexible governance structure

- Effective and artful relationship management

- Focusing expertise on specialist areas, such as fiscal, regulatory, and legal; for example, within the context of global sourcing.

The remainder of this chapter is devoted to exploring each of these risk mitigation strategies in further detail.

WHAT CAN GO WRONG IN THE CONTRACTING PHASE?

Contracts are written to reduce risk and to clarify the understanding between parties. Yet they present a risk themselves. By focusing on operation risk early in the process, the high level advantages and disadvantages can become unclear. Additionally, when considering potential failure, it is hard to develop the close relationship necessary to sustain a strong, long-term partnership. To mitigate this risk, an outsourcing arrangement should always be predicated on a strong and clear business case.

The contract should be prepared subsequently setting out the relative responsibilities of each party. The success of an outsourcing arrangement cannot depend on the contract. At the same time, a robust contract is essential. It will underpin and provide the framework for mitigating the commercial risks involved. These range from managing performance, to the clarification of intellectual property rights, to arrangement termination and the method of separation.

The level of detail in the contractual documentation will vary according to the circumstances; *too little detail* as to the scope and nature of the service to be provided can lead to problems in handling differences in expectations; equally important, *too much detail* may be premature and can lead to a myriad of subsequent disputes which may put the overall outsourcing objectives at risk. Consider the following:

- Preventing scope disputes

  In an outsourcing arrangement, the work is either 'in scope' or it costs extra. You need to make sure that the project scope in your contract matches the service that you expect. This is quite hard to do because the outsourcing candidate is often an undocumented and dynamic process. Work hard on a clear, complete, and tight scoping document and select end-to-end processes so that the hand-offs are clean. Prepare for a slight scope shift as the arrangement 'beds down' by pricing 'out of scope' services. Set the process for changing the contracted scope in advance. Consider the impact that changes in your business or markets may have and plan for those contingencies.

- Unexpected changes in the account team

Inevitably the account team will change over time. Make sure you are able to approve the replacements for key personnel, and specify minimum levels of experience, education or other competence factors. However, be careful – responsibility for delivery squarely rests with the outsourcer – how they fulfill their service obligation is up to them. The retained part of the function should behave as a service manager, focused on outputs rather than inputs.

- Intellectual property ownership

Intellectual property laws favor authors and inventors. As a customer, you won't necessarily have the right to use systems the outsource provider has created or improved, unless specified otherwise in the contract. Such property could include data about your customers and the software and processes that run the business. Work with the provider in advance to agree on a mutual basis for the ownership of intellectual property.

- Failure to perform

Once you have signed the contract, the emphasis switches from negotiation to delivery and both parties move into value maximization mode. The contract should contain mechanisms that motivate both parties to perform and to align with business need. These should be used judiciously and sensitively and include:

  - Clear reporting responsibilities and audit rights
  - Disciplined service performance management
  - Attuned risk/reward incentives and penalties
  - Flexibility to use judgment and override the contract where appropriate.

- Open-book audit provision

Contracts routinely contain a provision authorizing audit of the outsource service provider's invoices to confirm that you have been charged in accordance with the contract. In a highly regulated industry such as banking, contracts also allow the company regulators to perform audits. These sometimes include business unit satisfaction surveys. Such audits can reveal the underlying causes of problems at an early stage and accelerate issue resolution.

Figure 9.1 summarizes what typically can go wrong.

In the early stages of discussions between the contracting parties there is sometimes too much abstract discussion about *soft* issues like 'relationships' and 'partnerships'. The contract team should be able to have a clear dialogue on the business objectives, service scope, costs, pricing, performance, staffing, and other *harder* aspects of a potential long-term relationship. For this reason contracting is ideally conducted by a team distinct from business visionaries and relationship holders.

A material breakdown in the relationship regularly has its roots in a poorly defined contract, unclear objectives, and confusion regarding roles and responsibilities. Risk mitigation flows from a strong contracting process that is financially transparent, non-adversarial, and where all aspects of the arrangement are clear and unambiguous to both parties.

A well-constructed outsourcing contract is the result of a carefully, well-executed process. It enshrines the business case, and is developed after the high-level principles are established. It should clearly and precisely define all the significant aspects of the relationship, providing mechanisms to address changes in requirements and the tools necessary to manage performance effectively.

Statement of Work	Payment Terms & Conditions	Other Terms & Conditions
• Poorly defined responsibilities between the company and the service provider	• Unclear pricing structure	• Inadequate change control process
• Poorly defined responsibilities between the service provider and other third parties	• Insufficient variability for changes in volume and service	• Inadequate acceptance process
• Misaligned expectations	• Imprecise warranty terms	• Restrictive rights around intellectual property
• Insufficient clarity around baseline conditions and performance	• Inadequate visibility of the service provider charge breakdown	• Limited influence of outsourcer personnel
		• Inadequate protection in the event of termination

Figure 9.1   *What can go wrong in contracting*

In structuring the contract it is useful to think of the transaction in three phases:

Phase one – transition

- **Asset transfer** – during the transition phase people, facilities, equipment, software, and service contracts are transferred to the service provider. The contract should specify which party will be financially, administratively, and operationally responsible for each of these resources.

- **Service transfer** – consideration will need to be given to front-end systems integration, process re-engineering, and any transformation involving complicated infrastructure and process changes.

- **People transfer** – human resources are a particularly sensitive area; especially cooperation and continuity of the incumbent staff. They have vital knowledge about the business and technology and are critical to a successful transition. Consider employees who will receive employment offers, their salary and benefits package, and any employment guarantees. These should be discussed between the parties and addressed in the outsourcing contract.

Phase two – performance

- **Scoping** – the outsource provider performs a defined set of services at the agreed-upon economic and service levels.

- **Gain sharing** – agreeing on deal economics and clarifying how economic rewards are to be shared are the most challenging aspects of structuring a successful contract.

- **Fair compensation** – within the contract both parties should be entitled to fair and pre-agreed compensation should either partner fail to perform its responsibilities.

- **Adjustment mechanisms** – do not focus exclusively on the baseline charge quoted by the outsourcer. It will be predicated on the use of defined quantities of resources and will contain assumptions. Actual service usage may vary significantly over the life of the contract, so the mechanisms for determining adjustments to charges are essential.

Phase three – termination

- **Exit agreement** – an outsourcing contract makes provision for termination at any stage. Both parties should be able to exit under pre-agreed conditions, enabling the smooth transfer of service back in-house or to another supplier.

- **Exit economics** – the contract should contain a mutually agreeable set of economics that support such an exit eventuality.

Disagreements are inevitable at some point in any outsourcing relationship. This makes a dispute management and resolution process invaluable. The contract should provide governance arrangements that will robustly deal with problems without resulting in recourse to the contract itself.

SETTING UP THE RIGHT GOVERNANCE STRUCTURE AND RELATIONSHIPS

To manage risk as you enter the arrangement, the CFO will first need to ensure there is a **governance structure and methodology** in place, with the proper representation from both the company and the outsource provider. It is the governance structure that provides the mechanism for managing the arrangement, rather than the contract. It should reflect risks at strategic, tactical, and operational levels with a defined escalation process that raises any issues to an appropriate level within each organization.

The right governance structure is essential throughout the lifecycle of an outsourcing arrangement. It is one of a number of tools that can be used at various points to intervene between parties and resolve issues and disputes.

The design of the governance structure will depend on two key criteria:

1 **The extent to which the outsourcing is transformational** – what impact will process changes have on the overall direction and strategy of the business? The more change that will be effected within the retained business, the greater the need for senior representatives and the more controlled the governance structure needs to be.

2 **The stage in the outsourcing lifecycle** – at the beginning of the arrangement, issues are more critical. The transition needs to be han-

dled, as does the set-up and restructuring of the retained organization. Over time this settles into an ongoing operational routine. The issues will be the achievement of service level metrics, business change, and continuous improvement.

The art of governance is involving the right people, at the right level of seniority, at the right time. For example, while the CFO and other senior executives are critical participants at the beginning of the arrangement, and will need to be regularly involved, over the longer term C-level involvement may become quite rare.

Figure 9.2 sets out the key elements of an outsourcing arrangement and the risk issues that need to be addressed through the governance structure.

The governance arrangements must not lose sight of the original outsourcing objectives and benefits. These may be, for example:

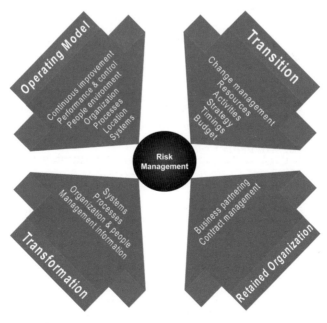

Source: Accenture, 2003

Figure 9.2 *Managing the risk components of an outsourcing arrangement*

- **During the transition** – To consolidate processes and systems from multiple locations into a single service delivery center with minimal disruption to the business and ongoing service delivery.

- **For the retained organization** – To ensure the right people, of the right caliber, are retained to fulfill the responsibilities within the retained function, with the right policies and procedures in place to facilitate the fulfillment of the outsource contract.

- **For the overall operating model** – To provide low-cost, outsourced finance and accounting services from within a framework that ensures control, quality service delivery, and high performance.

- **For the longer term** – To deliver continuous improvement of systems and processes within the outsourced operating model.

The governance organizational structures and events are crucial in managing risk. These include committees, functions, meetings, and communications. They are needed to plan, direct, and resolve matters arising from the outsource service agreement. However, they are not intended to replace the operational management structures on either side of the fence. Rather, the governance structures are there to manage the **interface** between the service provider and the company.

There are three levels to consider in the governance structure:

1 Strategic – to *decide what* to change

2 Tactical – to *make change* happen

3 Operational – to *deliver service.*

These three layers are supported by a contractual relationship management framework.

Figure 9.3 provides an illustration of three levels of governance – strategic (*through a joint review board*), tactical and operational (*through an operational committee and service review meeting*).

Consider the governance structure put in place by UK travel and leisure services company, Thomas Cook, to govern its newly outsourced finance and accounting operations.

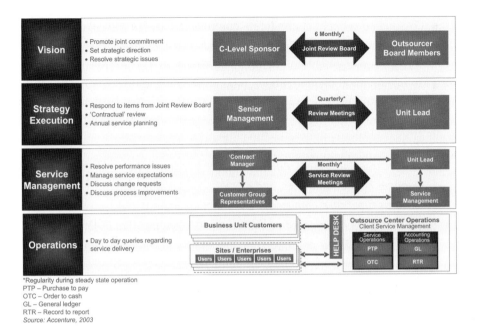

*Regularity during steady state operation
PTP – Purchase to pay
OTC – Order to cash
GL – General ledger
RTR – Record to report
Source: Accenture, 2003*

Figure 9.3 *Illustrative governance methodology*

CASE STUDY

Co-sourcing governance in action at Thomas Cook UK

This was a co-sourcing arrangement, so named to reflect the strong partnership between Thomas Cook UK and the provider. Both parties have a stake in both the risks and rewards – and this was reflected in the governance structure. It was decided that while Thomas Cook would have strategic control in respect of the co-sourced services, the outsourcer would have operational control. Both parties were to ensure that members of the governing committees were of appropriate seniority and empowered to make decisions and take the appropriate actions.

Thomas Cook UK and its outsourcing partner defined the following governance structure and guiding principles:

- *Co-sourced services committee – controlling body for the co-sourced services agreement, chaired by Thomas Cook. This committee is responsible for reviewing the relevance of performance metrics and major changes.*
- *Transformation projects steering committee – this established an appropriate communications framework that was implemented initially. It now sets priorities and ensures that the required business benefits are delivered, and that the strategic direction is sustained. This includes facilitating the necessary release of resources. Additionally, the transformation project committee manages budgets, bonuses, and escalation resolution.*
- *Business function committees – these include finance and accounting (F&A), HR, and IT. Each business function committee ensures that business requirements are captured, prioritized and delivered in accordance with agreed service targets and internal customer satisfaction levels. These committees also review and act on continuous improvement initiatives.*

Regular reporting occurs on a monthly or a quarterly basis, depending upon the committee involved. However, meetings were held more frequently in the early stages of the contract. Much emphasis is still placed on the communications program that covers ongoing organizational changes, amendments in services and the contact, as well as alterations in process and the activities of the finance function.

An outsourcing arrangement can sometimes be conceived through a protracted bid, evaluation, and negotiation process. Both parties take positions in this process and work to get the maximum economic advantage. The company may want the outsourcer to make an upfront investment and to assume financial and performance-related risk. The provider, on the other hand, wants the highest fee possible for the minimum amount of investment. During this negotiation phase, it is challenging to avoid mistrust and conflict.

The best means of doing this is to accommodate each other's needs. Both parties must work hard to sustain goodwill, emphasize teamwork, and push for a positive relationship between their staff.

In particular:

- Focus on business objectives, not the process;

- Appoint the right functional manager;

- Ensure high-quality knowledge management.

Figure 9.4 illustrates the relationship structure that should be forged between the service provider and the retained organization. The functional manager should not be seen as a barrier to this direct relationship, but as a facilitator in measuring performance, and managing and resolving issues that cannot be dealt with at the lower level.

Consider the following case study, where a member of the senior management team at a leading UK supermarket describes his team and how it functions.

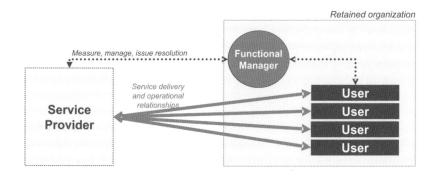

Source: Accenture, 2003

Figure 9.4 *Relationship management*

CASE STUDY
The challenge of understanding a new relationship

Sainsbury's supermarkets in the UK has outsourced its IT backbone to support the future growth of the company. John Palmer, the Head of Business Transformation Finance at Sainsbury's, is the financial controller for its outsourcing contract and a member of the financial leadership team. The arrangement has been in place since 2000 and has seen the implementation of award-winning information and financial systems. John, who has experienced the lifecycle of the arrangement, comments:

'Since the transition, the IT senior management team has changed considerably and the team now uses a different range of skills. Instead of managing resources, they now manage outputs. Many of the team were originally employed to transfer operations, but have been retained to manage the arrangement. Several had worked in the outsourcing industry and had strong contract management expertise. Many of us have "lived and died" by service level agreements before, so we know what the strengths and weaknesses of such arrangements are.

'One of the key activities during the early stages of the arrangement was establishing the outsourcer's credibility in the business. This required significant internal promotion of our outsourcing partner. The business did not initially understand the contractual nature of outsourcing. Our role was to be diplomatic during this learning process and to buffer the outsourcer from the business. It is really important to interface the right people, at the right time. We are now looking to drive this relationship throughout the business both in breadth and depth.

'The senior management relationship is now stable, successful and close. While there are occasional "spats" at local levels, overall IT systems are more stable than they ever were. By the first Christmas, system outages were down by 90%, despite using the same systems and people.'

John explains: 'Our relationship is based on delivery. The biggest challenges have been understanding where the responsibilities lie, driving change, and accepting responsibility where necessary.'

Sainsbury's has just signed a three-year extension with its service provider. The original deal was 7 years; so now it will run for a further 7 years to 2010. Sainsbury's has changed the pricing structure and achieved additional cost reductions, reflecting the growing confidence it has in its partner.

THE RISKS OF GOING GLOBAL

Globally sourcing business services and benefiting from cost arbitrage is a topic generating considerable interest in the CFO community. There are an increasing number of attractive locations in the global marketplace, which continues to expand. Yet, while offshoring offers incredible benefits, most senior executives are concerned about the very real risks.

When looking at the risks and potential benefits of going global, two options present themselves:

1 **Going global by yourself** – transferring services to an in-house shared service center abroad; owned, financed, and operated by the company.

2 **Going global with an outsourcing partner** – who transfers and transforms services for you, onto their global platform; which they own, finance, and operate for you.

The risk profiles for each of the options above are very different. Perhaps the biggest risk of all when globally sourcing is a poorly executed transition; this could lead to loss of control over the core business. Whether undertaken by an internal team or an outsource provider, it is essential that you are confident that your transition will be successful. Much of the risk inherent in international sourcing is actually passed on to the outsource provider, i.e. the risk you need to manage is less if you employ an outsourcer to transfer and deliver the networked service for you.

Some examples of the ways that networking with a partner mitigates risk are given in the table below.

RISK	
Global Risk	Mitigated by Outsourcing Partner
Painful or difficult transition offshore may result in interrupted service delivery	Transition expertise developed during experience performing previous transitions offshore
Unpredictable expense of cost incurred when building the offshore center	Outsourcer has existing offshore asset, and has multiple clients so is able to leverage scale and incur substantially less cost. Cost can be more predictably outlined in advance
Risk of service failure if offshore location suffers from disaster	Multiple offshore centers in different locations support service delivery

Thorough due diligence should be undertaken before executing a global sourcing strategy. Consider the case of a large German multinational telecommunications company that decided to opt for a nearshore solution in the short term when it outsourced a large proportion of its finance function two years ago.

CASE STUDY
Considering the risks and migrating to a nearshore location

The new owners of the business were in the process of returning the company back to profitability, aiming to reduce overhead and then sell the transformed business. To support this strategy, the management team of the Network Division needed full and timely business information that the controlling function was not able to provide. Inadequate decision support and management reporting were identified as pressing areas for improvement.

The Network Division was still reliant on its former parent providing systems and administrative services – and the service level agreements were both inadequate and temporary: A Europe-wide systems change project was under way to effect a complete separation.

The CFO decided to consider sourcing back-office operations with an external service provider, rather than building a new capability. He took advice from a specialist third party to identify potential complications in offshoring from Germany. His commercial lawyer conducted an investigation and discovered that only a limited scope of activities could be outsourced to an outsource service provider that is not authorized under the German tax consultancy act.

After identifying and selecting an authorized provider, the new partner conducted a study of potential locations for the service delivery center. Comparisons of economic indicators such as unemployment, price inflation, property, and other costs, and their likely movement in the future, also played an important part in the decision. Communications technology played a vital role in enabling the transition, facilitating the remote sourcing of services. Investigation of the cost and legal implications of document scanning and voice communications threw up unexpected difficulties. Nevertheless, the company decided to go ahead with full knowledge of the risks involved.

This country analysis revealed that the most likely choice would be the provider's existing center in eastern Europe where scale could be leveraged effectively. The provider's Indian center was discounted because the arrangement would have represented the first significant offshore outsourcing from Germany. Additionally, while English is a major language available in India, other European languages were discovered not to be as widely available.

Prague and Budapest were finally selected. High-quality German language skills, as well as other European languages, were easily available. The CFO was initially concerned that though costs in these eastern European centers were low, they might inflate as the countries integrated into the European Union. He gained peace of mind, knowing that if the nearshore location became too expensive, his outsource provider could successfully migrate service delivery across its global delivery network to a cheaper location – incentivized by the benefits that further cost reduction would bring.

In the case above, the Network Division had already been sourcing many of its operations externally, but was able to improve the service it received. Consider also the company's decisions were influenced by legal and commercial constraints. The financial, legal, and tax implications alter when an outsourcing arrangement is undertaken.

FINANCIAL, LEGAL, AND TAX RISK

Because shared service centers – be they insourced or outsourced – often encompass multiple jurisdictions, the CFO has to examine the key issues and risks associated with the legal and fiscal requirements involved. Consider the case study[1] of this large multinational agricultural and food company who wanted to outsource finance and accounting activities to a shared service center in South America.

CASE STUDY
Analyzing tax considerations in South America

A multinational agricultural and food company was involved in purchasing agricultural commodities from farms and trading, processing, and marketing food. It had established an internal shared service center in Brazil to provide services to subsidiaries and also had a center in Argentina. The company was keen to focus management attention on customers and decided that outsourcing non-core business activities would help achieve this.

The company decided to conduct a feasibility study with a potential outsourcing partner to consider outsourcing and expanding and developing these shared service centers, enabling them to service other South American countries. This would improve the cost and quality of the service beyond what had been achieved in-house. Another benefit would be the shift from a fixed to a variable cost base, providing structural flexibility.

Brazil was selected as the most appropriate country for a South American center. This was, in part, because of the large cost differential, relative to other countries. But, cost was not the only factor. Other issues considered were – availability of a skilled workforce, tax advantages, and solid local infrastructure.

Some factors worked against the chosen location. One problem was that Brazilian law requires physical invoicing. For example, an invoice has to be physically handed by the lorry driver to the inbound warehouse manager of the customer. This meant that some operational improvements were unviable. These included accounts payable; best practice processes like electronic billing, centralized invoice receipting, invoice scanning, and optical character recognition.

Ultimately, the decision favored Brazil because of the proximity to relevant pools of skills in the trading of agricultural commodities, involving complex contracts for purchases from farmers and their representatives.

Legal and fiscal requirements need to be understood in advance. If they are not, there is likely to be an adverse impact on the business case for change.

In Figure 9.5 an illustrative assessment is shown, with high-level summaries of the statutory and legal requirements in several European countries.

Ensure the early involvement of in-house tax consultants and the legal department. Also develop a communication and involvement plan for the relevant tax authorities. You may need to work at getting the acceptance of the authorities – explaining local controls, organization design, infor-

	Germany	Switzerland	Austria

General Information
  – Language
  – Currency
	– German
	– € (Euro)
		– German, French, Italian
		– CHF (Swiss Francs)
			– German
			– € (Euro)

Transaction Processing
  – Invoices
  – Method of Payments
	– Invoices kept as paper &
	  must comply with German
	  HGB. Records retained for
	  10 years.
	– Mainly electronic fund
	  transfer ('Überweisung')
		– Invoices kept as hard
		  copy, microfiche or disk
		– Method of payment is
		  Electronic Settlement (ES)
			– Invoices kept as hard
			  copy, microfiche, but not
			  on disk
			– Mainly electronic fund
			  transfer ('Überweisung')

Contracts	– Contracts have to be
	  retained up to 30 years
	  after expiry
		– Contracts have to be
		  retained over 10 years
			– Contracts have to be
			  retained over a period of 7
			  years

Accounting Records	– Records can be stored in a
	  foreign country
		– Records can be stored in a
		  foreign country
			– Records can be stored in a
			  foreign country, if
			  accessibility is guaranteed

Data Protection / Remote Data Processing	– There is no domestic law
	  preventing cross-border
	  credit checks by a non-
	  domestic company.
	– Customer databases may
	  be kept abroad if they
	  comply with the German
	  Data Protection Act.
		– There is no domestic law
		  preventing cross-border
		  credit checks by a non-
		  domestic company.
		– Customer databases may
		  be maintained overseas
			– There is no domestic law
			  preventing cross-border
			  credit checks by a non-
			  domestic company.
			– Customer databases may
			  be maintained abroad

Source: Accenture, 2003

Figure 9.5   *Illustrative assessment of statutory and legal requirements*

mation availability, and document archives. Systems and data should be fully accessible from the relocating country, so that there won't be any deterioration in the availability or timeliness of information.

Finally, consider also international developments in data privacy. If you plan to outsource any of your HR or technology functions you will encounter privacy issues. Employee records, medical and performance data may be subject to different privacy laws and regulations. There are also privacy issues regarding the collection, use, and disclosure of customer data. When you share data with third parties, like an outsource provider, then the laws and regulations apply to the privacy practices of these third parties too.

Employees affected by the outsourcing arrangement need to be handled sensitively, firmly, and in accordance with the law. Employment regulations vary country by country – with variations in requirement on matters from consultation, to the preservation of terms and conditions, to people transfer to the new outsourced entity, to redundancy.

SARBANES-OXLEY AND EUROPEAN INTERNATIONAL ACCOUNTING STANDARDS (IAS)

Near the top of the CFO agenda today is regulatory compliance – not only with national financial legislation, but also with emerging international financial reporting standards (IFRS), and with regulations relating to control and accountability and Sarbanes-Oxley, and with tax law.

Well-publicized accounting scandals and disasters have put CFOs and the finance function under the microscope. Institutional investors have increasingly higher expectations for corporate behavior. There is increased vigilance by rating agencies with more regular and faster credit downgrades. Additionally, there is increased public scrutiny of material corporate mishaps.

With the implications of recent US legislation still being felt, it is not surprising that 4 out of 5 of the hottest issues for CEOs and CFOs in a recent *Business Finance Magazine*[2] poll were accounting standard related:

1 CEO and CFO certification of statutory filings

2 Internal controls

3 Compliance with accelerated filings deadlines

4 Real-time disclosure of material events to everyone at the same time.

In addition, new IFRS regulations are coming into force in Europe in 2004–5. Key provisions include:

- Common consolidated accounts by 2005 for all European listed companies

- Harmonization of accounting and reporting standards

- Greater transparency and faster disclosure of additional material information

- Introduction of quarterly reporting as per the US

- Accelerated reporting deadlines.

The spate of new regulation is aimed at installing greater rigor and discipline in risk management and statutory compliance. These latest developments are reinforcing due diligence with respect to 'inspecting good quality in'. The end result is that one-time spend on compliance is rising fast, not to mention additional annually recurring charges of up to $8m. The heavy and costly burden of governance is frustrating senior executives and consuming valuable management bandwidth.

As the dust settles, more efficient, robust, and resilient alternatives to current processes will emerge. The key is in designing higher quality processes, rather than 'inspecting bad quality out'. By realigning people, new technology, and process, institutionalized performance reporting and management can increase the rigor in recording process failure incidents at the transaction level. This will establish higher levels of consistency in data reconciliation. New technology can remove dependency upon specialized people to interpret data and prepare reports, compressing the time needed to collect, synthesize, and format – enabling compliance with tighter filing deadlines.

What does all of this mean?[3] Future changes are expected in the following areas:

- Upgrade of fragmented accounting systems

- Improved forecast accuracy and better projection of future performance and volatility

- Better consolidation of enterprise data using a common data model

- Reliable digital record trails through the reconciliation processes

- Automated reconciliations – eliminating manually adjusted spreadsheets and related control risk.

CEOs and senior finance executives are demanding progress at pace and with certainty of outcome. Greater rigor in scrutiny and adherence with internal controls and governance is not a bad thing. Figure 9.6 sets out some of the benefits of Sarbanes-Oxley and IAS.

While internal control was not defined as such in the Sarbanes-Oxley Act, the US auditing standards provide a generally accepted integrated framework for control infrastructure. Section 404 of the Act addresses internal control over financial reporting – the key control components are illustrated in Figure 9.7.

Internal control is one of the highest potential risks on the agenda of the CFO when considering outsourcing finance and accounting processes.

Source: Accenture, 2003

Figure 9.6   *Sarbanes-Oxley Act – benefits*

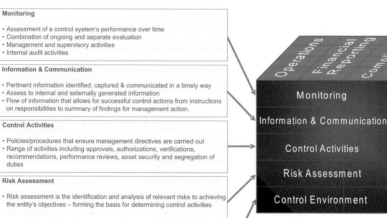

Source: Accenture, 2003

Figure 9.7   *Sarbanes-Oxley, Section 404 internal control requirements*

Virtually all of the CFOs interviewed for this book had an opinion on the relative merits of outsourcing from a control and regulatory viewpoint.

In an outsourcing arrangement, the service provider is engaged to execute processes, according to a defined scope, within the accounting and finance policies and procedures framework. Performance against the contract is measured, reported, and monitored by senior company management. Responsibilities between the parties are properly defined and there is improved segregation of duties.

In summary, as in the case of every major business decision, there are risks associated with outsourcing. In reality, however, outsourcing can actually *reduce* overall corporate risk by increasing control over resources through greater transparency and more disciplined business processes.

CFO INSIGHTS

- **Risks exist whatever you do!** Outsourcing can reduce, rather than increase, the risks associated with complex change; for example, service delivery interruption during a major transformation, such as a substantial SAP roll-out.

- Global sourcing may be considered to be a risky thing to do, but outsourcing to an established service provider with an existing network of SSCs in cost-efficient countries should improve your chances of success.

- Outsourcing is like diving into a swimming pool. Once your feet leave the platform, you are committed. It is not the time to discover the water is only a few inches deep!

- Emotional risk should be high on the CFO agenda. If senior management are seen to waver, then negative response to the outsource arrangement may build up within the ranks. Commitment at the C-level to the outsource arrangement and to the provider should be sustained from the very outset, throughout the transition to post-implementation.

- A strong governance framework can help in mitigating the risks. Clarify governance arrangements at key levels: strategic, tactical, and operational. Do not make the mistake of having a 'middleman'. Connect service providers directly with users to improve two-way communication where it counts: the front line.

- Remember, outsourcing is only a personal risk for the CFO if it doesn't work. If you choose your partner wisely, have a sound business case, and the sustained commitment of your CEO, then there is plenty of evidence in the market that you will be successful.

FROM INSIGHT TO ACTION

MAKE SURE THERE IS A *REAL DEAL* TO BE DONE
A clear vision of the strategic outcome is essential. There is a risk of confusion and misunderstanding if the time is not taken to clarify objectives and the endgame. The CFO and board member sponsors involved should be consistent in supporting the vision and keeping key stakeholders in the picture.

PUT IN PLACE A GOVERNANCE STRUCTURE FOR MANAGING *BOTH* STRATEGIC AND OPERATIONAL RISKS
Consider the organizational impact. Is it transformational? Where are you in the outsourcing lifecycle? Adapt the ongoing governance arrangements for the level of impact and the stage in the lifecycle you have reached.

BE PROACTIVE IN MANAGING YOUR OUTSOURCING ARRANGEMENTS
Make the internal outsourcing relationship manager a very important position. Emphasize teamwork and a positive relationship between your provider(s) and your staff. Rapidly create a process to perpetuate the knowledge and intent of the outsourcing agreement.

BE COMPREHENSIVE IN THE WRITTEN CONTRACT
This will facilitate a smoother relationship and reduce unpleasant surprises down the road. Build processes into the contract for unforeseen needs. Consider how you are going to measure results and how you manage the arrangement.

CONSIDER THE SPECIAL RISKS ASSOCIATED WITH GLOBAL SOURCING
Do your due diligence on the countries you have short-listed and the capabilities of the proposed outsource provider.

ASSESS THE RISK OF AN ADVERSE DECISION BY THE REGULATORY AUTHORITY
Develop a communication and involvement plan for the regulatory and tax authorities affected. Ensure early involvement of tax specialists, legal advisors, and external auditors in your outsourcing program.

SATISFY YOURSELF YOU ARE COMPLIANT WITH CORPORATE LAWS
Ensure you have in place the necessary processes, controls, and documentation. Consider your relative responsibilities and accountabilities in relation to your outsource provider for the certification requirements.

REFERENCES

1 S A Bond, *Offshore Outsourcing of Administrative Functions*, 2003.

2 Eric Krell, The CEO–CFO Relationship: Are New Regs Strengthening or Straining the Ties, *Business Finance Magazine*, 2004. www.businessfinancemag.com

3 Ian Baker, Founder and Business Development Director, riskHive Ltd, Risk is Not a Four Letter Word, Competitive Financial Operations. *The CFO Project*, Volume II, 2003. www.accenture.com, www.cfoproject.com

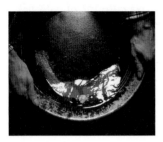

CHAPTER 10

Continuous Improvement: Keeping the Deal Working

BUILDING ON SUCCESS OVER TIME

John Coghlan
Group Finance Director of Exel

One of the world's largest global logistics companies, Exel has operations in 120 countries, and sales of approximately £5bn. Its customers include many of the world's largest corporations.

Exel specializes in providing outsourced supply chain services, so the arguments for outsourcing F&A are well understood. Some eight years ago, the company out-sourced its UK Contract Logistics finance function. A major success story, it offers a mature example of what can be achieved and the ongoing benefits that a strong outsourcing program can deliver.

Exel as we know it today is the result of a merger, between Ocean Group and NFC. The company divides its operations into two complementary segments: contract logistics, including ground-based supply chain services such as warehousing and distribution; and a freight management business, including air and ocean freight forwarding. In the mid-1990s the company had numerous, fragmented operations centers and outdated systems. It was seeking to improve both the quality of its financial systems, processes, and management information, and generate cost savings through the rationalization of its then network of 13 accounting and administration centers in the UK and Ireland.

In 1996, Exel signed a 10-year F&A outsourcing contract; included in the agreement was investment in a new Oracle ERP platform. The resulting value to Exel proved substantial: high-quality service delivered consistently across business units; a rationalized and reorganized backroom finance function; accurate and timely management information; increased flexibility; and a 40% operational cost improvement. John Coghlan, the group finance director, comments:

'At Exel, we operate in a very competitive marketplace and it is increasingly important to achieve excellence, efficiency, and control in our administrative functions. We need to continue developing our financial systems and processes so that they can support our growth in coming years. So cost reduction has not been the only objective. We've evolved from a country-driven to a customer-driven organization. Our original outsourcing plan was to implement a first-class accounting package supported by standardized processes, both in our shared service center and across 200 or so UK locations. We were successful in this, and significantly improved the quality of our financial operations, achieving our aspirations of actively supporting growth and reducing cost.'

The shared service center is located in Bedford within easy reach of Exel's UK headquarters in Milton Keynes, and prior to the recent switch of certain services to Bangalore (as explained below), employed 220 people. The services it provides include management reporting support, general ledger accounting, accounts receivable, accounts payable, and payroll. The transformation program took 18 months of concerted and collaborative effort between Exel management and the outsourcer. The existing 13 centers were decommissioned as the new shared service center began to ramp up.

In addition to implementing new integrated financial systems and processes, the service provider developed decision-support tools, including custom reports and an Management Information System solution using Oracle Financial Analyzer. John Coghlan comments:

'I appreciate the independent suggestions on improvements to the general business that the provider comes up with from time-to-time. They seem to have a genuine understanding of what is going on and can take a broader look. This

understanding is growing the longer they are with us and is one of the value-added benefits of outsourcing.' The service provider has helped Exel to develop innovative solutions for a number of complex functional requirements, such as contract billing, open book accounting, and inter-company processing.

The roll-out of a nationwide infrastructure and common accounting platform was a significant step-change for Exel staff. The outsourcing provider conducted training throughout the UK and Ireland, building employee confidence in handling often unfamiliar technology. Improvements such as the new purchase ordering system meant that remote logistics centers could generate their own purchase orders. At the same time, Exel benefited from a controlled purchasing environment that enabled them to increase procurement discounts.

Streamlined, coordinated financial information made it easier for Exel to track customer profitability and credit issues, gain a better idea of its costs and enabled Exel's logistics experts to make better-informed decisions. Over the course of the contract, both Exel and its outsource provider realized additional benefits. These included:

- *Improving the quality of information available*
- *Developing a service-oriented culture in the finance function*
- *Focusing internal resources on financial analysis and improving business results.*

In September 2002, John awarded another five-year contract to Exel's outsource provider to manage and operate its previously separate freight management pan-European financial shared services center in Dublin. In order to drive quality, John opted for a contingent-compensation arrangement, linking the provider's earnings to continuous improvement. He explains:

'Our recent contract initiates the next phase of our shared service program. Now we are going to transform our freight management financial processes. This agreement builds on our already successful and existing seven-year relationship with our provider. It will free us to focus on our core business of supply chain services.'

A year later, the Bedford contract was further extended to incorporate a transition of certain shared service activities to the outsourcer's delivery center in Bangalore. This introduced a further step-change in cost efficiency. The Dublin shared service center, along with the one in Bedford, is now part of a global network of delivery centers providing economies of scale through the use of repeatable solutions, processes, methods, and tools.

John Coghlan summarizes his experience: 'Outsourcing is not about sitting still. On the one hand, as CFO, you have to be in control and have the right control mechanisms in place. On the other, this is an evolving relationship where both parties feel empowered and energized to make a real difference in the business.'

Exel has had a particularly successful F&A outsourcing experience – one that has truly evolved and stood the test of time. During the outsourcing lifecycle, Exel's business has changed shape more than once and its outsourcing arrangements have changed in response. So have the contracts and relationships involved.

What are the ingredients of long-term success? How do you deliver continuous cost reductions while also making service improvements and adding value to *both* parties in the relationship? This chapter starts with lessons learned from experienced CFOs. It goes on to examine success factors for *keeping the deal working* – planning for the longer term, managing changing relationships, and sustaining service management discipline while enabling continuous improvement. The chapter concludes with some advice on contract renewal.

GETTING THINGS RIGHT FROM THE START

Here is what some of the CFOs who have experienced F&A outsourcing said to us when interviewed for this book:

'Once you sign up with your outsourcing partner it is like being married. At the beginning, it's like a honeymoon: The outsourcer makes a sales pitch and some ambitious promises. We commit, as the retained organization, to restructure and provide our partner with quality data so it can fulfill its part of the bargain. However, as with all marriages that last, there is a danger that you take each other for granted – this could result in divorce!

'I am a proponent of outsourcing, especially when downsizing. But you will hit issues that you never planned for – and when you do, the partnership needs to be good. We have tried working suppliers with brute force, and it has failed. You need to know the difference between squeezing out

the last buck and a real partnership. It is the **spirit** *of the deal that gets you through the difficult times.*

'When you outsource finance, you don't walk away from your responsibilities for making sure the accounts are right. Initially, outsourcing means that you have to do more work, not less – not only is there a learning curve, but you have to restructure and sharpen up what you leave in-house. I am satisfied my outsourcer has my accounting service unit under control, but my controller and his team still need to do their bit. An outsourcing partnership means that you are totally dependent on each other to make it work.'

CFOs with experience in F&A outsourcing partnerships talk about the importance of 'maintaining momentum' over the longer term; 'being fair,' and 'providing financial equilibrium.' Many executives bake the need for constant refreshment and renewal into the plans underpinning their contract to secure service cost reduction year after year. This continuous improvement mentality is vital for long-term success. Many such partnerships fund the investment necessary for the next generation of service delivery improvements from their initial savings. Our research reveals that this regenerative cycle has become a powerful incentive to embrace outsourcing rather than the internal shared service alternative. Figure 10.1 provides an illustration of how an F&A outsourcing contract can go through a cycle of change and renewal.

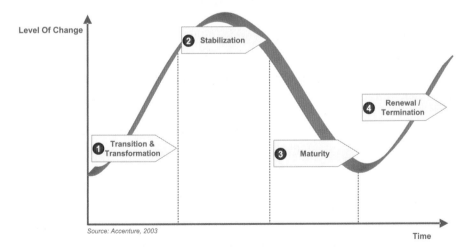

Source: Accenture, 2003

Figure 10.1 *Cycle of change over the life of a long-term outsourcing relationship*

Transformation is a journey over which expectations rapidly evolve as benefits are achieved and the performance bar is raised. Resilience is a part of the package; the unexpected is always just around the corner! No one-size-fits-all approach guarantees results; organizations have a better chance of succeeding with BPO if they craft a relationship that meets *their* needs. However, experience has shown that success is more likely if fundamental questions are properly addressed at the outset and throughout the life of the partnership:

- **How deep should the relationship be?** The answer depends on what is being outsourced and how critical it is to the future of the organization. Effective relationships can be purely contractual: arms-length relationships with clear performance expectations, but minimum contact. These are typical commodity-based relationships and have historically applied to narrowly focused processes such as payroll. However, outsourcing partnerships can also be much more collaborative, requiring greater dialogue between the parties to flex and respond to changing corporate strategy and business conditions. At the far end of the spectrum, some partners are highly dependent upon each other for success. Relationships at this deeper level will be the most transformational, the most rewarding, and the most likely to endure. The profiles of BP and Exel, offered earlier in this book, are good examples of these far-reaching arrangements.

- **How broad should the relationship be?** Some companies choose a different provider for each narrowly defined function or process. Others favor relationships that are broader in scope. The approach taken depends on *what* is being outsourced, on the company's management bandwidth, and on the value that the outsource partner can offer. A broader relationship requires a much greater degree of mutual interest, trust, and risk-sharing. Alan Eilles of BP stresses the strategic advantage of its dual supplier approach for F&A.

- **How much should you change your way of working?** Do you want to take advantage of your external provider's *best-practice* processes for transformation? Or is your goal to *lift and drop* your existing operations into its outsource center? The CFO of Rhodia based his strategy on making minimal changes to legacy systems, while the CFO of Thomas Cook wanted to transform business processes completely and standardize onto a common SAP ERP platform.

- **Whose assets should we use?** In terms of people, physical infrastructure, and technology? At one end of the spectrum, some companies use all their own assets and import only the outsource provider's management expertise; at the other end, the assets are provided by the outsourcer 'lock, stock, and barrel.' In most cases, however, a company's assets are pooled with those of its outsource provider.

Consider again what Alan Eilles, BP's vice president – group financial infrastructure, who is responsible for BP's F&A outsourcing says on this point: 'The only way to further better the scale is to give suppliers both process and asset ownership. This lets the outsourcer create cross-industry capability by enabling its service centers to cater to large companies from different industries simultaneously.'

Whatever you choose, to achieve consistent, long-term alignment, make sure that your outsource relationship can adapt to changes in corporate portfolio and business conditions.

MAKING THE COMMERCIALS MATCH THE INTENT

Most companies, when first entering an outsource agreement, want to reduce their cost-base both incrementally and by step-change. They wish to increase their effectiveness and efficiency using process re-engineering and, most important, they want to ensure that the outsourced business functions are, and remain, culturally attuned to their existing corporate 'credo'.

Some companies want a long-term business relationship in which benefits are delivered early, even though significant investment funding is required for transformation. A true partnership can emerge in which large-scale project costs are deferred and banked against future benefits. You work together with your partner to achieve and exploit process and technological advances.

One company has developed a 10-year 'co-sourced' business relationship. It was purposely designed to be different from traditional consultancy and typical outsourcing relationships. Flexibility and innovation were key goals. A co-sourced framework was established to manage the relationship through the three phases – transition, transformation, and continuous improvement. This is illustrated in Figure 10.2.

In Figure 10.2, the outsourced provider charges a service fee that 'flat-lines' over the course of the contract at a level substantially below the in-house baseline cost. Initially, extra costs are incurred by the service

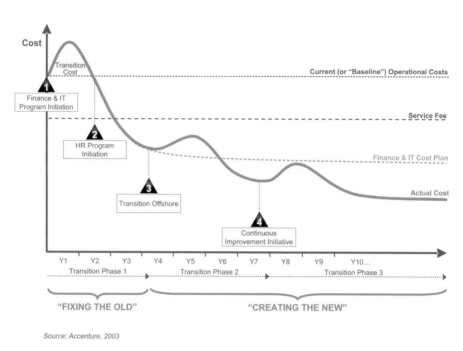

Figure 10.2 *Outsourcing transition over the long term*

provider because of the transition. Over time, however, the actual cost falls below the service fee, enabling recovery of the initial investment by the service provider. Later improvements also cause smaller, temporary peaks in transition cost. This is a good example of continuous improvement. The company adopted a phased approach by *'fixing the old'* before moving on to *'create the new.'* For the co-sourced business relationship to succeed, each party had to leverage its core skills, experience, and resources. Specifically:

- **The company** leveraged its market awareness of its industry sector and experience in its core business

- **The outsource partner** leveraged its experience in business process re-engineering, operational capability, and technology expertise to make step-changes in performance.

The spirit of co-sourcing encouraged each party to contribute its unique expertise and, ultimately, to co-brand the outsource service so that it could be marketed to other companies in the same industry sector, in the way that BP and Accenture did in the UK North Sea oil exploration industry. This mutuality of business interest should lead to a long and fruitful relationship.

When thinking about how best to shape and reshape a commercial relationship over time, consider the BP F&A contract – which started in 1991, was renewed in 1994, and again in 1999. The next renewal is in 2004. The Accenture delivery center in Aberdeen has grown from just servicing BP to a multiclient site serving the North Sea oil industry, including ConocoPhillips, Total as it is now called, and Talisman. BP's journey, from 1991 to today, in which it shed non-core assets and grew through acquisition, is charted in Figure 10.3. This figure also shows BP's F&A outsourcing activity with Accenture in a number of locations, together with a list of the other oil companies that have joined the delivery center alliance.

Alison MacKenzie, the Accenture business support services director of the Aberdeen outsource operation, has been involved from the beginning and comments on the challenges and learning points for *keeping the deal working*!

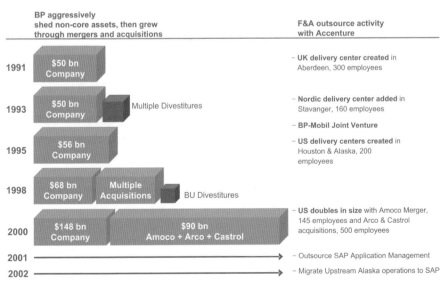

Figure 10.3 *The BP journey: moving from single to multiclient outsourcing*

CASE STUDY
Changing the commercials to keep the deal working

'Our first contract with BP, launched in 1991, was based on a guaranteed fixed price, with savings targets of 20%. At the time, BP wanted cost savings, because the prevailing oil price was low. It also wanted predictability, since outsourcing the finance function was a new and untested idea. In the end, we achieved a 30% cost reduction, and proceeded to work with BP to renegotiate the contract a year early within the first five-year term.

'In 1994, the original fixed-price contract was changed to include joint incentives, taking the business case to the next level. Accenture was to participate financially in driving additional service improvements through continuous process changes and a new systems implementation. At this point, BP was more interested in investing for the longer term. Accenture assisted BP in implementing a new SAP system based on a design, build, and run contract. This provided an excellent platform on which new leading-edge tools could be employed for performance management, Internet invoicing, and general accounting.

'In 1999, oil prices were dropping again – BP had also acquired Amoco – and the outsourcing contract was changed again to a fixed-fee structure. This time, the savings target was set from the beginning of the new contract – at 70% less than the original fee! This put enormous pressure on Accenture to make dramatic savings. Accenture was fully motivated to "add value," with a "quality" bonus and a share in the savings, and to focus on finding opportunities for continuous improvement. Examples of value initiatives include the introduction of a new contract compliance service which has generated major vendor savings for BP, and cost coaching for offshore management, which led to improved financial performance.

'Figure 10.4 shows the different commercial structures of the three BP contracts for F&A outsourcing in Aberdeen, covering the years 1991 to 2004.

'When the contract comes up for renewal, we expect the situation to change again. BP will want to benefit from another step-change by taking advantage of the latest leading-edge technology, the new global operating and delivery models and best thinking that we, as the outsource provider can provide. Such a service, which is designed to make processes faster not just cheaper, can best be provided on a global scale.

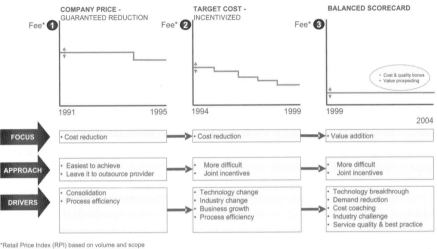

*Retail Price Index (RPI) based on volume and scope
Source: Accenture, 2003

Figure 10.4   *Changing F&A contract commercial structures*

'How have the relationships between BP and its outsourcer changed? Well, many of the senior people at BP are still involved. But, lower down in the organization there have been many changes and we are always working hard on building rapport. For those of us who have been involved for a very long time, we have the advantage of providing continuity, but the downside is you need to introduce fresh blood from time to time.

'We start contract renewal discussions at least one year ahead of the expiration date. We involve someone external to the delivery team to help bring new insight into the negotiations. By starting with a relatively clean sheet, you can see the value proposition afresh from both sides' viewpoint. Also look outside at what others are doing – re-benchmark against best practice – and think about collaborating with others to leverage new opportunities.

'What have I learned from my F&A outsourcing experience over the last 10 years or more? Firstly, be honest in all your negotiations and communications. From the provider viewpoint, accept responsibility when things don't go according to plan, don't make excuses, but come up with options for a solution. Sometimes you just have to apologize when there is a problem and move on. Regular contact, working *ever closer together, and getting to know each other better at the personal level – these are the keys to a good long-term relationship.*

'Then, remember that each client feels unique and wants a special service. Try to prioritize and keep focused on the business challenge – the stretch target. But also be realistic. Sometimes stretch targets are just not achievable in the time frame and this can put unnecessary stress on staff, and morale can suffer. Don't beat your outsource partner with a big stick. Use your buying power sensibly. Try not to take out the service level agreement and put it on the table every time there is a minor dispute, but build the relationship on trust.'

OUTSOURCING IS ABOUT RELATIONSHIPS

As noted earlier, in any outsourcing relationship, it is important to start well, with mutual understanding and agreement on objectives, service levels, responsibilities, and pricing. Inevitably however, long-term relationships are affected by external circumstances that can cause the parties' interests to diverge, putting pressure on their attitudes toward each other.

In Chapter 9, which focused on risk, we showed how important a good governance structure can be. A strong agreement will reflect the spirit as well as the letter of how the parties will communicate at various levels in the organization. Here are some best practices that we uncovered during our research for managing long-term outsource relationships:[1]

1 **Empower contract managers:** A relationship manager should be appointed on the client side for day-to-day operational issues; the counterpart on the outsourcer's side will work with this manager on problem solving, budgeting, and performance reviews. Both managers should be empowered to effect meaningful change, so that as few problems as possible require the CFO's attention.

2 **Foster senior peer-to-peer relationships:** In long-term contracts, experienced managers cite the development of strong relationships and understanding each other's company as key success factors. In the case of BP, such relationships have deepened and matured over more than 10 years.

3 **Communicate frequently and informally:** Outsourcing relationships thrive on frequent, informal communication. This is especially important when the service provider's employees are located on the company's premises. Such on-site outsource employees should be treated as an integral part of the organization.

4 **Maintain a governance board throughout:** Special boards or committees are useful in managing complex relationships successfully – especially those involving very large or multinational corporations. The joint review board, which meets quarterly at BP, for instance, oversees service-level performance and facilitates strategic discussions on new ideas, marketing, and innovation.

5 **Prioritize change initiatives:** Maintain a prioritized change agenda that both parties can shape together.

6 **Build skills and capabilities jointly:** Companies are becoming more involved in the selection of their outsourcer's key account managers – especially in cases where the outsource manager is based on the company site. Over a long-term contract, the people involved and their roles will necessarily change. In best-practice cases there is joint management of both retained and outsourced skills. Staff may well switch from the company to the outsourcer, and back again!

Make no mistake, challenges will occur and problems will arise, no matter how strong the outsource relationship. It is how you deal with these that matters. Be ready – have the right operating policies, mechanisms, and escalation routes agreed upon in advance, so that you don't have to invent solutions in the *heat of the moment*. When problems do crop up, address them quickly and with a spirit of openness. Make sure you and your partner understand any problems that occur and are sensitive to each other's interests and expectations. Where commitments to action are made, make sure that all parties follow through.

KEEP FOCUSING ON SERVICE MANAGEMENT

What is service management? It is the blueprint for starting new contracts and maintaining them over the longer term. It provides a framework for baselining outsourced activities, developing service-level agreements, and measuring performance. It is also the basis on which a contract can be adjusted as circumstances change. Equally important, a

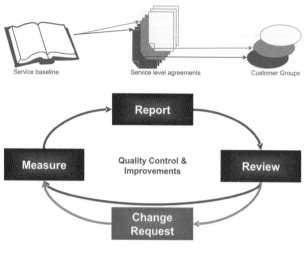

Source: Accenture, 2003

Figure 10.5 *Continuous improvement via service management*

good service management framework is an essential tool in communicating between the partners and employees.

Figure 10.5 provides an illustrative service management approach and sequence designed to encourage and facilitate continuous improvement through measurement, reporting, and reviews.

The service baseline, and supporting management framework, should be a *living* document; it should be reviewed frequently to ensure that service offerings remain accurate and up-to-date. The process of putting it together and the documentation involved provides a comprehensive database of knowledge – of business processes, roles, and responsibilities. *This proves invaluable in maintaining standards and continuity.*

INTEGRATION AND SERVICE MANAGEMENT

At the heart of every successful shared service center and outsource implementation is a *service management framework*. This brings together a framework and governance structure for measurable, high-performing, service-oriented business process delivery. In this final section of the chapter, we consider how all the different aspects of the transition process are integrated.

The service management framework should cover key implementation issues and offer clarity on:

- Service definition, including responsibilities, performance requirements and measures. *In effect the set of service level agreements (SLAs)*

- Responsibilities and reciprocal commitments of users. *In effect the set of operating level agreements (OLAs)*

- The process for managing change requests and driving continuous improvement.

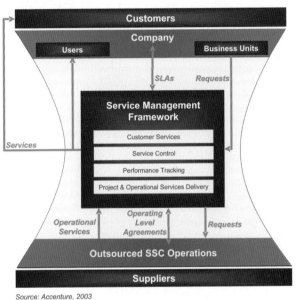

Source: Accenture, 2003

Figure 10.6 *Service management framework*

What are the benefits of developing a service management framework? It helps ensure that everyone involved on both sides of the fence – both service providers and end users – will perform according to pre-determined standards.

Figure 10.6 shows a more detailed example of a service management framework.

Performance can be aligned with both career development and incentives. The framework offers a platform from which both client executives and outsourcing staff can develop a high-performing and fully accountable profit center.

Figure 10.7 illustrates the level of detail required to document relative roles and responsibilities in the service baseline for some sample F&A

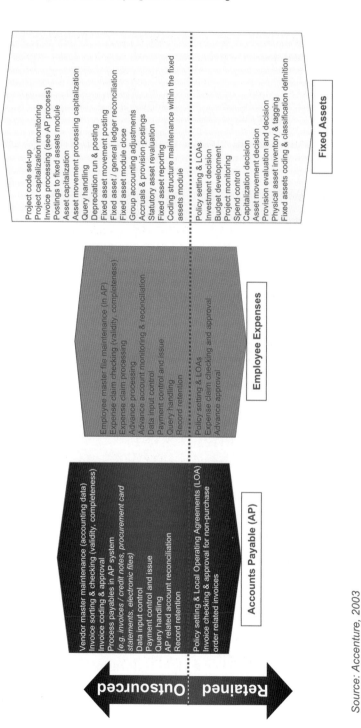

Source: Accenture, 2003

Figure 10.7 *Setting the roles and responsibilities boundary*

processes. This was taken from an actual example where the process landscape was constantly changing.

Why is service management important to keeping the deal working in long-term contracts? Simply because circumstances, people, and goals can change. And the disciplines seen to be so vital at the beginning of an outsource arrangement can, if neglected, lose their freshness and commercial bite – and ultimately degrade over time. The service management framework is at the *very core* of a successful outsourcing program. The longer the contract, the more likely the risk of complacency.

Lincolnshire County Council in the UK decided to outsource its finance, IT, HR, and property functions some six years ago. As a public service organization, it needed to ensure that the business case could withstand public scrutiny. The social consequences needed to be well thought through and the staff affected had to be treated sensitively. Peter Moore, the County Treasurer, was involved from the outset. Here, he comments on the arrangement.

CASE STUDY
Strong service management at Lincolnshire County Council

'We embarked on a 10-year contract, with an option to extend for a further five years. Both parties have geared up for a long-term partnership. Our outsourcing partner has invested £7m in IT and has created a service center in Lincolnshire. We transferred 1,100 jobs to this center, retaining only 70. Not only has the outsourcer saved us 22% in baseline costs, but it also managed to redeploy the staff.

'What has made the partnership work so well, so early on? Of course, we have had some problems. But we have overcome them through clear communication, highlighting performance problems early, and addressing them quickly. I try to avoid applying financial penalties; instead, we just sort things out. We have good contract mechanisms in place to monitor variances and our SLAs are managed tightly for volume variation. When necessary, we adjust the SLA targets to reflect reality.

'We have challenged each other on how things work; we share risk and benefits. New projects have been added that were not in the original contract, providing extra revenue to the outsourcer and value for us – a win-win arrangement. The contract could well be expanded in the future to include document imaging and management, the piloting of customer relationship management, and a telephone contact

center to service the public. If we don't think our partner is pricing competitively, we can put the additional work out to bid – but it gets "first bite at the cherry."

'Each party has taken a risk – we, at the Council, have tied ourselves to a supplier for 10 years, maybe more. An exit route, although viable, would be unattractive. The outsourcer, on the other hand, has made a big investment in us. So far, the arrangement has been a great success! Strong service management has meant that in the first three years more than 95% of the contract's KPIs have been met.

'One of the most rewarding aspects of this contract has been the openness with which financial discussions have taken place and the transparency afforded us in understanding the economics of the deal and how they have changed. Our partner has just recently broken even and then made a small profit on its heavy upfront investment. We take a mature attitude to the financials, rewarding our partner with high margin work to balance low service delivery margins.

'One point of detail to consider – make the performance indicators really "key". Initially we had 271 KPIs; we now have 110. But there are still too many. Our Council Members only need 15 to 20 KPIs, focused on service outputs, value, and quality.

'As you can imagine, this outsourcing arrangement was originally seen as radical and has had a very high profile. Today, it is regarded as best practice in the UK public sector – we have had more than a hundred local authorities visit to take a look. I have had to work hard at promoting and justifying the partnership. This ensures that we take a joint approach to everything we do. Internal and external communications are very high on the Treasurer's agenda in this respect. This keeps the deal alive and working!

'Would I ever take the services back in-house? No. It would take a serious service failure for this to happen. Our first major contract review happens in year seven and we will need to start this review early since we have the option of extending deal to 15 years. What would I do differently? I would have involved the directors of our internal customer departments earlier in the contract negotiation process. This would have assisted in service requirement definition and engendered a feeling of "ownership." I would have also involved other stakeholders, particularly the elected politicians on our council, at an earlier stage in the outsourcing strategy. Generally, however, I am very pleased with the progress we have made.'

As this case clearly shows, successful service delivery is the cornerstone of a robust outsourcing agreement. The ultimate continuation of any contract is contingent upon meeting and delivering on the service levels agreed. Therefore it is imperative that you have a clear baseline. Only then can you measure the quality of service and exactly what has been delivered.

PUSHING FOR CONTINUOUS IMPROVEMENT

Continuous improvement can lead to benefits ranging from increased compliance to elimination of manual hand-offs, automation, and enhanced data quality. It can also result in enterprise-wide reductions in administration and bureaucracy. **It's a process, so treat it like one.** As with all good processes, there has to be a clear objective with a measurable and clear series of steps. It does not just happen by itself. Here are some guidelines for making it happen:

- **Do it together** – ongoing improvement is most likely when both the outsource provider and the company commit the resources required

- **Measure, measure, measure** – tracking progress is critical for continuous improvement; if you don't track results, you won't be able to tell what does and doesn't work

- **Focus on the outcome** – don't forget the reason why you support continuous improvements... you're doing it to drive specific, measurable outcomes. Make sure these are defined from the start

- **Focus on end-to-end processes** – think outside normal boundaries; change can still happen in another part of the organization

- **Get the right resources** – it may not be sufficient just to have finance resources involved. Bring in individuals from other parts of the business – for example, operations, sales and marketing.

Ultimately, a structured approach to continuous improvement will encourage a spirit of partnership over the long term. A road map for continuous improvement will not only set out a menu for change, but also a mechanism for *keeping the deal working*. In Figure 10.8, we show, for illustrative purposes, the road map in use on the Exel F&A outsourcing contract referred to in the CFO interview at the beginning of this chapter.

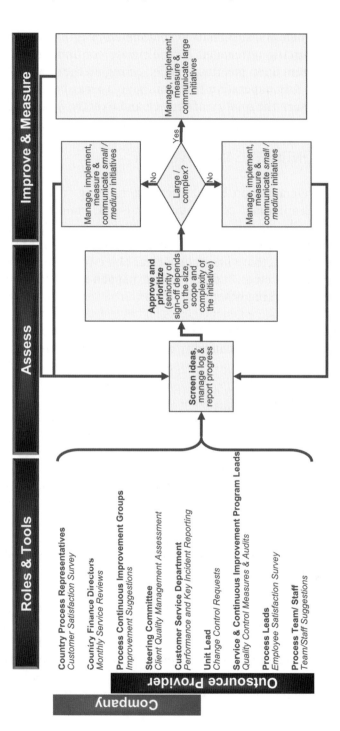

Source: Accenture, 2003

Figure 10.8   *Exel continuous improvement road map*

Keep at it and don't give up! Continuous improvement is not a project with a detailed plan. Often it can take some time, so be persistent. If you have an idea, then pilot it; trial and error is often the secret to continuous improvement. Innovation rarely is planned. Promote a culture that empowers, recognizes, and encourages ideas from all employees. This is most likely to drive successful change and deliver future benefits.

REFRESHMENT THROUGH CONTRACT RENEWAL

Outsourcing agreements are altered for a variety of reasons including expiration, changes in the customer's business or dissatisfaction with pricing. How does the renegotiation dynamic differ from shaping of the original deal? How can renegotiation revitalize your outsource arrangement and push performance to the next level? Here, we look at renewal strategies, tactics, and some of the pitfalls to avoid as contracts mature:

Think of restructuring, not renegotiation: The term 'renegotiation' implies that the original deal structure remains the same and is simply re-priced. The reality is that most companies will want to move beyond re-pricing and restructure commercial mechanisms. As the outsourcing contract matures, services are often added, removed, and changed. Pressure to reset the cost baseline at a lower level always exists, but some companies will be prepared to pay new or higher prices to achieve additional flexibility or faster time to market. Remember, the leading service providers continue to invest heavily in the next generation of service delivery capabilities. We recommend that you monitor these developments closely and take advantage of them.

The emphasis should be on added value: Initial negotiations are like a 'courtship;' both parties need to get to know each other. When you renegotiate, the honeymoon is over. You know your outsourcers' hot buttons and they know yours. Contractual discussions at this stage are not so much about minimizing supplier performance risk, as they are about building added value into your agreement.

Relationship, not price, is key: Price will always be a key consideration; it can also be a danger zone. There will always be a provider willing to work for a lower price – sometimes just to displace your current partner. But do you really want to go through the learning curve with another supplier and undergo a disruptive transfer? Remember, your provider has made a substantial investment; now that it knows your company well, it may have more to offer.

Start with a blank slate: Define the new, restructured relationship in terms that both sides can agree on. If the business has changed structurally, the existing contract may be less workable. Redefine objectives to clarify key issues and create a solution that is aligned with your new business goals.

Generally, the more flexible the parties are in dealing with each other, the more likely they are to develop long-term relationships based on trust. Consider the case of BT, explained below, which wanted to streamline its HR function and then changed direction, redefining the structure and ownership of its outsource solution.

CASE STUDY
Restructuring and renegotiating the deal at BT

When BT wanted to outsource its HR function, it formed a joint venture with Accenture. Within a few months, it was obvious that there was a better solution. The joint venture was dissolved and BT's stake was sold to the service provider. To quote David Clinton, President of Accenture HR Services:

'Like many telcos, BT was saddled with significant debt as a result of acquisitions and 3G licenses – and wanted to set up a shared service center to improve service delivery, enhance cost flexibility, and increase savings. At Accenture, we wanted to broaden and deepen our service offering in HR. Both Accenture and BT established early on that a joint venture would not fully deliver for either of us, so we opted for a straightforward outsource arrangement based on an arms-length service contract.'

Has service improved? Immeasurably! The full range of service performance indicators have all been exceeded. BT now benefits from increased responsiveness, flexibility, and innovation. The service is 'transformed, both in perception and in substance'. Costs have been reduced by 5% every year. Problems are fixed quickly, queries are turned around faster, and there is a perceived improvement in overall service. Financial rigor has also improved. The introduction of advanced portals has also led to a transformation in HR. David comments on the contract renewal process:

'This has been brought forward a year or so earlier, so that we can work on the issues together. Many things have changed since we first started working with BT

and the current 5-year contract has been overtaken by events. Things are going very well at the moment, so this is a good time to start negotiations for renewal.'

These are some of the changes since the outsourced contract started:

The telecommunications industry has changed. *This has had an impact on the relationship. Telecom companies have suffered increasing competition, reduced demand, and increased debts. The pressure has increased on operating cost and there is a trend to outsource more and more and at a lower cost. Furthermore, there are now greater opportunities to leverage scale as other companies outsource as well.*

Now, we have moved from just servicing BT – a one-to-one model – to providing an HR service for other telecommunications companies using the one-to-many model.

The service relationship has changed. *Because the joint venture structure has shifted to a straightforward outsource relationship, client expectations, governance arrangements, and performance levels have also changed. Greater reliance is now placed on the outsource provider's service management framework. Although the two parties work together in partnership, their roles are underpinned by clear KPI targets that influence commercial pricing and payment policy.*

The people involved have also changed. *BT no longer has the chair or direct management involvement in the outsourcing provision. The retained HR function in BT continues to be responsible for matters of policy, strategy, and industrial relations. The outsourcer is operationally responsible for processing. BT has appointed a contract manager to manage its side of the deal. Accenture has appointed a dedicated account manager to ensure customer satisfaction, service coordination, and development.*

David comments: 'Many of the BT constituencies we serve have changed. At times we ask ourselves – who is the customer? Not only the end users – be they either active or retired employees – but also the retained HR function itself. As a fully independent, commercial operation we at Accenture HR Services would advise the following:

From a client perspective ...

- **As outsource arrangements change over time, work to the original business case**. *Focus on business outcomes and track your achievements over the longer term. Don't be constrained by the initial contract; keep the 'prize' at the forefront of your decisions on service and cost.*

- **Subject your retained organization to the same disciplines**. *It, too, has a part to play in transforming itself and in delivering its side of the bargain. Ensure that the appropriate service management and operating disciplines are in place for both sides of the deal.*
- **Take governance seriously**. *Fully involve your representatives in the governance committees and reporting arrangements. Have them resolve disputes early and quickly. Know when to be tough with your outsourcer and when a compromise can work in your best interests.*

From a service provider perspective ...

- **Keep a handle on client expectations**. *Expectations can skyrocket soon after a deal is signed. They always exceed what is in the contract. As the outsource provider, you walk a fine line in behaving responsively – and going off-contract when necessary and not pandering to uncalled for, unpaid extras.*
- **Always have operational excellence highest on your agenda**. *Delivering the service on target is crucial. As problems emerge, analyze them fast. Set out the options for resolution. Involve the client at an early stage. Quite often, remedial work is required on the retained side of the organization to fix the problem.*
- **Provide transparency across service operations**. *This will avoid misunderstandings and build trust. Hiding problems does not help. Be transparent on all matters – scope changes, commercial and financial implications, and operational difficulties need to be viewed from both sides of the fence. Not all service providers are prepared, or should be expected to reveal their profit margins, but virtually everything else can be made available to the client. This will help provide a partnership approach to problem resolution.'*

David Clinton goes on: 'We started talks in late 2003, in preparation for contract renewal although our contract does not require such talks until 2005. It is like picking a date for a government election long before its parliamentary term has expired. You don't leave it to the last minute and negotiate at the 11th hour. You need sufficient time to re-baseline the outsourced function, revisit the benefits case and drive for a new set of outcomes, and then reconsider the contractual implications.'

In the next section we consider how to evaluate and monitor results.

KEEPING SCORE

As a part of the services agreement, it is essential that you develop a balanced scorecard that defines your target objectives and key performance measures. This tool will be used as a monitoring mechanism within the contract and will be subject to change throughout the contract lifecycle. If possible, the scorecard should be implemented prior to service transfer; this is critical in comparing pre- and post-transfer service performance. The balanced scorecard should be formally reviewed, ideally, at the end of each quarter of each contract year. The agenda for such reviews should be defined at a high level in the governance schedule of the contract. The balanced scorecard links to service credits and bonus payments.

Here are some best-practice guidelines for performance management on long-term outsource contracts:

- **Start early with what you can** – Performance measurement starts before service delivery starts. Provide factual evidence on the baseline so that improvements can be measured easily. Without this early quantification, there will be a lot of 'hot air' around whether service has improved or not – it becomes too emotional.

- **Performance measures should be flexible** – They evolve with the service over time. You need regular checkpoints, maybe once a year, to make sure that the performance measurement system is not out of sync with customer requirements.

- **Tie to incentives and penalties to make it bite** – Quality of service is just as important as cost, so you need the ability to penalize bad service. Remember, most organizations want to buy only good service – not something that's 'gold plated'.

- **Don't just measure the service provider's performance** – You should seek to focus on end-to-end processes, measuring the performance of *both* the service provider and the end user (or customer).

- **Drill measures down through to the individual** – Tie everyone in the organization to service and the contractual performance measurement system. The more you can link career models to performance measurement, the more individuals will be motivated to excel.

- **Don't go overboard** – Performance measurement can easily become a cottage industry if you are not careful. Consider what you are trying to achieve and don't over-engineer. Think about where you are in the outsourcing lifecycle and what is really important.

- **Automate as much as possible** – The more you can eliminate manual intervention the less effort-intensive and the more accurate the measures will be. Service reporting through a portal can provide an immediate web-based view of service performance.

An outsource provider should provide you with a performance information system and come up with the processes and tools that support decision-making. Figure 10.9 illustrates a balanced scorecard for a major company's F&A outsourcing contract.

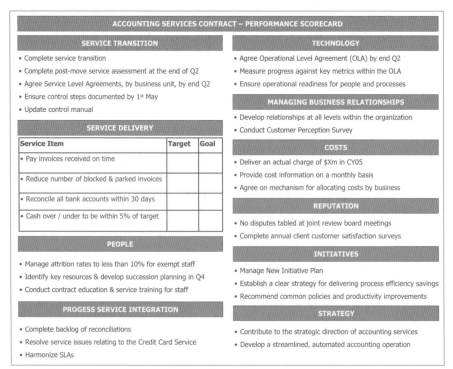

Source: Accenture, 2003

Figure 10.9 *Balanced scorecard for a major F&A outsourcing contract*

The challenge after the initial honeymoon period is over is to maintain the momentum in achieving results – *and being seen to continue achieving results*. An outsourcing scorecard should measure the following five dimensions:

1 **Business value delivered:** Is the client organization becoming more successful?

2 **Financial growth:** Does delivery match financial targets?

3 **Service:** Are the internal customers satisfied?

4 **People:** Are the staff motivated, trained, and satisfied?

5 **Process:** Are business processes and service delivery improving?

Perhaps the most difficult areas to measure are client and customer satisfaction. Take a balanced view of what service level is necessary to meet customer expectations and agree on this with your outsource partner. Survey regularly. Relative, modest improvement over the longer term is usually what is required. As we said earlier, dramatically exceeding customer expectations at a high cost can be as dangerous as not quite meeting your targets.

CFO INSIGHTS

- Keep the deal alive and working. Outsourcing is not about sitting still. As CFO, you have to be in control and have the right control mechanisms in place. Strong service management is the bedrock of your deal. It ensures that the outsourcing KPIs are met as circumstances change. Strong service discipline also provides a solid foundation for continuous improvement.

- Don't leave contract renewal to the last minute and negotiate at the 11th hour! Leave sufficient time to re-baseline the outsourced function, revisit the benefits case, and drive for a new set of outcomes. Then reconsider the contractual implications.

- Be honest in all your negotiations and communications. Work hard at promoting and justifying the partnership. Both you and your provider should accept responsibility when things don't go according to plan.

- Don't whip out the contract every time you have a problem! Focus on achieving the original business case and working together to make a strategic impact. Be realistic – don't over-stress staff with unachievable objectives. Sometimes stretch targets are just not achievable in the time frame and can put unnecessary stress on staff.

- Don't be constrained by the original contract. Keep the 'prize' at the forefront of your decisions on service and cost. Expectations can sky-rocket soon after a deal is signed. Focus on business outcomes and track your achievements over the longer term.

FROM INSIGHT TO ACTION

FLEX AND RESPOND TO CHANGING BUSINESS CONDITIONS

Your business doesn't stand still, neither should your outsourcing arrangements. Work together in the spirit of partnership for a 'win-win.' Don't be afraid to realign the relationship – if necessary take the plunge and restructure the deal.

PLAN FOR THE LONGER TERM

Remember, expectations at the beginning can change rapidly as benefits are achieved and the performance bar is raised. Plan for step-changes interspersed with periods of stability and incremental improvements. But, prepare to deal with the unexpected!

EMPOWER RELATIONSHIP MANAGERS IN BOTH ORGANIZATIONS

Make provision for escalating unresolved issues – these should be few and far between! Encourage peer-to-peer relationship building and informal communication.

SUBJECT YOUR RETAINED ORGANIZATION *AND* YOUR OUTSOURCER TO SERVICE MANAGEMENT DISCIPLINE

Both parties have a part to play in delivering on the deal. Install a service management framework. Differentiate between the management and the users. Set up customer services and service control.

> **KEEP SCORE**
> Measure business value, financial growth, and performance improvement. Survey internal customer and staff satisfaction. Rationalize the number of KPIs to between 15 and 20, remembering to focus on outputs not inputs.

REFERENCES

1 Kathleen Goolsby, White Paper: *Governing Attitudes: Best Practices in Managing Outsourcing Relationships*, Outsourcing Center, 2002.

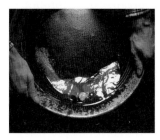

CHAPTER 11

Finance BPO
– the Future

Finance executives around the world are intrigued by the explosive growth of outsourcing, the impact it is having on businesses, and how it is influencing strategic investment. In this book we have sought to provide answers to the fundamental questions that CFOs are raising.

So far, we have focused on what is happening today. In this chapter, we look to the future. If current trends continue, we will see a finance and accounting outsourcing industry worth $110bn take shape over the next decade. CFOs want to know the **end game** – where the trends are leading – and whether they should be participating in the outsourcing phenomenon.

As we were writing this book, some of the questions most frequently asked of us were:

> '**How far do you go** with outsourcing and where do you draw the line? Are new entrants to our industry – the guys that don't have the baggage that we have – moving faster and more nimbly than we are? How can we compete with these new players?'

> '**Does it make sense for us to continue to invest in technologies** aimed at improving the efficiency and productivity of our administrative processes – or is there an another way to achieve the same results so that we can refocus our investment dollars on innovation?'

> 'Our finance function faces more challenges today than ever before due to a combination of stricter statutory regulations and pressure for greater transparency. **How do I do more for less – with lower risk?**'

We hope you've found the answers to questions like these in this book. One thing our research has underscored is the vital importance of adaptability. The key to responding to the unstable world we now live in is to deploy a flexible business model – one that enables you to tackle twin problems: being too asset intensive, and a high fixed-cost infrastructure.[1]

INNOVATION INSIGHTS

Cost cutting and refocusing management attention will always be important. Executives in high-performing businesses are increasingly deploying business transformation outsourcing as a powerful vehicle for rapidly realizing superior results across end-to-end business processes. Finance process outsourcing can help achieve mastery of core competencies, spurring renewal. It can also help deliver current earnings, while laying the groundwork for future growth.

Figure 11.1 is an example of how high-performance consumer goods companies demonstrate mastery of core competencies as part of this accelerating evolution.[2]

As we discussed in Chapter 2, high-performance businesses have the ability to identify the most important industry drivers of present and future value. They develop strategies aimed at building both current and future value – and are relentlessly focused on efficiency and the pursuit

Clear Strategic Intent			
Obsessive Customer Focus	Innovation & Execution to Value	Operational Excellence	Alliance & Collaboration Capability
Clearly articulated and differentiated customer value proposition Customer & consumer insight and interaction	Strong culture of innovation (anticipate and lead) Agile commercialization and execution of innovation	Well-defined operational efficiency program Productivity & functional excellence IT appreciation & leverage	Competence in selecting, structuring & managing strategic alliances & partnerships Expert at capturing internal synergies & promoting internal collaboration
Talent Management			
Performance-oriented culture Effective talent lifecycle management			

Source: Accenture, 2003

Figure 11.1 *Core competencies in consumer goods*

of new sources of value creating opportunity. Integral to their superior performance is the ability to harness technology – investing in it to ensure long-term success and zoning in on advances that will generate most business value. Such companies use a combination of technology and business process outsourcing to standardize delivery approaches and guarantee expected returns on investment.

Growing numbers of medium-sized enterprises are accumulating the critical mass necessary for shared services to be a realistic proposition. Many will become nimble, high-performance companies in their own right – able to benefit from the scale and flexibility previously enjoyed only by larger organizations.

It is increasingly important to manage and leverage intangible assets to sustain competitive advantage. This is leading senior finance executives to develop new processes, capabilities, and tools. The goal is fourfold:

- Increasing scalability in former high fixed-cost support functions

- Improving capital efficiency

- Creating transparency in, and focus on, underlying performance drivers

- Enabling 'out-of-the-box' decision-making by providing insight into the dynamics of demand and supply.

Companies are adapting their operating models to support the reconfiguration of their capital structure. Additionally, they are redesigning their finance processes to take advantage of 'lights out processing' – no longer a Holy Grail, but rather an attainable goal. CFOs are seeking structural resilience so they can weather economic cycles and continue to prosper even in the face of disruptive industry events. They want the financial capacity to fuel the innovation engine – the key to sustaining growth over the long term.

Nimbly reconfiguring assets, infrastructure, technology, and intellectual capital to adjust quickly and smoothly to new market conditions is a fine aim. But concentrating on core competencies, entering new markets, and adopting new ideas takes enormous energy and focus. Knowing that it is hard to achieve everything independently, high-performance businesses are adept at setting up effective business partnerships and forming alliances to gain access to new capabilities and expertise. They are highly motivated to seek out help in managing and sharing risk.

Over the next 10 years, the technology investment model in particular will no longer be based on unilateral corporate activity. Instead, business process outsourcing mega-service providers (MSPs) will emerge and consolidate. Independent industry commentators forecast that they will take ownership of the corporate ERP backbone of many companies and will spur innovation and the creation of new capabilities by adopting successive waves of new technology. The end result? Dramatically reduced labor intensity in transaction processing and an exciting new array of analytical and decision support tools.

ACCENTURE FINANCE SOLUTIONS: WORLDWIDE INTERCONNECTIVITY

Bill Gates' prediction of the 'death of time and distance' has become a reality. Digitalization means that knowledge-based activities can be delivered from anywhere on the planet. Freer trade and newly expanding economies are accelerating the advantages that global sourcing can offer. Stewart Clements, President of Accenture Finance Solutions, has a bold vision for the future:

'Today, for many people, outsourcing is simply about transferring current F&A processing operations to someone else based on the fact that they can perform them better and cheaper. To others, it involves fundamental improvements in service and quality. CFOs are quite understandably cautious about outsourcing large chunks of their business because of their perceived exposure to risk and feelings of vulnerability.

'In the future, we at Accenture believe that the very nature of the demand for outsourcing will change. As the broader business process outsourcing (BPO) market (in particular, the BPO F&A market) matures, clients will be less preoccupied with having direct control of the inputs (or assets) of an accounting or finance process – the resources, the technology, the location, and operational activities – and will be more concerned with outcomes. Outsource providers will be evaluated based upon service levels, pace and certainty in the delivery of results, continuous investment in technology innovation, and the ability to offer highly tailored solutions from globally scaled assets.

'We are already seeing signs of this change in mindset and evidence of clients who are beginning to make their selection of partner based on these parameters. For example, many of the case studies described in this book are focused on achieving outcomes such as improved conversion of customer orders to cash, "accurate cash forecasting with reduced float", "improved management information" and "operating model transforma-

tion". The more discriminating buyers of these services will be looking for zero defects in their outsourced processes.

'Companies will also seek to do all their trading electronically – buying and selling goods and services over the Internet – and will require third parties to handle payments and settlements. We envision a business environment in which trading exchanges have matured and the economic benefits achieved – for example, procurement and bill consolidation both within and across industry sectors. Settlement exchanges will dramatically speed up business cash flow and provide options for trade debt financing. The infrastructures and capabilities of outsource providers such as my own company, Accenture, will grow to support such exchanges.

'In the near future, we anticipate that new business models will emerge as a result of the revolution in wireless technologies and Web-based services with remote identity tracking technologies at their core. We expect exciting developments in the burgeoning field of business analytics – a key area of growth for the refreshed, redefined finance functions of the future. Our own company, for example, is on a fast track to create an array of assets that we can tailor and apply to specific company needs. This will provide vital value-added information to clients so they can transform deep customer and competitive insights into action more quickly and decisively.

'The provider's development of scalable and standardized business processes, systems, data, and reporting – all tailored to clients' individual needs – is rapidly gaining global acceptance. Consequently, buyers of outsourced services will be purchasing complete solutions to distinct business processing requirements. They will be less tied to any one software tool, sourcing approach or provider – and will have the freedom to shop around to see who can deliver on the most demanding service performance metrics for particular business processes. The drive to increase "transactional liquidity" will reinforce this focus on purchased outcomes.

'The more successful outsource providers will increasingly "bundle" their offer – their assets, people, and technology together with processes and supporting applications – into sophisticated, fully integrated suites of F&A BPO services (see Figure 11.2).

'Accenture Finance Solutions offers a prime example of a mature and rapidly growing business in this market. We have spent 12 years developing our people, processes, and practices in F&A BPO. Today, we serve more than 40 F&A outsourcing clients in 29 languages and provide services to more than 30 countries. According to a recent Gartner forecast,[3] there is a 70% probability that by 2005, two mega-service providers will have broken away and distanced themselves from the pack.

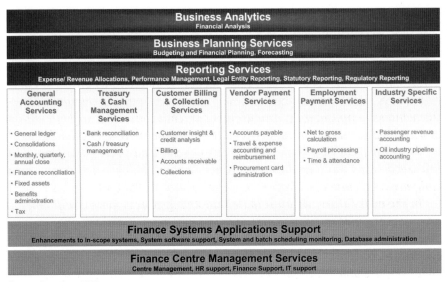

Business Analytics					
Financial Analysis					

Business Planning Services					
Budgeting and Financial Planning, Forecasting					

Reporting Services					
Expense/ Revenue Allocations, Performance Management, Legal Entity Reporting, Statutory Reporting, Regulatory Reporting					

General Accounting Services	Treasury & Cash Management Services	Customer Billing & Collection Services	Vendor Payment Services	Employment Payment Services	Industry Specific Services
• General ledger • Consolidations • Monthly, quarterly, annual close • Finance reconciliation • Fixed assets • Benefits administration • Tax	• Bank reconciliation • Cash / treasury management	• Customer insight & credit analysis • Billing • Accounts receivable • Collections	• Accounts payable • Travel & expense accounting and reimbursement • Procurement card administration	• Net to gross calculation • Payroll processing • Time & attendance	• Passenger revenue accounting • Oil industry pipeline accounting

Finance Systems Applications Support					
Enhancements to in-scope systems, System software support, System and batch scheduling monitoring, Database administration					

Finance Centre Management Services					
Centre Management, HR support, Finance Support, IT support					

Source: Accenture, 2003

Figure 11.2   *Accenture suite of finance and accounting BPO services*

'*If current growth rates and trends are maintained, then each of these mega players will have invested significantly in physical infrastructure and technologies, and employ over 20,000 employees in the F&A market. We expect Accenture to be one of those players as today's fragmented outsource industry consolidates around a full-service, integrated delivery model that is globally and regionally scaled.*

'*The trend towards bundling process and technology is taking root in a number of industry sectors. Consider financial services, for example. Accenture and SAP recently signed an agreement to develop and deliver IT solutions for banks and insurance companies worldwide. Together, they will offer the financial services industry expanded options for delivering IT products and services – including standard solutions, custom solutions, and BPO. Banks and insurance companies can take advantage of a shorter, less expensive SAP implementation with a greater degree of certainty by bundling SAP software into their BPO infrastructures. To support this strategy, Accenture uses a global delivery model (a combination of onshore, near-shore, and offshore centers of expertise) that provides accelerated implementation, with lower up-front costs and faster benefit realization, coupled with the ongoing business process execution.*

'*Our earlier experiences with F&A outsourcing were based on dedicated facilities focused on one client; initially these were located either in existing client operations or nearby. Today, clients are moving away from the one-to-one model to the one-to-many model in which a number of organizations use the same shared service facility. This new model lets companies benefit from mass customization – an approach in which tailored service solutions and scalability coexist and reinforce one another. In parallel with this approach, we are carefully selecting the locations of our centers to optimize both skill and cost. Today, our network of delivery centers spans India, China, North and South America, and East Europe.*

'As companies exploit the economies of scale and process/systems specialization available in these outsource centers, the one-to-many model will become more and more popular, particularly with medium-sized enterprises. Within a few years, we are going to see outsource providers like Accenture offer increasingly specialized process-based services from dedicated centers. Airline reservations processing, such as that provided by Navitaire[4] and Web-based HR services provided to the UK Telecom industry, are good examples of process sharing at an industry level.

'Specialist processes at a more granular cross-industry level are also gaining momentum. Accenture's "Credit Management Workbench," for example, tracks the status of receivables and related customer activities to speed up cash collections. Another example: We are currently introducing our newly launched wrap-around technologies, which provide higher levels of process integration with client-hosted ERP systems. These new technologies provide clients with deeper insights into the dynamics of their day-to-day operations. Eventually, we expect a change in ownership of the ERP backbone itself. Companies will find that it no longer makes sense to invest in automating administrative functions when they could be focusing scarce resources on activities that offer greater differentiation from a competitive perspective.

'The trend towards global sourcing via a network of outsource centers will continue for some time. Increasingly, companies will take advantage of such networks for load balancing and business continuity – and as a means of spreading geopolitical risk. Supply and demand is spurring the growth of new delivery locations around the world. As transaction processing becomes ever-more efficient, the number of staff required per client company organization will steadily decline. Increasingly sophisticated process automation, for example, in purchase-to-pay – will lead to declines in manual error correction and reconciliation work. I envision that a new outsource industry will emerge to take its place – information and analytics.

'The physical work in low-cost offshore locations will increasingly focus on higher value-added activities connected with access to, and vis-

Source: Accenture, 2003

Figure 11.3 *Relationship between value levers and buyer values*

ibility of, data for decision support. Technology innovation will lead to the industrialization of labor-intensive transaction processing and diminish the initial importance of labor arbitrage. Maintenance of processes and systems could well remain an offshore activity, but finance's capabilities for analyzing and interpreting data will have to be as close to the front-line of the client company management as is physically possible.

'Relationships with client executives will change too, as the strategic impact of BPO on their businesses deepens. Solutions will be highly complex; scale and reach will be prerequisites for provider selection. Brand equity, trust, and advocacy skills will become crucial differentiators for outsource providers. Figure 11.3 illustrates the relationship between buyer values and how these are met.

'We could well see strategic finance processes such as planning and forecasting fully integrated with the more traditional finance outsource service. Suppliers such as Accenture will rise to the challenge by deploying highly skilled and effective finance specialists to meet this demand. Buyers will focus on outsource contracts that offer higher quality outcomes – carefully scrutinizing providers' staff education and training, analytical capabilities, and communication skills – necessary to support effective decision-making. Ultimately, however, judgment and interpretation will remain the responsibility of client company management.'

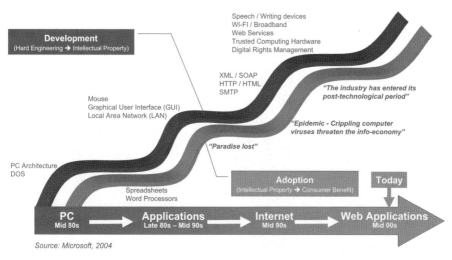

Figure 11.4 *Successive waves of innovation*[5]

THE IMPACT OF NEXT-GENERATION TECHNOLOGIES

At the beginning of the 1990s, who could have envisioned the profound changes that have swept across virtually every industry, from digital entertainment and communications to financial services and healthcare? The mobile phone has rapidly become the centerpiece of a global, digitally interlinked economy. Handheld devices connect to the Internet and already have partial ERP functionality. Consumer product companies can check stock levels and take orders on the move. Figure 11.4 illustrates the incredible evolutionary path that has recently unfolded.

No new wave of technology is poised to revolutionize business; however, existing technologies will continue to make it easier to gather, communicate, and process information. The deconstruction of the vertically integrated company and its replacement by the globally networked company will dramatically reshape the industrial and economic landscape.

Here, we highlight a few of the breakthrough technologies that will embed themselves in business infrastructure over the next decade.

- **Finance executives will benefit from new tools:** In the near future, it will be possible to carry out analytics and make value-added decisions using profitability analysis and pricing models that take advantage of real-time data delivered from the point of sale. Most data today is formatted in tabular form, and is unintuitively presented. This will change as

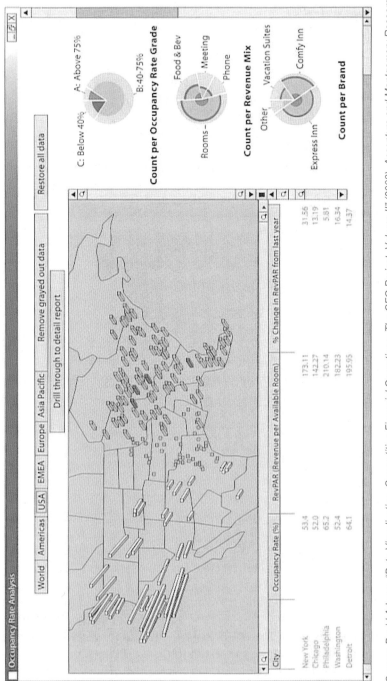

Source: David Adams, "Data Visualisation, Competitive Financial Operations: The CFO Project, Volume II" (2003), Accenture and Montgomery Research, supplied by ADVIZOR Solutions, www.cfoproject.com

Figure 11.5 *Illustrative example of a multidimensional, animated data-representation tool*

executives access a host of increasingly interactive, multidimensional, and animated data-representation tools – all instantly available in the palm of the hand!

An illustration of the user interface for an executive data representation tool is shown in Figure 11.5.

- **Electronic collections will expand:** Mega-service providers will be instrumental in creating a financial electronic ecosystem. Rapid growth in e-commerce collections will deliver significant cost savings – enabling almost real-time cash conversion between buyers and sellers. Between 2000 and 2001 almost 40% of non-cash retail payments were already made electronically.[6] Based on current trends, electronic volumes will surpass check volumes by 2006.

- **Lights-out processing is on the horizon:** Electronic check conversion will help to further automate the collections process. Checks presented for payment will be the source of payment information – not merely a method of payment. Line item information, including the bank routing transit number, the account number, and the check number, is captured electronically and then used to make a one-time debit from the customer's account. The consumer receives a convenient digital record of the payment on the monthly checking account statement. Information reporting and account reconciliation will be fully automated.

  Benefits will abound; because the transaction is digital, funds will be available faster, normally on the same or the next day. There will be faster notification of returns, two days after settlement rather than a week or ten days. Another major benefit is reduced exposure to fraud and less cost incurred in preventing check fraud and bad debt.

  The increased reliability of automated systems and processes will increase the confidence of companies considering outsourcing electronic collections. Best-practice, technology-intensive solution providers will have pre-established and tested operations with sophisticated capabilities. Figure 11.6 illustrates a comparison of a paper-based accounts receivable (AR) collection timeline with that offered by Wells Fargo, a leading US Internet banking services provider.

- **Declining demand for working capital:** As companies continue to automate, the need for high levels of working capital will decline. Corporate treasury and accounts receivable departments will know exactly when debits are due to be posted to the company accounts. The transparency of the future daily cash position will enable operation with much leaner levels of working capital. Funds will be available

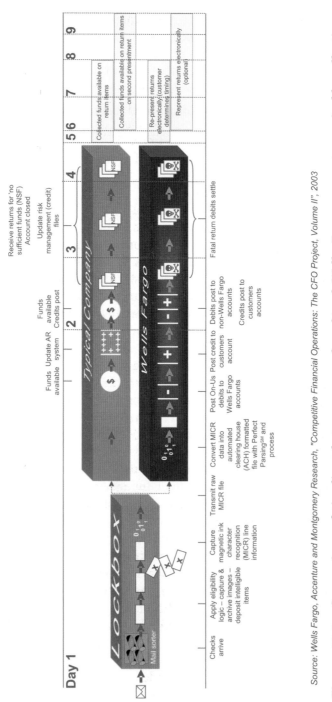

Source: Wells Fargo, Accenture and Montgomery Research, "Competitive Financial Operations: The CFO Project, Volume II", 2003

Figure 11.6 *Comparison of timelines between paper-based and Wells Fargo accounts receivable collections process*

faster and there will be quicker notification on returns. Determining daily cash positions will become far easier. Exposure to fraud will be reduced and less money will be spent on managing bad debt.

- **Silent Commerce will make everyday objectives intelligent and interactive:** Sensing technology and radio frequency identification (RFID) tags will transmit information about their location and condition using short wave radio frequencies. This technology is already being used for asset management and warehousing. Retailers and other supply chain members will be able to monitor transactions from truck to warehouse, warehouse to shelf, shelf to trolley. Information will be dynamically available on customer preferences, loyalty, and profitability, making instant data on consumption a reality.[7]

    Wireless technology will revolutionize connectivity: We are moving into a world in which wireless bandwidth is abundant and cheap. Fast data transfer will be available to users on the move. Telecommunications, financial service, and utility companies are all early adopters as they push relentlessly to improve field and sales force productivity.

    User-friendly Internet services and superior system interfaces: More closely interfaced software applications will communicate with one another over the Internet using open standards. This will enable organizations to share data – and even software processes. Communication between systems has been technically feasible for years, but until open standards emerged, it was limited by reliance on proprietary languages. In the near future, interconnected software applications will communicate with each other via the Internet using open standards – enabling organizations to share data and even software processes. One result: A rapid increase in industry-wide collaboration.

    In outsourcing, mega-service providers will focus on ensuring that their prime asset – their global service delivery networks – benefit as fully as possible from these advances in technology and innovation. They will expand the scope of their services beyond simple transaction processing – and will become the engine room behind analytics. With technology innovation as a key driver, mega-service providers will provide much more than cheap back-office service delivery. Consider the following International World Rally Championship (WRC) case study that demonstrates how technological innovation can radically transform a fairly static business model.

CASE STUDY
wrc.com – driving the future

The World Rally Championship (WRC) is a series of motorsport events staged around the world – poised to rival the popularity of Formula One. It is watched by over 550 million television viewers, while 10 million fans attend the events worldwide.

International Sportsworld, which owns WRC, knew that the only way to communicate with the widest possible audience was to turn a spectator sport into a participatory activity by putting viewers as close as possible to the driver's seat. With this in mind, the company turned to the new media capabilities of Microsoft .NET Web Services and telemetric tracking devices – using them to provide compelling content for its website, mobile phone service, and game consoles. A screenshot of the WRC website is illustrated in Figure 11.7.

During each rally, devices in the cars transmit information about their position and operating conditions. This information is sent from a Global Positioning System (GPS). Without actually being present, fans can 'see and experience' the rally wherever, and whenever it is happening. David Richards, chairman of ISC, says, 'Keeping

Figure 11.7 *WRC website screenshot*

pace with innovative new media applications is critical to transforming the image of WRC, enabling us to win the hearts and minds of new enthusiasts around the world.'

This new communications capability has been built and delivered by an external service provider – an example of an outsource provider taking on high value-add responsibilities. It demonstrates how simple, discrete technologies are being woven together to create new industries, new business models, and new processes that CFOs have to come to terms with and adapt to.

So, what will the future finance BPO landscape look like? Michael Donnellan, a partner at Accenture and author of this book, explains his vision.

'We at Accenture fundamentally believe that we have arrived at a watershed point in history in the way that finance processes are sourced – from in-house or open book outsourcing (with the client managing all the inputs to secure an output) to the client buying the output (the results) by purchasing a flexible, as-needed service (giving the provider complete control over people, technology, and the processes needed for delivery). Going forward, clients will source everything required to deliver the business results that they need. Ultimately, this will encompass people, software and processes, and shared investment. The debate I have with many CFOs around the world is no longer framed within the context of their giving something away and losing control. It now focuses on changing their delivery model so they can gain even more control as a result. To take advantage of this fundamental change, companies will have to alter the way they do business. They will have to think differently and deploy far-reaching alliance management techniques instead of using arms-length relationships with their suppliers.

'We think that the outsource market will become dominated by a few scale players and we expect that Accenture will be one of them – a mega-service provider. As the market leader, we are continuing to build a global network of interlinked delivery centers to balance risk and work load so we can offer our clients maximum flexibility. Global sourcing strategies (the decision on where to deliver service from) will quickly move away from debate about specific location options and service will be provided from everywhere on the planet.

'This implies common pools of management supporting multiple clients, the use of shared service delivery resources, universal standards, networks and systems all dedicated to providing interoperability across multiple geographies. Standardization and scale economics will prove increasingly attractive to mid-market companies and subsidiaries of global corporations who don't require customized solutions.

'We intend to develop successive waves of next-generation technologies and incorporate them as part of our service offering to help our clients transform their

business models. Sustainable high performance is the goal. Our initial investment focus is on efficiency and management tools surrounding the core ERP platform and service, but over time, we expect to move into the core ERP system area itself.

'Process performance and error handling will steadily improve with technology innovations. Ultimately, end-to-end "lights out" processing will become an everyday reality. The finance service ecosystem will quickly mature, offering clients a tantalizing value proposition – the chance to unlock working capital from the balance sheet and reinvest it back into the competitive core of their businesses. This will be supported by sophisticated technology and intelligence tools aimed at information manipulation – insight-driven credit and collections, vendor and employee compliance, business analytics, and so on. We are already using leading-edge technology in our centers to connect customer relationship management processes to working capital management processes, enabling our clients to deploy their capital more effectively. We intend to extend these capabilities by developing Web-based tools that integrate mission-critical processes such as supply-chain management with finance operations.

'Companies will, of course, continue to acquire, merge, and divest. BPO will be seen as a means of extracting synergies, off-setting the usual delivery risks that companies have historically shouldered on their own. The importance of this is revealed by a study that we recently completed of 50 of the largest US M&A deals in 2003.[8] Our analysis shows that in the deals where Accenture was involved the company share price outperformed the S&P500 24 months after the merger announcement (108% versus the index). This is compared to a performance of 94% versus the index for the other companies. We expect a new way of thinking about post-merger integration planning and execution to emerge with BPO at its core.

'Ultimately we believe that mastery of finance and performance management will be viewed as a necessary component in building a high-performance business – and we are excited about helping to shape this vision with our clients.'

FINANCE AND PERFORMANCE MASTERY IN THE FUTURE

Finance executives are managing growing complexity across multiple stakeholder groups – investors, analysts, regulators, internal customers – and dealing with day-to-day competitive pressures. As explored in Chapter 2, high-performance businesses do not view the finance organization as a controllership; rather, finance is seen as a dynamic function charged with infusing a value-centered mentality throughout the corporate culture. Finance contributes insight into how and where value is created and supports strategic thinking around the value chain or value network. To manage their enterprise as a value network, CFOs and their finance teams will need the following capabilities:

- **Capital stewardship:** the ability to consistently generate superior rates of return from invested capital by maximizing flexibility and operating businesses with ever-lower levels of working capital.

- **Earnings transparency:** close scrutiny of the composition of earnings, business volatility and material events will fuel demands for greater predictability and transparency in reported results.

- **Risk management:** the ability to analyze exposure to all types of risk – business and financial – and determine how to mitigate such exposure or turn it into a sustainable competitive advantage.

- **Finance operations***:* competitive pressures demand lower cost structures, especially in 'non-differential' functions and processes. Superior finance and accounting operations are the bedrock of efficiency and cost-effectiveness.

- **Business performance management:** the need for tightly integrated strategic, financial, operational, and external information that delivers predictive insights to decision makers so that they can make timely decisions that make the difference between success and failure.

The changing role of the CFO demands a sharper focus on value creation, and the smart allocation of capital and resources.

CFOs will need to adopt a capability framework for their finance functions to enable them to coach and develop new competencies and skills (Figure 11.8).

Source: Accenture, 2003

Figure 11.8 *Finance capability framework*

This long-term vision of F&A outsourcing must be balanced with the realities of recent events and the furor caused by Enron and WorldCom in the US – and, more recently, by Parmalat and Ahold in Europe. How will the growing globalization of international accounting and regulation play out over the longer term? During our research, many CFOs commented on the increasingly expensive, unnecessary, and distracting growth in bureaucracy and compliance – and voiced doubt about corresponding increases in real transparency and shareholder value.

What does all this mean for you now, today? CEOs and senior finance executives will demand progress at pace and greater certainty of outcome. Partnering with outsourcers will increasingly be seen as a vital strategic move.

We started out in Chapter 1 with the hypothesis that *'the equation of higher quality service at ever lower prices is irresistible, especially when outsourcing enables executives to focus on the core competitive attributes of their businesses'*. This has been tested in various CFO interviews, cases, and research studies – and, in this final chapter, against the long-term vectors of change.

The logic is simple and compelling: If someone else can complete mission-critical processes faster, more cheaply, and at higher performance levels while providing stringent standards of security and control – then why not make the leap into outsourcing? We have met many executives on our travels who remain to be convinced. We hope this book has helped you reach your own conclusions.

CFO INSIGHTS

- Executives in businesses that are considered high performers are increasingly deploying outsourcing as a powerful means of swiftly achieving superior results across end-to-end business processes.

- Inherent in high performance is the ability to harness technology – investing to ensure long-term success and zoning in on what will generate most business value. Using a combination of technology and outsourcing, companies can standardize delivery approaches and reap projected returns on investment.

- Concentrating on core competencies, entering new markets, and adopting new ideas takes great energy and focus. Knowing that it is hard to achieve everything independently, high-performance businesses are adept at setting up effective business partnerships and forming alliances to gain access to new capabilities and expertise.

● The mega-service provider's core focus will be on developing its prime asset (a global service delivery network) by fully exploiting advances in technology. Industry leaders will expand the scope of their services beyond simple transaction processing – and strive to become the engine room behind analytics.

REFERENCES

1 Scott McGregor, President and CEO, Philips Semi-Conductors, *World Economic Conference*, 2003.

2 Accenture High Performance Business research, *High-Performance Business Research Collection*, 2003. www.accenture.com

3 Frances Karamouzis, *Gartner Symposium ITXPO*, Lake Buena Vista, Florida, 2003.

4 Accenture's wholly owned subsidiary company focused on transaction processing and airline ticketing administration. www.navitaire.com

5 Terry Smith, Director Public Sector, Microsoft, *The World in 2004 – Priorities for Sustaining Business Success*, closing address.

6 Wells Fargo, The Electronic Financial Ecosystem, Competitive Financial Operations: *The CFO Project*, Volume II, 2003. www.cfoproject.com

7 Accenture, *The Innovator's Advantage: Using Innovation and Technology to Improve Business Performance*, Accenture, 2003. www.accenture.com

8 Michael J. May, Patricia Anslinger and Gary A. Curtis, *Managing for Today & Tomorrow: Strategy & the High Performance Business*, Accenture, 2003. www.accenture.com

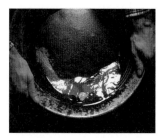

Biographies

CHAPTER 1: THE FINANCE OUTSOURCING LANDSCAPE
CHAPTER 11: FINANCE BPO – THE FUTURE

Stewart Clements is president of Accenture Finance Solutions (AFS), the unit responsible for Accenture's finance and accounting outsourcing business. In this role he is responsible for AFS business strategy; development of Accenture's delivery center network; finance- and outsourcing-focused assets and tools; and the management and development of organizational capabilities. Mr Clements is a Chartered Accountant and has a degree in Accountancy from Glasgow University. Based in London, he has been with Accenture for nearly 20 years.

CHAPTER 1: THE FINANCE OUTSOURCING LANDSCAPE
CHAPTER 7: STAKEHOLDERS: ACHIEVING BUY-IN
CHAPTER 11: FINANCE BPO – THE FUTURE

Mike Donnellan is a lead partner in Accenture's outsourcing and consulting business. He has more than 20 years' experience in the professional services industry. Mr Donnellan has also worked extensively on the research, development, and deployment of innovative operating models. In 1997, he co-authored *CFO: Architect of the Corporation's Future*, which resulted in the adoption of new finance and accounting organizational models by numerous corporations around the world.

CHAPTER 2: CREATING AN OPERATING MODEL FOR HIGH PERFORMANCE

Michael R. Sutcliff is the global managing partner for Accenture's Finance and Performance Management group. In this role, he develops new service offerings and alliance relationships, and manages Accenture consulting services of interest to senior finance executives. Mr Sutcliff has extensive experience in strategy, business architecture, systems integration, business transformation, and business process outsourcing; and has assisted companies from most major industries, including automotive, chemicals, consumer goods, and transportation, with their finance transformation programs.

CHAPTER 3: SUPPLIERS: OPTIONS FOR SERVICE DELIVERY

Adam Johnson is the global lead for Business Process Outsourcing (BPO) growth in Accenture's Products operating group, which includes the automotive, health and life sciences, industrial equipment, retail and consumer goods, and transportation and travel industries. In addition to more than a decade of specialized experience in outsourcing, Mr Johnson has a strong background in sales and general management. Based in London, he is focused primarily on European BPO deals and was part of the teams that closed outsourcing deals with Thames Water, the London Stock Exchange, and La Rinascente, a leading Italian retailer.

CHAPTER 4: SCOPING: DECIDING WHAT TO OUTSOURCE

David Rowlands is a partner with Accenture Finance Solutions, Accenture's finance and accounting outsourcing business. Mr Rowland's particular strengths are providing finance shared services and transformational outsourcing assistance to clients in the travel and hospitality industries (key clients include Thomas Cook and Forte Hotels).

He also has extensive experience in managing cross-European accounting operations, finance strategy and post-merger integration, and core financial process re-engineering and has worked across a range of industries, including chemicals, construction, and aerospace and defense. Mr Rowlands is a Chartered Management Accountant and has a Masters degree in Economics from Cambridge University.

CHAPTER 5: GLOBAL SOURCING OF SERVICE DELIVERY

Daniel Lipson is vice president of product development for Accenture Finance Solutions, Accenture's finance and accounting outsourcing business. He specializes in architecting pan-European finance and accounting outsourcing and enterprise resource planning solutions and has deep expertise in most financial arenas, including budgeting and forecasting, profitability and cost analysis, and management reporting. Mr Lipson has more than 11 years of experience in the consumer goods and services industry, as well as experience in the automotive, travel and transportation, and aerospace industries. He is a Chartered Management Accountant and has a Masters degree in Chemical Engineering from Cambridge University.

CHAPTER 6: PRICING AND SHAPING YOUR DEAL

Steve Ferneyhough is a partner in Accenture's Consumer Goods and Services industry group. His specialty is developing, selling, and delivering large-scale business transformation outsourcing engagements; he also oversees the development of Accenture standards for outsourcing solutions in the Products operating group, which encompasses the airline, automotive, consumer goods and services, health and life sciences, industrial equipment, retail, and travel services industries. In addition to outsourcing, Mr Ferneyhough has extensive experience managing projects for supply chain re-engineering, supply chain planning, network optimization, and systems integration.

CHAPTER 8: ENSURING A SUCCESSFUL TRANSITION

Scott Laughner is a Chicago-based partner with Accenture Finance Solutions, Accenture's finance and accounting outsourcing business. In his position as vice president of solutions and sales for North America, he supervises client service delivery, manages the national sales force, and oversees operations. Mr Laughner's client experience includes the design, development, and deployment of shared services capabilities for two major telecommunications providers, a global steel manufacturer, a national water utility, and a global packaging and automotive parts manufacturer. Mr Laughner has been with Accenture for fifteen years and holds a BS in Industrial Management from Purdue University and an MBA in finance from the University of Notre Dame.

CHAPTER 9: REDUCING RISK WITH OUTSOURCING

Alan Healey is the lead partner for outsourcing delivery in Europe for Accenture's Products operating group, which includes the automotive, health and life sciences, industrial equipment, retail and consumer goods, and transportation and travel industries. He developed the overall design for a late 1990s outsourcing contract with Sainsbury's which, at the time, was the world's largest transformational outsourcing agreement. He also oversaw contract negotiations and transition management for Accenture's first financial business process outsourcing agreement with BP Exploration in 1991. Internally, Mr Healey was responsible for developing Accenture's best-practice approach to IT transformation.

CHAPTER 10: CONTINUOUS IMPROVEMENT: KEEPING THE DEAL WORKING

Anoop Sagoo is a London-based partner with Accenture Finance Solutions, Accenture's finance and accounting outsourcing business. Mr Sagoo specializes in finance change programs for multinational organizations and has deep expertise in shared services and outsourcing. His more than nine years of experience with Accenture spans numerous industries, and includes the design and implementation of best-practice operating models and processes. As vice president of sales for Europe, Mr Sagoo has also been heavily involved in the evolution of Accenture's finance and accounting BPO strategy. Mr Sagoo has a joint honors degree from Manchester University in Accounting and Computer Science.

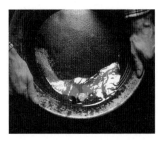

Index